Connect the Dots

Connect the Dots

*How to Build, Nurture, and Leverage
Your Network to Achieve Your Personal
and Professional Goals*

Inga Carboni

College of William and Mary

INFORMATION AGE PUBLISHING, INC.
Charlotte, NC • www.infoagepub.com

Library of Congress Cataloging-in-Publication Data

A CIP record for this book is available from the Library of Congress
http://www.loc.gov

ISBN: 978-1-64113-366-1 (Paperback)
        978-1-64113-367-8 (Hardcover)
        978-1-64113-368-5 (ebook)

Printed in the United States of America

Contents

$$1$$

Introduction

What do sticky rice, bridges, rangers, and weirdos have to do with your professional success? They are all critical aspects of *networking*.

Most people think that networking means attending networking events, collecting business cards, and getting a lot of LinkedIn followers. Certainly, those are the activities that are promoted by most career coaches and counselors. Literally hundreds of books have been written on how to make a favorable impression by crafting a memorable elevator speech, dressing to impress, working a room, and projecting your "personal brand" in-person and on-line. But will these activities really build a network that will get you jobs, promotions, salary increases, and other indicators of career success?

The answer is a resounding, *No!*

The truth is that networking is not about managing impressions (although managing impressions *does* a play a role). Effective networking is about managing relationships, *real* relationships built on genuine connection and not superficial relationships built on smoke and mirrors. Effective networkers *build, nurture,* and *leverage* professional networks.

For nearly twenty years, I have studied the science of networks and networking. I have taught thousands of undergraduate and MBA students—in the United States and abroad—and worked with hundreds of executives at all levels to improve their networking skills. I have seen people undergo life-changing transformations in the way that they view networking—from an unpleasant but necessary chore to a core part of their professional identity. I have also seen people get jobs, raises, and promotions as a direct result of creating ethical, empowering, and effective networks.

When I first got the idea to write this book, I did a little digging. I knew that there were many networking books on the market and I didn't want to repeat what someone else had already said. I was surprised by what I found. On the one hand, most of the existing books on networking are written by self-professed experts, based primarily on personal experience. While some of these offered useful tips, none were grounded in the network science I knew.

When I looked through the books written about the science of networks, none of them provided practical guidance for networking. As I well know, a growing body of research on networking—in addition to a well-established literature on its close cousin, relationship-building—provides many evidence-based recommendations for networking. I saw a need for a book that shares what is known about networks *and* networking and that gives practical advice on how to use that knowledge to create networks designed specifically to meet personal and professional goals.

The result is this book.

What is a network? A network is a collection of relationships. Below is a picture of a network. The dots represent people and the lines that connect them represent relationships. The lines connecting the dots might represent how often the people talk to each other, how much they like each other, if they give each other advice or not, if they have heard of the other person or, even, how much they dislike each other. There are as many different kinds of networks as there are kinds of relationships.

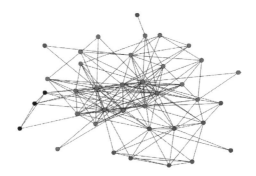

All of us have networks, although we might not realize we do. The trick is to recognize what you have—and what you don't have!—and to connect the dots that will turn your network into a tool for achieving success. In this book, we will explore networks and networking as they relate to the fulfillment of *your* personal and professional goals. I'll show you exactly how and why networks and networking matter and help you develop a network and networking approach that fits your personal style and needs, according to where you are in your life and career. Together, we'll start you on your networking journey.

Why do we need networks? Networks are important because they connect us to *social capital.*

Social capital is the complement to human capital. Our human capital is the unique set of knowledge, skills, and abilities we each have as a result of our education and experience. Many of us spend our early years investing heavily in our human capital by studying, working hard, and by engaging in experiences that stretch our capabilities and prepare us for ever more challenging experiences. We do this because we've been taught from a young age that the more we know—or know how to do—the higher we will rise in our professions, workplaces, and communities. We invest because we know that one day we'll leverage our investment to our personal and professional benefit.

Of course human capital is important. We need certain skills and abilities to succeed in our personal and professional lives. You can't be a carpenter without knowing something about carpentry. But human capital is only part of the success equation. Success is a function of human and *social* capital.

> These days, it's not enough to keep your head down and produce A-plus work. You need to connect with others, be vocal about your interests and career goals, and build relationships with people you might not otherwise have met.
>
> —Madeline Bell
> President and CEO, The Children's Hospital of Philadelphia[1]

Perhaps you've heard the phrase *social capital* before. The term exploded in popularity with the publication in 2000 of Robert Putnam's bestseller, *Bowling Alone: The Collapse and Revival of American Community.* In his book, Putnam argued that Americans have diminished their social capital with disastrous results. Since then, politicians, educators, academics, and pundits around the world have used *social capital* to explain everything from the support for democracy in post-Communist states to income inequality in the United States.[2]

But what exactly *is* social capital? Just like our human capital is the advantage we gain as a result of our skill sets, experiences, and knowledge, our *social* capital is the advantage we gain as a result of our networks. Unlike human capital, which is built through investments in ourselves, social capital is built through investments in our *relationships.* Our relationships provide us with social capital. More specifically, *social capital includes all of the visible and invisible resources that you can access—directly or indirectly—as a result of your relationships with other people.*

You have social capital when someone you know lends you money for your start-up. You have social capital when someone you know tells you about a job opportunity. You even have social capital when someone you know puts you in touch with someone else who can help you. Your social capital get you higher returns on your *human* capital because it'll put you in a better position to see and take advantage of opportunities.

To visualize how this works, imagine a household plumbing system in which pipes carry water from one place to another. The way that the pipes connect to each other determines the flow of the water.

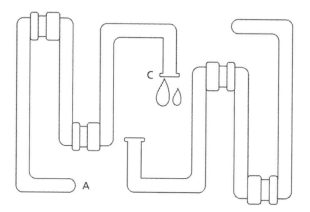

Water cannot flow from A to C if there's no pipe connecting A to C. In the same way, a network is a system of links between people. Flowing through the links is all the tangible and intangible stuff that people give to each other, such as information, advice, or money. The structure of the links determines how—or if!—stuff flows from one person to another. For example, A may have information that C needs but that information can't get to C if there's no person or pipeline connecting A to C.

The more effectively your network is structured, the greater your social capital. Decades of scientific evidence have established conclusively that social capital is as valuable—and often *more* valuable!—than human capital when it comes to determining personal and professional success.

Examples of human and social capital:

Human Capital	Social Capital
• Education	• Information
• Skills	• Support
• Experience	• Ideas
• Talent	• Advice
• Money you have	• Money you can borrow

Networks matter, sometimes much more than we realize. We know, for instance, that people who have more effectively structured networks receive more positive performance evaluations, faster promotions, and higher salaries. Not only that, they are also more likely to be tapped as top talent, propose good ideas, be involved in innovation, and receive venture funding for start-ups. Networks are also good for your health. Networks increase the odds of surviving cancer, having lower levels of depression, and being less likely to catch the common cold. Social capital can even add years to your life!

Having an effective network is not just a matter of being lucky enough to be in the right place at the right time or to be born into the right family (although those things certainly help!). An effective network is something that you purposefully build over time by making thoughtful and strategic investments in your relationships. Although early investments can pay off handsomely later in life, investments made at any point in your life or career will provide you with significant advantages.

The first step to maximizing your social capital is to understand what an effective professional network looks like. Effective networks are structured differently than ineffective networks, and they have different characteristics. Despite all the prevailing advice to judge the quality of your network by its size, bigger is not necessarily better. As you will learn, quality trumps quantity. Having five thousand Facebook friends or LinkedIn contacts won't do you any good if none of them are willing to give you the support, advice, or information you need. Once you know what an effective network looks like, you can design and adapt your network accordingly. This book will help you do that.

The second step to maximizing your social capital is learning how to network effectively. Networking is the single most powerful activity you can undertake in terms of developing your social capital. Networking is *building, nurturing,* and *leveraging* your personal relationships to create advantage. The research shows us that managers' networking ability is the strongest predictor of the career success, far ahead of their ability to undertake traditional management activities, routine communication, and human resource management.[3] Understanding the principles of effective networking will give you the tools you need to maximize your social capital.

It may be that your reluctance to network stems from your beliefs about what networking *is*. Perhaps you imagine that networking means acting phony or pretending to be nice to people just so you can get something from them. Many of us have had the experience of meeting someone at a professional event who scans the room while talking to us, presumably looking for someone more important to talk to. Or—and this tends to be a particular bugaboo for introverts—perhaps you think that networking means going to a lot of networking events for the sole purpose of meeting someone "important." For many of us, the very word *networking* brings a chill to our hearts.

When done correctly, networking is not manipulative, unethical, or labor-intensive. As you'll see in the upcoming chapters, networking can be *empowering*—for you, for all the people in your network, and for the organizations and communities in which you reside. As one manager noted,

> I have to actively manage my relationships. I can't wait for them. It's in my interests and it is my career. If you don't manage your career, someone will manage it for you. And maybe not in the way you would like . . . .You have to make it your business to be visible and interact.[4]

By networking more effectively, you can increase the amount and quality of stuff flowing in your network, even if you don't change *who* is in your network. This is because networking isn't just meeting people and getting their contact information. Networking is developing those relationships through small but significant actions. It's also about leveraging those relationships appropriately and ethically. Networking effectively can provide you with increased professional support as you learn to create powerful and mutually rewarding relationships that advance your personal and professional goals.

Networking effectively can even help you overcome some of the disadvantages of not being born into privilege. As you will see, one of the biggest benefits of being born into privilege—for example, as a result of your parent's socio-economic status or your ethnicity or even your gender—is having greater and more effortless access to social capital. Just as education and effort can help equalize the human capital "penalty" for being born into a historically disadvantaged group, networking effectively can help level the social capital playing field.

Networking effectively can also further the goals of the people in your networks as well as the goals of the organizations and industries to which you belong. Most people when they think about networks—if they think about them at all!—think only about who they know. That makes sense if you view your network as belonging to you and you alone. But everyone in your network is also connected to other people. Those connections can influence you, just as your connections can influence others. The more social capital you have, the more is available to the people in your network. On an organizational level, the pattern and strength of individual networks can provide a competitive advantage. On a community or societal level, networks can reduce conflict, increase prosperity, and promote well-being.

Networks are powerful.

Most people know that networking can be helpful and want to do more of it, but either don't know how to do it or—even if they know what to do— feel uncomfortable doing it. Maybe you're one of those people. Maybe you want to network but you don't know how. Maybe you're afraid of doing it wrong. Maybe that's why you picked up this book! If so, relax. By the time you finish this book and work through the exercises at the beginning and end of every chapter, you'll be a networking pro.

The good news is that there are actions that you can take to make your network work for *you*. The principles and methods discussed in this book will enrich your career and professional skills for years to come by developing your ability to build, nurture, and leverage effective networks. By completing the self-assessment snapshots at the beginning of each chapter, answering the reflection questions presented at the end of each chapter, and by following the simple steps and guidelines presented throughout the book, you will create your personal action plan for networking effectiveness.

In this book, we'll focus primarily on your *professional* network. Your professional network includes all the relationships that you have with people who have the potential to assist you in your work or career. The people in your professional network may be people you work with on a regular basis or people with whom you worked at previous jobs. They may also be colleagues, friends, and even family members that you contact when you need work-related advice, a sounding board, or just want to blow off steam from work.

If you're just starting out your career, you may think that you don't have a professional network. But, think again. You almost certainly already have a professional network, although you may not realize it. If you have ever held a job, interned, volunteered, been part of a social or religious community, attended college, been on a team, joined a club, had a group of friends, or belonged to a family, you have a professional network. These people are your network.

Of course, professional networks have a direct impact on our professional development. But they also have a huge impact on our general health and happiness. At the same time, our professional networks often include people that we also identify as friends or community members. For both of these reasons, we will also frequently consider other types of networks—such as those based on friendship—to get a better sense of how networks can support or derail career and job-related goals.

Who should read this book? This book is written for anyone who wants to create the most effective network possible, to nurture and feed productive relationships over time, and to reap the maximum rewards from their network. It's for people who have no problems striking up a conversation with strangers and for people who hate making small talk. It's for people who don't think that they have a network. (Spoiler alert: *Everyone* has a network. This book will show you how to recognize and then leverage it.) This book is also for people who don't have time to waste on meeting new people. (Spoiler alert: Networking effectively takes a lot less time than networking ineffectively. This book will show you how to maximize network effectiveness *and* efficiency.)

If you work with women, people of color, or other members of historically disadvantaged groups—or if you are one yourself—this book will help you recognize and address common barriers and challenges to creating effective networks. No matter where you are in your career—just starting out, a senior manager, or CEO—this book will help you develop a networking strategy that fits your specific career stage.

Who's this book for? This book's for you.

How to Read This Book

This book is organized into two sections. Section I grounds you in a firm understanding of networks and networking, and prepares you to develop the networking skills and action steps that are the focus of Section II.

At the beginning of each chapter are self-assessments for you to take before reading the chapter. I highly encourage you to take a few minutes to work through them. At the end of each chapter are some reflection questions to help you distill and clarify what you have just learned. Lastly, I have included three additional exercises in the Toolbox at the end of the book. Each exercise is designed to give you insights into your current professional and organizational network. Use them as the starting point for developing your personal networking strategy.

Section I is comprised of Chapters 2 through 4. In Chapter 2, we tackle head-on the perception that networking is unethical. Many people despise networking as superficial and dishonest. If this describes you, you are not alone. I've come across hundreds of students and professionals who feel the same way. There are three main reasons that people hate networking—because it's using people, because it's cheating, and because it sows conflict. We'll delve into each one in turn and, along the way, explore new frameworks for approaching networking, ones in which networking is not inherently selfish, deceptive, or divisive.

In Chapter 3, we'll start to look at some of the science underlying the magic of networks. In particular we'll talk about *sticky rice* networks, those tightly knit networks in which everyone knows everyone. Most of us live entirely in sticky rice networks. And no wonder! Sticky rice networks feel great. But sticky rice networks come with some disadvantages, too. If you want to increase your individual performance at work, and especially if you want to innovate, you have to step out of some of your sticky rice clusters and into a different network position.

In Chapter 4, we'll examine the critical network role of *bridge-builder.* If you've ever wondered why some people seem to do better than others—even though they're no smarter or better at their jobs than other people—it may be because they are bridge-builders. Compared to the rest of us, bridge-builders get promoted faster, make more money, are more involved in innovation, and are more likely to be identified as top talent by the organizations in which they work. Managing the bridging position for advantage is challenging and calls for a unique set of interpersonal skills and emotional abilities.

In Section II, having set the foundation in place, we begin to outline the specific steps you can take to establishing and leveraging networks. Chapter 5 begins that process. Whereas Chapters 3 and 4 focused on the structure of effective networks, Chapter 5 helps you start to figure out who is in your network and who *should* be in your network. Chapter 5 introduces the concept of *range* and how range can trigger creativity and innovation, reduce conflict, improve the quality of decision-making, and increase knowledge-sharing. We'll look at four ways you can increase range in your networks as well as specific steps that you can take now to increase your network's range.

Chapter 6 focuses on the quality and strength of the relationships in your network. We'll explore the advantages and disadvantages of strong, collegial, and dormant relationships. For each relationship type, we'll look at strategies for building the right relationships. We'll learn, for example, that quantity is good for some types of relationships but not for others. We'll also identify the *three crucial characteristics* of strong relationships and five strategies for building the right collegial relationships. Lastly, we'll look at negative relationships and the damage that they can do.

In Chapter 7, we start to develop your personal networking strategy. First step? Building relationships. In order to *build* relationships effectively, you need to learn how to optimize the context for relationship-building, prepare to engage in interactions, and then to actually engage in interactions that are both meaningful and positive for both people. I'll take you through each of these aspects of relationship-building. Along the way, I will give you tips and specific steps you can take to start your networking efforts off on the right foot.

Chapter 8 takes you further along your networking journey by focusing on how to *nurture* a network. We'll cover eight ways to nurture professional relationships that range from straight-forward tactics for turning an initial interaction into a budding relationship to broader and more holistic strategies for deepening and strengthening existing bonds. At each step, I'll provide specific examples of things you can do to nurture relationships.

In Chapter 9, we'll look at networking challenges for people who are members of historically disadvantaged groups or who work with people in these groups. We'll focus particularly on challenges facing women, people of color, and people from lower socio-economic backgrounds. We'll take a look at why these groups face networking challenges and what individuals can do to maximize their networking outcomes. In particular, we'll cover the *Magnificent Seven*—seven strategies that women and other historically disadvantaged people can and have used to successfully create effective networks.

Chapter 10 rounds out Section II. It covers the trickiest aspect of networking: *leveraging*. Leveraging your network releases its potential and makes it available to you and others. To leverage effectively, you'll need to develop three skills: knowing, asking, and bridging. I'll cover each of these skills in detail and provide examples, advice, and specific tips on how to foster these critical skills.

Earlier, I said that networking was a journey. In Chapter 11, we look at your networking needs at six different stages of your career. Your career goals will shift as you develop professionally and your networking strategy should change accordingly to meet your goals. What you need to accomplish when you are first starting out is very different from what you need to accomplish as CEO. We'll take a look at how to shake up staid networks and feed the relationships that bring you the most personal and professional rewards.

The final chapter, Chapter 12, reviews what we've learned throughout the book and pulls it all together. By the end of this book, you will have a personal plan of action for building your strategic network—strategically, mindfully, ethically, and comfortably—and for developing the networking skills that you need to maximize your personal effectiveness.

Reflection Questions

Why are you interested in networking?

What do you hope to get out of this book?

SECTION I

2

The Slime Factor

SELF-ASSESSMENT SNAPSHOT

1. Write down the first 5 words that come to mind when you think of "networking":

   _____

2. What is the goal of networking?

   _____

3. Why do most people network?

   _____

4. Which of the following *best* describes your attitude toward networking?
   a. Networking is an important part of my job and my career. It's an opportunity to build strong and supportive relationships.
   b. Networking is a necessary evil. I don't like it but I know it has to be done.
   c. Networking is inherently unethical. People who do it are just out for themselves.

Connect the Dots, pages 15–35

The Networking Genius

He was an American success story. His grandparents immigrated to the United States from Poland, Romania, and Austria between 1900 and 1905. They ran a Turkish bath on the Lower East Side of New York City that did well enough to allow their children to live in a middle-class area of Queens. He grew up in a modest three-bedroom home, swam for the high school swim team, and married his college sweetheart.

In 1959, a year before he graduated from college, he founded his own Wall Street securities firm, listing his assets on the SEC application as "cash on hand: $200" and liabilities as "none." Within ten years, he would be worth nearly $600,000, an amount roughly equal to 3.5 million in today's dollars. By 2008, his estimated net worth was $17 billion. He lived in luxury, owning shares in two private jets, a penthouse apartment in Manhattan, a home on the French Riviera, a yacht in the Bahamas, and a mansion in Palm Beach.[1] His collection of antique watches included two dozen custom vintage Rolex watches.

But the walls soon came crashing down. In December of 2008, his sons told the authorities that their father had confessed to them that the asset management unit of his firm was a massive Ponzi scheme. The following day, he was arrested by FBI agents for securities fraud. In June of 2009, he was convicted of committing the largest financial fraud in U.S. history, bilking his clients out of $65 billion dollars. The judge sentenced him to 150 years in prison, the maximum sentence allowed.

His name?

Bernie Madoff.

The success of Madoff's Ponzi scheme depended upon the continual investment of new clients, clients that flocked to Madoff, despite the fact that his investment wasn't publicly traded or even widely publicized. It's estimated that more than 2,200 people invested roughly $20 million with Madoff, including celebrities such as Steven Spielberg, real estate magnate Mort Zuckerman, actors Kevin Bacon and Kyra Sedgwick, and Hall of Fame pitcher Sandy Koufax. But most of his investors were personal friends who entrusted him with their entire life savings.[2] Most of them lost everything.

The U.S. Securities and Exchange Commission (SEC) regulators were supposed to be overseeing securities fraud. But Madoff was a fixture on Wall Street, a well-regarded financier and an acknowledged investing guru. He was held in such high regard that—despite plenty of warning signs, such as a ten-year campaign by one whistle-blower, a number of expository articles in financial trade journals including *Barron's*, and multiple SEC investigations—his firm was never found guilty of fraud. Instead, in a show of trust, the board of NASDAQ—the second-largest stock exchange in the world—named Madoff to serve as its chairman.

How did Bernie Madoff convince so many people to trust him?

By networking.

Beginning sometime in the early 1960s, Madoff started quietly taking on investors in the surprisingly lucrative branch of his investment business that he ran with a handful of co-conspirators. The first investors included a limited group of family and friends, and then spread outward in larger and larger circles as each person whispered to the next about their phenomenal returns. Up until the very last years, the marketing of the business was solely by word of mouth. You had to know someone who knew Madoff to get an "invitation" to invest in his fund. The vast majority of investors had no idea that they were financing a Ponzi scheme.[3]

Madoff cultivated his relationships carefully. By all accounts, he was an affable and charming man. University of Wisconsin professor of management Denis Collins wrote, "Elderly clients treated Bernie as a son, peers treated him like a brother, and younger clients treated him like a friendly uncle." Madoff was quiet yet charismatic and did not boast about his financial success. "He appeared to believe in family, loyalty and honesty," said one former Madoff employee. "Never in your wildest imagination would you think he was a fraudster."[4]

One person brought into Madoff's orbit was his father-in-law's partner, Michael Bienes. According to Bienes, Madoff invited him to the bar mitzvah of one of his sons. As Bienes recalls,

> It was a lunch, a buffet lunch. And I was very impressed because he didn't go over the top. He was a wealthy guy, you know, but he did it in a very moderate way. And I remember my partner, Frank Avellino, and myself and Bernie meeting in the middle of the dance floor, and we were saying, "Thanks for having us," and he said, "Hey, come on—we're family, aren't we?" And at that moment, he had me. He had me. We were family. Oh, my God! I was in! It really took me because he had a presence about him, an aura. He really captivated you.[5]

Madoff targeted wealthy American Jewish communities, using his in-group status to obtain investments from Jewish individuals, many of whom were his friends and neighbors in Palm Beach. In 1995, he paid the $350,000 initiation fee and became a member of the tony Palm Beach Country Club, using it as a means to build an even larger network of wealthy clients. One-third of the Club members eventually invested with him.[6] One longtime friend noted after the arrest, "He was part of the family for so many people. There was this quiet culture of people, slightly older-money, who maybe weren't that interested in the market, who kept saying to each other, 'Just give Bernie your money, you'll be fine.'"[7]

At the same time, Madoff understood the power of networking with the people who were supposed to be regulating him. He began building key relationships with regulators as early as the mid-1970s. "He was the darling of the regulators, without question. He was doing everything the regulators wanted him to do," says Nicholas A. Giordano, the former president of the Philadelphia Stock Exchange. "They wanted him to be a fierce competitor to the New York Stock Exchange, and he was doing it."[8] Madoff served as chairman of the board of directors of the National Association of Securities Dealers (NASD), a self-regulatory securities industry organization. Later he served on its board of governors.[9] Madoff also served on the board of directors of the Securities Industry Association, a precursor of SIFMA, and was chairman of its trading committee.[10]

In the late 1980s, Madoff began to spend a considerable amount of his time in Washington, D.C., building relationships with SEC regulators. "He was smart in understanding very early on that the more involved you were with regulators, you could shape regulation," one individual who knew him at this time noted. "But... he was doing something much smarter. If you're very close with regulators, they're not going to be looking over your shoulders that much. Very smart."[11] Madoff indicated the extent of his relationship-building in a 2009 interview, noting that SEC Chairman Mary Schapiro was a "dear friend," and SEC Commissioner Elisse Walter was a "terrific lady" whom he knew "pretty well."[12] Although they claimed that they were not influenced by their relationship with him, SEC regulators later came under fire, accused of failing to adequately supervise Mr. Madoff and being too cozy with him.[13]

Bernie Madoff built, nurtured, and leveraged relationships to get what he wanted and didn't care much about what happened to the people in his network. Some would say that he was a networking genius.

Would you?

Networking is Slimy

At this point, I'd like to pause for a moment and reflect a bit upon the word, *networking*. My guess is that—for at least some of you—*networking* triggers some uncomfortable thoughts and feeling along the lines of *networking is slimy* or *networking is unethical*. Networking, you're thinking, is for people like Bernie Madoff. Perhaps you've resigned yourself to the idea that networking is important for your career but dread the thought of actually doing it.

If you find networking offensive, you're not alone. I've worked with many community and organizational leaders, as well as hundreds of students, who find distasteful the very idea of *thinking* about building and nurturing their social relationships (not to mention leveraging them!). Many people go so far as to say that networking—and especially professional networking—makes them feel dirty.[14] They despise networking as superficial and dishonest. Getting to know people, they say, should be a natural process, not a calculated means to an end.

> When anyone says "networking," it makes me think of slimy people, networking over a business lunch, all being totally insincere and basically in it for their own. And I don't like insincerity and I don't like two-faced people, and so it has bad connotations to me.
>
> —Naomi, managing director of a UK PR agency[15]

Over the years, I've heard three main arguments against networking. The first is that networking is wrong because it involves *using* people—like Bernie Madoff did!—as a means to a selfish end. The second argument is that networking is wrong because it is *cheating*. Networkers try to get ahead based on who they know instead of on who they are and what they can do. The third is that networking is wrong because it is *political*. Networking is just a fancy name for sticking one's nose into office politics. In this chapter, I'd like to consider each of these perceptions in turn and, along the way, suggest new frameworks for approaching networking, ones in which networking is not inherently selfish, deceptive, or divisive.

Networking Is Using People

That which you hate to do be done to you, do not do to another.

—Egyptian papyrus,
Dated between 1080 and 332, B.C.

Let's take the first knock against networking first: *Networking is using people.* Most of us have a negative feeling about the idea of using people. Bernie Madoff clearly used his friends and family to enrich himself. Pretending to like someone in order to get something from them or pretending to be someone's friend in order to get something from them, is to dupe others into thinking that they are liked (when they are not) or have a friend (when they do not). This lie, this pretense, is something few of us would want others to do to us. All of the world's great religions and philosophies include some version of the Golden Rule, *Do unto others as you would have them do unto you.* Our belief in the wrongness of duplicity has a long history.

But, you may be saying to yourself, isn't the whole point of networking to build social capital—in other words, to use our social relationships to enrich ourselves?

My answer is, No, it's not. That kind of networking is not what this book is about. That kind of networking is not only wrong, it doesn't work. Even in the case of Madoff, it didn't work. Sure, Madoff lived in the lap of luxury for many years but, in the end, he lost it all. His son committed suicide in the wake of the scandal as did several investors and he himself—called "the most hated man in New York" by the *New York Post*—will live the rest of his life in jail.[16]

Not long ago, I talked with an undergraduate student who was adamantly opposed to networking because it was "using" people. During the course of our conversation, she revealed that she would be spending the following summer waitressing a restaurant owned by her boyfriend's family and living with a friend of her roommate. I couldn't help poking her a little. "But aren't you just using your boyfriend to get a job and your roommate to find a place to live?"

"Of course not," she huffed in response, "I like them for who they are, not for what I can get from them."

Exactly my point.

We like who we like because we do. If they want to help us out, fine. Because it is not just the idea of pretending to like someone that we don't really like that makes the prospect of networking so distasteful, it's the reason *why* we want to form a relationship in the first place. That is, it is the *motivation* for forming a relationship that makes it feel right or wrong. When we form a relationship for the purpose of getting something out of it, it feels wrong.

In fact, we tend to view any action that is undertaken solely for the purpose of our personal benefit—rather than the benefit of others—as morally suspect. This is certainly true in the case of Bernie Madoff. But it's also true even when the action leads to an outcome that clearly benefits others, such as charitable giving. We still judge it negatively if we *perceive* the act to be motivated by self-interest. Mark Zuckerberg found this out the hard way when he was roundly criticized just seconds after he announced that he and wife Priscilla Chan would be donating 99% of their Facebook stock to a new nonprofit organization that would "advance human potential and promote equality in areas such as health, education, scientific research, and energy." At the time, their Facebook stock was valued at $45 billion, instantly making the new nonprofit organization the biggest in the world.[17] What could be morally suspect about that?

Yet, many people viewed the move cynically. Some saw it as a tax avoidance scheme or, at best, a clever way to separate good intentions from the social network's more realpolitik actions. In other words, perceiving the motivation for the charitable gift to be self-serving made some people judge it as morally suspect.

> Zuckerberg is not "giving away" 99% of his FB wealth. He's "donating" his FB shares to an LLC that he controls, for minimizing taxes.
>
> —olliander (@ollieblog) December 3, 2015

In an article entitled *How Mark Zuckerberg's Altruism Helps Himself,* reporter Jesse Eisinger made clear his views on Zuckerberg's motivations, noting that "[t]he superwealthy buy great public relations and adulation for donations that minimize their taxes."[18]

Networking is morally suspect for the same reason. Our *motivation* for forming relationships is what makes networking feel either okay or, well, *slimy.* The reason for this perception has deep roots in our psychological make-up.

Humans have always—and will always—form relationships with each other. We are social animals and forming social relationships is part of the human condition. Social capital is the product of those relationships. Our social relationships may result in personal benefit regardless of whether or not that was our intention when first forming the relationship. The undergraduate student benefited from her social capital even though getting access to social capital did not motivate her to *build* relationships with her boyfriend or her roommate.

Many people purposefully seek out and nurture relationships with friends or romantic partners. They want to "meet someone." Although attending an event, such as a party, for the purpose of "meeting someone" may strike a few people as distasteful, most people aren't bothered by it. Indeed, hundreds of thousands of people regularly go to sites such as meetup.com, Tinder, match.com, and eHarmony to find potential mates, and thousands more seek out friends by joining online communities focused on common interests such as Reddit, StumbleUpon, and Facebook. We don't usually accuse these people of being selfish for wanting to build relationships. In fact, most of us recognize that building relationships is an essential part of a healthy lifestyle.

Usually the goal of *personal* networking is to find a *mutually* rewarding relationship based on personal interest and affection. In that sense, friendship IS selfish. Because, of course, there is always some self-interest involved in forming relationships. It is clear that we benefit from our relationships. Our friends and acquaintances bring us happiness, support, and stimulation. My life would be much poorer without the many times I've shared laughter, tears, and wine—sometimes all at the same time!—with my friends.

But friendship is not *only* selfish. Part of being in a relationship is caring about the other person. We care about the other person and we want what's best for them, just as we expect that they want what's best for us. In this way, our relationships are as much about the other person as they are about ourselves. I know I've tried to be there for my friends, in good times and bad, and that they've been there for me. Our motivation in forming and staying in a relationship might be partly self-serving but it is also about caring for the other person.

Networking—that is, relationship-building—feels morally correct only when we aren't motivated *primarily* by self-interest. So, if we want to build and nurture relationships that feel right and not wrong, all we have to do is make sure that we are genuinely motivated as much by the other person's best interests as we are by self-interest. All we have to do is search our hearts and we'll know our true motives. Are we forming a relationship—at least in part—to benefit the other person or are we simply in it for ourselves? By answering that question honestly, we can discern our true motives for networking.

Easy, right?

Unfortunately, we are surprisingly poor judges of our own inner attitudes and feelings. In a funny quirk of human wiring, we often infer our inner motivations from our outward behaviors, instead of the other way around. Smiling, for example, reduces our stress level![19]

We also infer what we think by observing what we do. Years ago, attitude researchers found that if individuals were randomly asked to give a scripted speech in support of one of two political candidates, that they would come to feel more positively toward the candidate. This was true even when the scripted speech didn't include any new facts or information about either candidate. More interestingly, the individuals in the study were particularly adamant that reading the scripted speech had not influenced their attitude. They were completely unaware of the effect of their action on their subsequent attitude.[20]

This quirk becomes problematic when we are trying to examine our motivation for forming a particular relationship. Given the choice between perceiving ourselves to be acting out of pure self-interest or out of what is good for the other person, most of us would feel better if we believed—at least in part—that building a particular relationship is also good for the other person. At the very least, we're more likely to feel morally pure. It's usually not hard to do that when it comes to our personal relationships. But interpreting our own behavior when it comes to *professional* relationships is trickier.

It turns out, compared to perceiving our motivation for personal networking—such as going to parties or online sites with the express purpose of finding new friends or romantic partners—we are much more likely to perceive ourselves to be building *professional* relationships purely out of self-interest. And that's not a self-perception we like. In a clever study by researchers Tiziana Casciaro, Francesca Gino, and Maryam Kouchaki,[21] more than 300 adults were asked to think about times when they engaged in either personal or professional networking. They were then given the task of completing word fragments, such as W_ _ H and S _ _ P. Participants who had thought about professional networking were more likely to complete the fragments with words such as *wash* and *soap* whereas people who had thought about personal networking were more likely to use words such as *wish* and *step*. In other words, people who believed that they were engaged in professional networking were more likely to feel that they needed cleansing than people who believed that they were engaged in personal networking. Professional networking literally makes us feel dirty.

There are two reasons why we tend to believe that professional networking is motivated primarily by self-interest: Expectations regarding *balance* and expectations about *giving*.[22]

People have different expectations regarding the *balance* of exchange in professional relationships. In personal relationships, we usually assume that if one person feels close to someone than the other person feels similarly close. (Of course, some personal relationships are unbalanced but these are usually called dysfunctional!) However, in our professional relationships, we are much more comfortable with a lack of balance. Just because Kevin Bacon turns to Bernie Madoff for financial advice doesn't mean that Bernie also turns to Kevin for advice. For the most part, this type of unbalanced relationship feels okay. We don't expect an advisor to necessarily reciprocate by asking a protégé for advice.

But pursuing a potentially unbalanced relationship seems to suggest that one is angling to be on the receiving—rather than the giving—end of the relationship. Otherwise, why would Kevin seek to build a relationship with Bernie? It must be because he perceives that he will get some benefit for doing so. If we find ourselves seeking to build a professional relationship that we perceive as unbalanced—in our favor!—then we are likely to believe that we are motivated by self-interest rather than by a desire to help, nurture, or otherwise give to the other person. This feels wrong.

The second reason why we are more likely to believe that professional networking is motivated by self-interest concerns the different ways people *give* to each other in personal versus professional relationships. In personal relationships, each person responds to another's needs or well-being over a prolonged amount of time without the necessity of repayment. Typically, these relationships occur between close friends, family, and romantic partners. Parents, for example, take care of their children's needs for years without expecting any "pay-back."

Professional relationships, on the other hand, are more often expected to be transactional. In transactional relationships, each person expects benefits to be equally distributed and directly reciprocated. If I give you something you want, I expect you to give me something I want. *If you scratch my back, I'll scratch yours!* Normally, transactional professional relationships don't bother us. After all, being paid in return for performing work is normal. But they can pose a problem if we are trying to understand our motivation for building a relationship. If professional relationships are more likely to be transactional and we're pursuing a professional relationship, then it must be because we expect to get something out of it. Professional networking is again more likely to be interpreted as motivated by self-interest because we assume that the only reason to form the relationship is to get *our* back "scratched."

As if our self-perceptions weren't enough of a barrier, our attitudes toward professional networking are also affected by our beliefs about how *other* people perceive us. Even if *we* believe that our professional relationships didn't arise out of pure self-interest, we may feel guilty or ashamed if *others* believe or suspect that we are engaging in professional networking. We worry that other people will think we were being slimy or insincere.

And we'd be right.

Other people judge self-interested motives more negatively—*just like we do!*—and they're more likely to consider our professional networking as motivated by self-interest. Because sometimes networking IS motivated solely by self-interest, as it was in the case of Bernie Madoff. People like

Madoff are another reason why we worry that others will view *our* network-ing as motivated by self-interest.

It all adds up to making professional networking feel "slimy."

Networking Without the Slime Factor

At this point, it may seem like the only available ways to approach profes-sional networking are (a) to just accept the moral impurity and schmooze away, or (b) to avoid networking at all. I suggest a third way: Think about networking as a way to *give* to others.

Most people when they think about professional networks think only about who they know. That makes sense if you view your network as belong-ing to you and you alone. But everyone in your network also has a network. And the people in those networks also have networks.

Visualize your professional network as embedded in a vast web of re-lationships. Notice how it connects and intersects with dozens, hundreds, even thousands of other networks. Your network is bigger than just you. It belongs to a lot of people. Once you realize this, you also realize that the people and resources flowing through your network influence the people and resources flowing through the networks of everyone to whom you are connected and to whom they are connected and to whom they are con-nected and so on and so on and so on . . .

If you establish an effective network, you increase the effectiveness of *all* those networks, too. Your contribution to the pool of available resources enriches the pool for everyone. The conclusion is obvious. If you want to help others live in a vibrant and resource-rich network, then the best way to do that is to build a vibrant and resource-rich network yourself.

If you go about it in this way, professional networking can be an altru-istic endeavor.

Networking to benefit others includes benefitting the person in front of you. It is impossible to perceive yourself as interested in the well-being of another person if you're building a relationship with him or her for the sole purpose of benefitting yourself. Instead, build a *mutually* rewarding relationship.

So, how do you do that? *You do it by giving first and giving as generously as you can.* "The best networkers are people who start by seeing what they can give to somebody," said Arianna Huffington, former editor-in-chief of *The Huffington Post.* "It's not because you want something back, but because you want to help—it's a state of offering."[23] Giving first makes you a more effective networker in four ways:

1. Helps you (and others) avoid seeing you as self-interested
2. Encourages *other* people to give
3. Builds authenticity
4. Stimulates generalized reciprocity

One, giving helps you (and others) avoid seeing you as self-interested. No one wants to be—or be perceived to be—a person who is scheming to benefit from an unbalanced or transactional relationship. Giving makes it easier for you to look beyond pure self-interest. Moreover, it helps other people see you that way, too. "Being altruistic is often seen as 'good,' and being greedy or selfish is not," writes Duke behavioral economist Dan Ariely with two colleagues, so giving is "a way to signal to others that one is good."[24]

Two, your giving encourages other people to give. Seeing you give makes it more likely that someone observing you will "pay it forward" by giving to someone else. We learn behaviors through role modeling and vicarious learning. We are particularly responsive to behaviors that express core values and emotions. Just as neglect and ill treatment can be learned by observing neglect and ill treatment, so can kindness be learned by observing kindness. For those of you who question whether paying it forward exists in the cold, cruel business world, a study by researchers Wayne Baker and Nathaniel Buckley may alleviate your doubts. Their multi-method study tracked requests for help and actual helping behavior of 125 people in two organizations over the course of three months. Their findings demonstrated strong support for the "paying it forward" principle. The more help the people in their study received, the more likely they were to help someone *else*.[25]

By giving first you create a virtuous cycle of giving, unleashing resources into the larger network far beyond your initial contribution. Paying it forward builds everyone's social capital.

Three, giving builds authenticity. Thinking about networking as a way to give means that you don't have to worry about acting fake or insincere. You're not looking to *be liked*, you're looking to *help*. That said, more helping IS likely to result in more liking. Helping someone will make that person like you more because we tend to like people who help us. Moreover, given our tendency to infer our motivations from our behavior, helping someone is likely to make you believe that *you* like the person more. Ben Franklin understood this principle when he told this story of leveraging helping to build liking:

[I] did not like the opposition of this new member, who was a gentleman of fortune and education, with talents that were likely to give him, in time, great influence in the House, which, indeed, afterwards happened.... Having heard that he had in his library a certain very scarce and curious book, I wrote a note to him, expressing my desire of perusing that book, and requesting he would do me the favour of lending it to me for a few days. He sent it immediately, and I return'd it in about a week with another note, expressing strongly my sense of the favour. When we next met in the House, he spoke to me (which he had never done before), and with great civility; and he ever after manifested a readiness to serve me on all occasions, so that we became great friends, and our friendship continued to his death.[26]

In other words, the more you give, the more you like.

Four, giving stimulates generalized reciprocity. Savvy networkers know that networking is a mixed-motive situation. You can network to benefit others AND network to benefit yourself. Somewhat surprisingly, focusing only on helping others achieves both ends. In fact, networkers who focus first on *giving* to others are more likely to benefit from networking than networkers who focus first on *getting* from others.

Why?

Because of the principle of generalized reciprocity.

Reciprocity means expecting back from someone the same level of resources that you gave that person. It's one of the principal components of our moral codes. The urge to give back to those who have given to us is so strong that marketers take advantage of it by giving us free samples of a product in order to provoke our urge to reciprocate the favor by buying the product.

Generalized reciprocity means expecting something back from your network *but not necessarily from the same people.* As Adam Grant writes in his excellent book, *Give and Take,* giving "enlarges the range of potential payoffs, even though those payoffs are not the motivating engine."[27] Once these investments are made, there is a return on that investment—though not on every relationship and not all the time. Have faith. While there may be a significant lag between the initial investment and a later payoff, eventually, givers will receive as much as they give.

Trusting in the principle of generalized reciprocity means relying upon the old saying, *what goes around, comes around!* Many people in your network will never give you anything but some will. Because you cannot predict the future, you never know exactly who these will be. Five years from now, you may be in desperate need of something that is unimaginable today. And the people you meet at one point in time may have different things to give at a later point in time. For example, the young woman with few tangible resources who interned for you last summer may one day become a Fortune 500 CEO.

Networking works if you are continually contributing to the network by giving to others when you have something of value to give. Sooner or later—directly or indirectly—someone else's contributions will affect you for the better. Networking effectively for yourself means networking effectively for others first. I once had coffee with a woman who is well-recognized in her field as an expert on personal branding. While ordering, she chatted amiably with the server, an energetic teenager whose chatter was lively and quick. As we paid our bill, she turned to the server and asked, "What do you think you are going to do with your life?" The teen smiled and explained that she wanted to be an English professor.

"That's terrific," my colleague replied. "Learning how to communicate effectively is something everyone needs." Then she added, "I am so impressed by your smarts and your attitude. I know you're going places." She handed the teen a business card. "If you ever want to talk about schools, personal branding, or anything, contact me." The teen smiled.

This was networking at its best. I knew my colleague well enough to know that she would indeed help out this girl however she could. It was equally clear to me that this girl had lots to offer, both in the present and in the future as her career took off. Just watching this exchange inspired me to make the same offer later that day to the impressive young Uber driver who drove me to the airport. I could tell that she was going places.

For those of you whose toes curl at the mention of the word *networking*, let me suggest that you reframe the way you approach networking. Try to think of networking first and foremost as an opportunity to give. Professional networking—at least *effective* professional networking—is not a purely selfish endeavor. Instead, it's as much about others as it is about you. It's about the person in front of you, the one you're talking with right now. It's also about the other people in your network and the other people in this person's network. Done correctly, professional networking builds the social capital of everyone, including you.

Thinking differently about how you approach networking is not as hard as it sounds. A number of studies by Stanford University Professor Carol Dweck demonstrates that our ability to change the way we approach challenges is much more malleable than we once thought. Her research tells us that the main barrier to change is our *belief* that we can't change. If you believe that your motivation for professional networking and your ability to form satisfying professional relationships can't change, then they probably can't. But, if you *believe* that you can change, then you can.[28]

Okay, you may be saying, I'd like to build my professional network by focusing on what other's need but what do I have to offer?

The answer: More than you think.

Many people believe that they have nothing of value to offer other professionals. This can feel especially true when you are just starting your career, if you are unemployed, or if your job and income are insecure. As my students often lament, "I'm just starting out, they have the jobs and I have nothing." First of all, to avoid feeling needy in the first place, it helps to develop your professional networking long before you "need" something like a job or start-up funds. But even more established professionals may feel that they also have nothing to offer, because they have little or no access to staff, budget, or other tangible resources.

Feeling like you have nothing to offer is another way of saying that you feel powerless. Feeling needy makes you feel even more powerless. People who feel powerless believe that they can't possibly give as much as they get. For them, networking feels all-too-clearly to be motivated by self-interest.

If you think you have nothing to offer in a professional relationship, don't despair. Most people have a very narrow conception of what they have to offer. There are many ways in which so-called "powerless" people can give to "powerful" people. Many powerful people, for example, seek appreciation, idealism, and the opportunity to give back to their industry, alma mater, or home community. The trick is to start thinking less about what *you* want and more about what *others* want. What does this person in front of you right now value and want?

Alumni, for example, often say that they volunteer to mentor students as a way of giving back to a community to which they feel attached. Their protégés "give" them a feeling of greater closeness to an institution that is important to them. If you are a student, is this something you can give a powerful alumnus? Of course you can. Perhaps you can provide updates about current university events, share information about professors whose classes you both have taken, or talk positively about your recent university experiences. Figure out what kind of "currency" speaks to someone.[29] If it's a currency that you can and would like to offer, then offer it.

Another way to help yourself move from perceiving professional networking as overly self-serving to one in which networking also benefits others is to consider networking as a way to support a cause that you believe in, one that's greater than yourself. If you have trouble determining a cause greater than yourself, one that you are passionate about, think about your core values. What motivates you? Are you passionate about helping people get access to high-quality health care? Creating beauty through the thoughtful design of everyday items? Helping investors keep and grow the money that they've worked hard to earn? Raising healthy, happy children? All of these are admirable goals. Achieving any one of them will require unlocking the support and resources of others. The more effectively you do that, the more you can further your cause

Finding or reading about a role model who networked in a way that you admire can help you change your mindset. Musician Bob Geldof may be one such role model. In October 1984, deeply moved by images of starving children in Ethiopa, Geldof called fellow musician Midge Ure and together they quickly co-wrote the song, *Do They Know It's Christmas?*. In less than a month, Geldof persuaded members of his network, which included some of the biggest British and Irish musical acts at the time, to record and produce the song for free.[30] Geldof said,

> I then rang Sting and he said, yeah, count me in, and then [Simon] Le Bon, he just immediately said tell me the date and we'll clear the diary. The same day I was passing by this antique shop and who is standing in there but Gary Kemp, just about to go off on tour to Japan. He said he was mad for it as well and to wait 10 days till they [Spandau Ballet] got back in the country ... suddenly it hit me. I thought, "Christ, we have got the real top boys here," all the big names in pop are suddenly ready and willing to do this. ... I knew then that we were off, and I just decided to go for all the rest of the faces and started to ring everyone up, asking them to do it.[31]

Do They Know It's Christmas? became the fastest-selling single ever in Britain, raising £8 million for famine relief.[32] Acting on a suggestion from Boy George, the lead singer of Culture Club and one of the singers on the single, Geldof again leveraged his network to stage a dual-venue charity concert the following year. *Live Aid*, as the concert was called, was one of the largest-scale satellite link-ups and television broadcasts to date. It also inspired other musicians to host concerts in their countries on the same day. As a result, an estimated global audience of 1.9 billion, across 150 nations, watched the live broadcast and contributed more than $100 million in famine relief for African nations.[33] Bob Geldof's network and his networking literally saved thousands of lives.

A role model doesn't have to be a single person. Perhaps you admire the way your co-worker Theo seems to genuinely enjoy his interactions with everyone he meets and the way your friend Serena takes the initiative to post LinkedIn testimonials for her employees and contractors. Its fine to create an ideal role model based upon a set of observed best practices.

As you shift your motivations to the concerns of others, make sure that you don't lose sight of the person standing right in front of you. Even if you are networking for a greater cause, you are still interacting with another human being. That person matters too. You will find it nearly impossible to convince yourself that your motivation for building or nurturing a particular relationship is out of a concern for that person's interests and welfare if you continue to view the person as a means to an end, no matter how noble the larger cause.

Networking Is Cheating

Let's turn to the second reason why people dislike networking: Because it is *cheating*. Career success, some say, should be a function of character and competence, not connections. This argument has its roots in two fundamental Western values: equality and individualism. On the one hand, we believe that we are all created equal and should have an equal opportunity to pursue the goals that are important to us. To this end, we have legislation in place to reduce discrimination and bias in hiring and recruiting. Colleges, for example, will sometimes remove an applicant's name from his or her file to reduce the likelihood that admission decisions will be made on the basis of race or gender.

At the same time, we believe that successful people "pull themselves up by their own bootstraps." According to this view, human capital in the form of talent, effort, and relentless persistence inevitably leads to success. Everyone has the opportunity for a better future—if only they work *harder, smarter, faster*. To receive any personal gain from networking is to unfairly stack the deck in your favor.

> Some people like to come to their boss and ask questions, but I'm the opposite. I do it on my own. I go through every possible way that I can and then go for a quick discussion, meaning I am independently handling all of those myself, *like a real professional* [emphasis added].
>
> —Kim, AuditCo[34]

Of course, we already know that social capital *is* as important as human capital in determining important career outcomes such as performance evaluations, pay, and promotions. But purists argue that, whether or not it is true that social capital trumps human capital, it *shouldn't* be true. Accomplishments should speak for themselves.

From this perspective, leveraging a network to gain power and influence is akin to seeking an unbalanced power distribution, with yourself on top. Again, the argument goes, networking thwarts the principle of equality and rewards social connections instead of human capital.

But this argument misses the point.

Networking isn't a short-cut to success. It's not a way to avoid doing your real work. It IS your work. Networking is a critical leadership skill. "The capacity to connect with people is absolutely essential for leaders," says Carlos Ghosn, Renault-Nissan CEO.[35] That's because, as we've seen, effective networking releases resources and generates knowledge flow that benefit individuals, teams, organizations, and even industries.

If you don't know how to create an effective network, then you can't lead. You need an effective network that you can mobilize to strategize and innovate, make and implement high-quality decisions, and influence others to get work *done*. Effective networkers influence people over whom they have no formal authority by building and nurturing relationships with people who have the resources they need as well as with people who need the resources they have. Groups whose managers have influence tend to get what they need; other groups don't.

To avoid feeling like networking is "cheating," it may help to reframe your ability to connect to others and to leverage those connections as part of your human capital. Networking effectively is a leadership skill. The skill of networking is critical for anyone who is in a leadership position or who aspires to be. The *results* of your networking efforts are your social capital. In other words, when you network effectively, you enhance your human capital with your social capital. Your social capital, in turn, increases the social capital of the organizations and communities to which you belong. By building a resource-rich network, you enhance your value to the organization.

Networking Is All About Office Politics

Now, what about the argument that networking is simply playing the game of "office politics"? Office politics is that nasty game that some people play to get what they want. Madoff engaged in "office" politics by building relationships with key securities industry regulators in order to get what he wanted. And he was successful . . . in the short-term. Although his network contacts claimed that they were not influenced by their relationship with him, they later came under fire for failing to adequately supervise him.

Even when people play office politics for a supposedly good cause— such as getting their department the resources it needs—the *way* they do it can be reprehensible. They cozy up to powerful people and backstab the people who get in their way. They use their connections to pick up gossip which they then whisper into the right ear at the right moment. Tensions erupt, people get hurt, and careers are damaged. And these so-called networkers just sit back, smile, and reap the benefits.

Sounds all too familiar, right?

But what if we redefine the game of office politics? Instead of seeing it as inherently a game of war, consider the possibility that it could also be a game of diplomacy. While it is true that office politics can *heighten* existing tensions, the truth is that the underlying tensions existed long before the office politicians started to fan the flames. Office politics are often the *result* and not the *cause* of existing conflict. If you avoid engaging in office politics, you may be limiting your ability to lead and manage effectively.

Conflict arises because organizations—by their very nature—always contain a diversity of opinions, interdependent units, and limited resources. Sooner or later, these differences lead people to disagree over ideas, courses of action, or distribution of resources. As a result, conflict is an unavoidable fact of life in all organizations. One long-time scholar of organizational conflict says that he used to believe that conflict was an aberration before he realized that the *lack* of conflict is the real aberration.[36]

While conflict is inevitable, it isn't inevitably destructive. *De*structive conflict occurs when initial differences become inflamed with animosity, tension, and outright hatred. Unchecked, destructive conflict can lead to acts of sabotage, derision, back-stabbing, and even crime. Very little good comes out of destructive conflict.

In contrast, properly managed conflict can become <u>constructive</u>— sparking innovation, creativity, problem-solving, and higher quality decision-making. *Constructive* conflict leads political players to consider multiple viewpoints, goals, and interests to develop the best solution. The positive force of conflict is why so many organizations are matrixed at some level. Individuals and units that are matrixed are asked to be responsive to two conflicting sets of priorities, such as needs for global standardization of products and needs for customizing products to appeal to regional markets. The thinking behind matrices is that when individuals or units must be responsive to opposing needs, they will determine the solution that best satisfies *everyone's* interests and, in so doing, the organization's best interests. Of course, that's not how it always works out in practice!

At their roots, destructive and constructive conflict are not different. They both arise in response to naturally occurring differences. The negative outcomes begin to occur when the disagreements over ideas and behaviors become increasingly attributed to negative aspects of a person's character or personality (e.g., *He wants the company to go in that direction because he lacks common sense* or *She takes that position because she doesn't care about my department*).

Of course, if we were all purely rational decision-makers, conflict would be resolved through the thoughtful consideration of the facts that led to agreement on the most rational course of action. But we are not rational animals. Instead, we interpret facts as parts of a story that we know very well, a story informed by our experience, personal history, and any number of other things. We are inherently biased in favor of our own stories because we tend to think that all rational people see the world as we do. If others don't agree with us, it must be because they are irrational. The point at which we begin to seek reasons for the other person's "irrational" behavior is the point at which constructive conflict becomes destructive conflict.

Keeping the conflict conversation focused on promoting mutual understanding and collaborative problem-solving is hard. But if we don't contribute our story and genuinely seek to understand the stories of other people, we cannot help to resolve conflict.

And here's where the networking of individuals becomes critical to organizational success. Effective networkers—acting with integrity and for good ends—can proactively create the conditions for success. Yes, they are playing the game of office politics but they are playing for the good of the organization and not for their own personal good. They know that resolving conflicts is best done through diplomacy, not war. To do that, you need to build an effective network.

An effective network allows you to influence others to consider what you have to say when making decisions. It also helps *you* genuinely and deeply understand the view of *others*, making it easier to collaborate effectively to resolve organizational conflicts.

To become an office "diplomat," start by taking a look at your department or organization. Are there some conflicts that occur regularly—for example, over budget allocations? Is there a way that you could help address the conflict more effectively the next time it erupts? The critical question you should be asking yourself is not how can I *avoid* office politics but how can I build, nurture, and leverage my network to influence the nature of organizational conflict so that it leads to *productive* outcomes—such as collaboration and innovation—rather than *destructive* outcomes such as bickering and turf-protecting?

If you are an employee of an organization, network on behalf of what's good for your team, your department, *and* your organization. If you are in a freelance or consulting role, focus on the value you and your network bring to your clients and your industry. If you are consistent in your active involvement on behalf of others, you will gain the trust of the people in your network, making it easier to develop the mutual understanding and collaboration required to address organizational conflicts.

To Recap...

Bernie Madoff networked unethically. He—and many others like him—give networking a bad name. But I hope I have convinced you that, networking is not inherently selfish, deceptive, or divisive. Networkers—acting with integrity and for good ends—can positively influence the outcomes of everyone in their networks. Ethical networkers enrich the networks—and lives—of all the people they work with, as well as the organizations and communities to which they belong. As you read further in this book and learn more about how to network effectively, never forget that networking should be first and foremost an ethical endeavor.

Reflection Questions

What can you give to someone in your network today?

Do you spend as much time and energy developing your networking skills as you do your other critical leadership skills?

What conflicts can you anticipate occurring in your department or organization? How can you use your networks to manage the conflicts constructively the next time they occur?

3

Sticky Rice Feels So Good

SELF-ASSESSMENT SNAPSHOT

1. Which of the following *best* describes your attitude toward the people in your professional network?
   a. I like it when my friends like each other.
   b. Whenever I can, I introduce the people I know to each other.
   c. I don't like it when the people I know also know each other.
2. Which of the following best describes the people in your professional network?
   a. Few people in my professional network know each other well.
   b. Some people in my professional network know other people in my network well.
   c. Almost everyone in my professional network knows each other well.

The Nut Island Plant[1]

To begin with, Nut Island is not actually an island at all. It is a small peninsula located at the southern entrance to Massachusetts's Boston Harbor.

Connect the Dots, pages 37–53
Copyright © 2019 by Information Age Publishing
All rights of reproduction in any form reserved.

When it opened in 1952, the Nut Island sewage treatment plant was promoted as the solution to Boston's overwhelming wastewater problem. At the time, raw sewage from much of Boston and the 43 towns and cities of eastern Massachusetts was transmitted directly into the harbor, polluting local beaches and fisheries and posing a serious health hazard. Heralded in the local press for its "modern design," the Nut Island plant was built to treat all of the sewage produced in the southern half of the Boston metropolitan area and then to release the safely rendered sludge about a mile out into the harbor.

Workers in the Nut Island plant fell into one of three categories: operations, maintenance, and the plant's laboratory. When Superintendent Bill Smith arrived at the plant in 1963, he noted the animosity between the different groups of workers. "The maintenance guys thought that the lab guys were a bunch of college students. And the guys in the lab said the maintenance guys were just grease monkeys."[2] Smith took it as his mission to bind the organization into one cohesive group.

Along with Operations Chief Jack Madden and Laboratory head Mac Kinnon, Smith began weeding out the plant's "shirkers" and "squeaky wheels" and hiring instead people like themselves—"hardworking, grateful for the security of a public sector job, and happy to stay out of the limelight."[3] Many were veterans of World War II or the Korean War. Within a few years, the plant went from an environment of hostility to one of harmony. One of the men recalled how he felt on his first day in 1968. "I can remember walking down those first stairs and saying to myself, 'I'm going to like this,' because I felt right at home."[4]

The plant workers quickly because a closely knit group, bonded by common values and a shared cause. Smith and his colleagues made job satisfaction a priority and, as a result, plant workers developed a strong sense of ownership and a deep commitment to the organization's mission. For example, even though few workers made more than $20K—low wages even in the 70s—members would reach into their own pockets to purchase needed equipment when there was no money for spare parts. As Paul Levy—executive director of the Massachusetts Water Resources Authority from 1987 to 1992—put it:[5]

> They were every manager's dream. They performed difficult, dirty, dangerous work without complaint...They needed virtually no supervision, handled their own staffing decisions, cross-trained each other, and ingeniously improvised their way around operational difficulties and budgetary constraints.

In the process of working together, they developed a deep trust in each other. Coworkers felt like they were part of a large, caring family. In an interview with Smith, Madden, and Kinnon more than 30 years after they first met—and nearly five years after the Nut Island plant transferred its operations to newer facilities on Deer Island—Levy noted that the strong bonds that connected the three men were still evident.

> They laugh often as they tell stories about the old days, featuring characters with nicknames like Sludgie and Twinkie, and they seem cheerfully oblivious to the hair-raising conditions that were part of daily life at the plant. When Smith talks about once finding himself neck-deep in waste water as he worked in the pump room, he speaks without a hint of horror or disgust. It's just a good story. "It was fun," Smith says, and his two friends nod in agreement...[6]

In January of 1976, an event occurred that bonded the plant workers even more closely to each other. Politicians—who gain votes by investing in skating rinks and swimming pools and not sewage treatment plants—had rarely allocated sufficient funds for plant maintenance. Not surprisingly, the plant's four enormous diesel engines finally shut down. For four days, the plant released millions of gallons of untreated sewage into the harbor while plant workers frantically worked around the clock to get the engines running again.

The workers blamed the incident on an indifferent management at MDC—the regional infrastructure agency responsible for Greater Boston's water supplies and sewers. The people in the plant had warned the bureaucrats that a breakdown was going to happen and they had done nothing. Plant workers decided that the plant was now *their* responsibility. If headquarters wasn't going to listen to them, then they would do whatever needed to be done to keep the plant running.

From that day forward, Nut Islanders avoided contact with management whenever possible. As Paul Levy noted,

> When the plant ran short of ferrous chloride, a chemical used for odor control, no one from Nut Island asked headquarters for funds to buy a new supply. Instead, they would contact a local community activist and ask her to complain to her state representative about odors emanating from the plant. The rep would then contact MDC headquarters and Nut Island would receive a fresh supply of ferrous chloride.[7]

Nut Islanders took immense pride in the plant. They worked hard and believed that they were doing important work. Unlike other plants in the area, the Nut Island plant had no more breakdowns for the next 20 years.

Workers were 100% committed to keeping the water in Boston Harbor clean and safe. In some ways, life at the Nut Island Plant sounds like a fairy tale.

... but this is only half of the story.

By the mid-1980s, Boston Harbor was recognized as one of the nation's dirtiest waterways and the Nut Island plant was one of the reasons. In 1980, the Water Pollution Federation found that only *two* percent of Boston's sewage flow met Federal standards established in the 1977 Clean Water Act. [In comparison, one *hundred* percent of Chicago's and Washington D.C.'s sewage flow met the standards.] In a single six-month period in 1982, the Nut Island plant released 3.7 *billion* gallons of raw sewage into the harbor. Beaches closed due to the amount of human feces washing up on shore; fishermen threw back fish with tumors. In a crushing blow, Presidential candidate George H.W. Bush criticized his opponent, Massachusetts Governor Michael Dukakis during the 1988 presidential race for overseeing "the filthiest harbor in America."[8]

What had happened?

A number of things that the Nut Islanders did suggest that the very strength of their connections to each other and to the plant may have constrained their ability to take effective action. In their eyes, they were heroic outcasts joining together to do whatever had to be done to keep the plant operating. They were "[h]olding an old sewer plant together with chewing gum and baling wire" and having the time of their lives while they were doing it.[9]

The Nut Islanders were not bad people. On the contrary, they were diligent, hard-working individuals, who—with the best of intentions—undertook actions that were diametrically opposed to their organization's mission to create safe and clean water in Boston Harbor.

What went wrong?

The answer has to do with the *structure* of the Nut Island network.

Balancing Act

In the last chapter, we touched upon the idea that our networks are embedded in larger networks of relationships that can include whole organizations, industries, communities, and societies. Your position in these larger networks offers opportunities for action as well as constraints upon your behavior. Knowing your network position helps you understand how the network can benefit you and also how it can work against you. It explains why the Nut Islanders loved their jobs and also why they ran into trouble.

If your network isn't supporting *your* professional goals, you may need to change your network position.

To understand your network position, you have to look at the structure of your relationships *and* the structure of the relationships of the people to whom you are connected. Ask yourself, *Are the people in my network connected to each other?*

Social scientists have long known that we act differently if our friends are friends with each other than we do if they are not. Early observers of friendship patterns among elementary school-age children noted that friends who had a friend in common were much more likely to maintain their friendships. In contrast, when one child had friendships with two different children, neither of whom were friends with each other, the relationships soon changed so that either all three children became friends or only two remained friends.[10] We seek what researchers call *structural balance* in our relationships.

Structural balance among three people happens when people share similar feelings towards each other. Balanced relationships tend to stay balanced. We like to like the people our friends like and we usually dislike the people our friends dislike. It is very uncomfortable for us to dislike our friends' friends or to like our friends' enemies. In fact, if two of our friends dislike each other, we are likely to either try to repair the negative relationship to achieve balance or, if that fails, begin to like one of our friends less. Researchers have gone so far as to call the relationship pattern in which a person has two friends who are either not friends or who are downright enemies, the "forbidden" triangle.[11]

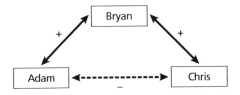

The "forbidden" triangle.

So strong is the urge to maintain structural balance that we often perceive balanced connections when those connections don't exist! A number of studies show that when asked to report the relationships among our friends and colleagues, we are likely to see positive relationships where none exist.[12] Even when asked to simply memorize a picture of someone else's network, we are far more likely to mistakenly "remember" balanced relationships than we are to forget existing ones. For some people, this tendency—often referred to as a *need for closure*—is particularly high, making it extremely difficult for them to accurately perceive their own or their organizations' network.[13]

The tendency to seek out balanced relationships makes us more likely to introduce our friends and colleagues to each other and to weaken relationships with people who are not friendly with other people in our network. Since we are all seeking structural balance, over time, most organizational or community networks develop tight clusters of interconnected people with few relationships between clusters, a pattern that looks like this:

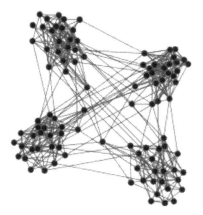

Notice the many clusters of balanced relationships and how they are relatively unconnected to each other. I call this pattern of clustering, *sticky rice*. In a sticky rice cluster, every person has a positive relationship with everyone—or almost everyone—else. The Nut Island plant was a particularly dramatic example of the sticky rice pattern, with some predictable results. Understanding sticky rice—and the extent to which your network resembles a sticky rice cluster—is your key to creating an effective network.

Sticky Rice!

The term *sticky rice* comes from a trip I took to Thailand and a tour guide who instructed us that when she called out *Sticky rice!*, we were all to gather around her, like a popular regional dish of the same name. Sticky rice means sticking together. Sticky rice grains cling together to form clumps or clusters that are more easily eaten by hand or chopstick. Sticky rice that doesn't cling with the other grains is harder to eat. Sticky rice is a great way to keep track of a tour group in a crowded city street. But as a professional networking strategy, sticky rice is a dead end.

Call it a clan, call it a network, call it a tribe, call it a family. Whatever you call it, whoever you are, you need one.

—Jane Howard[14]

Most of us—like the Nut Islanders—work and live almost entirely in sticky rice clusters. This embedded position is not only extremely common, it has deep roots in our human history and psyche.

To understand why, think about the first humans. They didn't have strong teeth or sharp claws or great speed with which to outrun prey. In the world they inhabited, they were decidedly not at the top of the food chain. To protect themselves, they gathered with other humans and, together, kept each other from harm. Even if a predator charged a large group, the group could disband in many directions, confusing the predator just long enough to allow at least some members to survive. These early human groups not only offered protection, they also provided food, shelter, mates, and help caring for offspring.

Even now, the perception that we might be in danger from illness, violence, or disaster, increases our desire to be with others. In one experimental study, individuals were asked to think about the emotional and physical aspects of their own death. The researchers reasoned that thinking about death would feel threatening. The individuals were then offered the opportunity to sit with a group of other people or by themselves. Compared to individuals who were asked to think about watching television, the individuals who thought about their mortality were much more likely to choose to sit with other people.[15]

Although many of us no longer face unpredictable and potentially deadly dangers every day, the desire to belong to a group has survived as one of our basic drives. Sticky rice clusters help us achieve that sense of safety and belonging. As a result, being embedded in a sticky rice cluster increases our feelings of validation, trust, and acceptance.[16] Sticky rice just plain feels good.

No wonder the Nut Islanders loved their work! Nut Island was one big sticky rice cluster.

Sticky Rice Is Good for You

Sticky rice offers profound and mostly positive effects on our health and material well-being.[17] Being embedded in a sticky rice network has been shown to reduce stress, depression, disease, and even poverty. Sticky rice clusters positively influence the onset, progression, and recovery from illness, including the common cold, cancer, HIV infection, cardiovascular diseases, and cardiovascular reactivity. One study of more than 12,000 French workers found that employees in sticky rice networks were nearly three times less likely to die when compared to colleagues not in sticky rice networks.[18] Another study of more than 16,000 individuals over 65 years old, tested over the course of six years, found that individuals with less densely connected networks showed significant decline in memory compared to individuals living in sticky rice clusters.[19] Sticky rice not only feels good, it's good for us.

Why do sticky rice networks have such a strong effect on our socioemotional and physical health? The answer has to do with the strength of connections within the cluster and the protective shield those connections form between our cluster and other sticky rice clusters.

Sticky Rice Is Strong

Inside the sticky rice cluster, relationships tend to be strong. Strong relationships are a great source of social support. The perceived availability of social support, especially emotional support, has direct effects on health. A number of years ago, cardio researchers noted that people were less likely to suffer from heart attacks and cardiovascular disease if they regularly ate meals with friends and family.[20] Similarly, a large Swedish study of people ages 75 and over concluded that dementia risk was lowest in those with a variety of satisfying contacts with friends and relatives.[21]

Today, many physicians encourage people, especially older people, to keep healthy by maintaining strong connections with friends, family, and community members. Strong relationships even support longevity. One meta-analytic study, which examined data from more than 300,000 people, found that a *lack* of strong relationships increased the risk of premature death from all causes by 50%—an effect on mortality risk roughly comparable to smoking up to fifteen cigarettes a day, and greater than obesity and physical inactivity![22] As Holt-Lunstad, one of the authors of the study noted, "We can all benefit from taking our relationships just as seriously for our health as we do other lifestyle factors."[23]

Members-Only Benefits

If you're in a sticky rice cluster, you reap all kinds of members-only benefits. For one thing, the interconnectedness of sticky rice networks means that information and resources circulate rapidly to members. Members quickly learn what resources are needed and easily mobilize to supply them. The

Nut Islanders, for example, rarely filed for overtime pay, although they put in thousands of hours of overtime. Claiming the extra time was even considered slightly shameful. They literally gave their most precious resource—time—to the cluster for free!

Members of a sticky rice cluster also benefit from their ability to help each other. They can rely upon each other. Because of their interwoven connections, it is relatively easy for one person in a sticky rice cluster to learn about the needs of someone else in the cluster. Individuals can even join forces to help or support one another. For example, if your friend Pat needs money to pay an unexpected medical bill, you can reach out to your mutual friends Darren and Clarence and suggest that the three of you pool together their money to give Pat the money she needs.

Being inside the protective shield of a closely linked network also means that everyone is likely to know about the actions of everyone else. If Pat asks Darren directly to lend her money, Darren will be more likely to lend her the money—even if he doesn't want to—because he knows that the way he responds to Pat's request has implications for his relationships with you and Clarence. You and Clarence may become upset with him if he doesn't help your friend Pat. You may even stop spending time with him. Conversely, Pat is more likely to pay Darren back because short-changing Darren is likely to negatively impact Pat's relationships with you and Clarence. You and Clarence may be less likely to lend Pat your own money if Pat doesn't pay Darren back.

Having friends in common means that Darren and Pat can trust each other because their common friends serve as guarantors. Knowing that their friends will find out about what happens between them makes them more likely to act positively toward each other and less likely to act negatively. This is why people who are embedded in a tightly knit web of relationships are more likely to receive help and, when they do, to receive greater levels of help than people in more loosely knit networks. Put another way, sticky rice networks are incubators of trust and cooperation. For people in frequent need of significant resources, a sticky rice network can be—quite literally—a lifesaver.

Suzanne Morrissey, a professor at Whitman College, knows this well. She studies low-income single-parent families. Increasingly shorter time limits and greater work requirements have made it harder and harder for low-income individuals to receive welfare, food stamps, and other benefits. As she notes, single moms with few resources have trouble making ends meet without their sticky rice networks. "They trade, they bargain, they strategize, they give each other daycare help, they share housing and food—women learn to strategize their way through all of these resources."[24] Without their sticky rice networks, they wouldn't survive.

Sticky Rice Is Comforting

The protective shield of the sticky rice network also works to buffer the negative effects of events *outside* of the sticky rice network, including the destructive effects of stress and negative emotions.[25] One study of more than 250 members of the Royal Canadian Mounted Police (Mounties) looked at the role of coworker support on the relationships between workplace anxiety, emotional exhaustion, and job performance.[26] Mounties regularly deal with many high-stress situations involving violent offenders, crime scenes, traffic accidents, victims of abuse and neglect, and fatalities, as well as public suspicion.[27] Over 80% of police officers report that they interact with angry and/or unpleasant individuals on a daily basis.[28]

Researchers asked the Mounties to report their levels of workplace anxiety and emotional exhaustion. They also asked the Mounties' co-workers the extent to which they provided social and emotional support to each Mountie. Lastly, they asked the Mounties' supervisors to rate their job performance. Not surprisingly, the researchers found that workplace anxiety led to emotional exhaustion which, in turn, negatively affected job performance. More surprising was the finding that social support weakened those links. Mounties whose co-workers gave them higher levels of support had *lower* levels of emotional exhaustion. In effect, social support reduced emotional exhaustion and, ultimately, improved job performance.[29]

In addition to negative events and relationships that arise outside the cluster, sticky rice networks also protect against negative relationships that arise *inside* the cluster. Given human nature, it is inevitable that conflicts will arise, even among friends. There will be times when even members of your sticky rice networks have a falling out. But in a sticky rice network, if one person starts to dislike another, a number of other relationships rapidly become affected. Imagine that two of your friends don't like each other. Suddenly, your relationships are unbalanced and you may even find yourself caught in a "forbidden" triangle. You will probably change your relationships to adjust, thereby causing another set of relationships in the sticky rice cluster to become unbalanced. In this way, one negative relationship has the potential to create a destructive ripple effect throughout your entire sticky rice network. It can even threaten the survival of the whole group. In order to maintain balanced relationships, friends—and friends of friends—will usually exert pressure on the disagreeing members to get along. A third party may step in to act as a mediator, arbitrator, or even judge in a particularly tense sticky rice relationship.

Sticky Rice and Friendship Go Together

All of these positive socioemotional outcomes, combined with the protective shield against negative socioemotional outcomes, make sticky rice networks a healthy way to build friendship and social groups. In fact, at least one study suggests that people who *don't* have sticky rice friendship groups have lower levels of emotional stability.[30]

Because members of sticky rice networks tend to act in ways that the group will accept—or at least not reject—sticky rice clusters can also reinforce healthy behavior. This increases the likelihood that healthy norms of behavior are adopted and unhealthy ones are abandoned, helping people who need to be safeguarded from negative behaviors. The success of groups such as Weight Watchers, Alcoholics Anonymous, and Gamblers Anonymous in helping their members avoid unhealthy behaviors and engage instead in healthier behaviors is a direct result of building, nurturing, and leveraging sticky rice properties.

Sticky rice networks can also control other types of negative behavior more directly. For example, the extent to which neighbors are willing to exert social control over deviant behavior plays an important role in preventing crime and delinquency.[31] A similar process might operate to prevent other forms of unhealthy behavior, such as adolescent smoking, drinking, and drug abuse. In *Bowling Alone: The Collapse and Revival of American Community*, author Robert Putnam observed that children benefit when their parents, teachers, and other community members form sticky rice networks. If a child is observed by one adult engaging in deviant behavior—such as skipping school or shoplifting in a neighborhood store—the other adults in the child's life can band together to more closely supervise and redirect the child's actions.

Sticky Rice Gets the Job Done

Sticky rice can also be an excellent way to get work done. People in a sticky rice cluster already have positive and often strong connections with each other so there is less friction to slow down work efforts. Knowing each other's ways and habits makes it easier to coordinate schedules. Knowing each other's strengths and weaknesses makes it easier to assign work appropriately. The Nut Islanders leveraged this sticky rice strength to work together efficiently and effectively. After the 1976 engine failure, they made sure that the engines never broke down again.

Sticky rice networks are a particularly good way to organize any group of people that needs to solve a complex problem without a clearly defined solution. Because people in clusters are motivated to help each other, they are more likely to share what they know or have with each other, expanding the pool of resources available to all. Having access to more perspectives, opinions, and information encourages team members to consider new ways of combining resources to solve problems.

Expertise is also more easily located and shared in sticky rice clusters. The likelihood of strong relationships increases the amount of encouragement and persistence in transferring information. Members work harder to transfer knowledge, especially when information is difficult to understand and may require detailed explanations. Instead of giving up at the first blank look, they'll draw on greater reserves of patience to repeat, explain, and repeat again.

Lastly, sticky rice networks heighten the efficiency of the decision-making process, by making it more likely that everyone will contribute to decision-making, will feel more committed to the final decision, and will be more likely to implement the final decision. Increases in coordination, knowledge-sharing, and decision-making explain why a meta-analysis of 37 studies of teams in real organizations found that sticky rice teams attain their goals better and are more committed to staying together.[32]

Even entrepreneurs benefit from being in sticky rice teams, contradicting the image of the entrepreneur as "lone wolf." Although slightly more than half of all ventures in the United States are founded by single individuals, entrepreneurs who work in teams are more likely to be successful than entrepreneurs who found ventures alone. Firms founded by more than one individual have higher revenue and are more profitable than similar firms founded by single individuals.[33]

But ... Sticky Rice Isn't All Good

Being embedded in a sticky rice cluster can feel great but it has its downsides, too. Paradoxically, the very thing that makes sticky rice relationships pleasant and productive is the very thing that limits their usefulness in other ways. On the one hand, members of sticky rice networks look out for each other. But looking out for each other is another way of saying that members are constantly being monitored. If someone threatens a relationship in the network, pressure may be applied to repair the relationship. This has the desired result of reducing destructive conflict and maintaining status quo. But it also can have the *un*desired result of reducing *productive* conflict and limiting innovation. Disagreement is perceived as so threatening that it is squelched before it can ever be expressed.

Some credit lack of productive conflict with one of the largest automobile recalls in history—the 2014 recall of 17.1 million cars by auto manufacturing giant, General Motors. The origins of the recall date back to the late 1990s, when GM safety engineers became aware that some of their cars had major defects, including issues with gasoline leaks, steering linkage, and most problematically, faulty ignition switches. In response to customer complaints that the old switches "felt cheap," the company had manufactured new switches with a more substantial mechanical feel. But the new switches sometimes unexpectedly slipped out of position, causing engines to stall. That shut off the power steering—making the cars harder to control—and disabled air bags.

Despite knowing about this defect and a rising death toll—13 deaths according to GM but other estimates put the count nearer to 100—no action was taken. The company's sticky rice culture didn't allow for disagreement. Years later, former GM Manager Bill McAleer simply described it this way,

> In 1997 something happened internally in GM where no problem could be admitted. Whether it was safety or any kind of problem. We couldn't have a problem. That's what happened with the ignition switch. People knew there was a problem, but problems were not acceptable. They just ignored it.[34]

In GM's case, avoiding conflict literally cost lives.

Another major downside of being in a sticky rice cluster is the tendency for members to see the world through a similar lens. This generates a subculture in which the same beliefs, values, and standards of what is considered appropriate behavior are widely shared and agreed upon. Sticky rice clusters may even develop their own slang or shorthand. These tendencies have the desired result of easing social interaction—people in sticky rice clusters know that they can interact without worrying about offending each other. Everyone interprets what is said in the "right" way. But being surrounded by people who see the world in the same way can also have the undesired result of shutting out new ideas and perspectives.

When everyone we know thinks like we do, we can fall prey to the *echo chamber* effect in which we all come up with the same ideas—not necessarily because the ideas are good but because we all approach the same problems the same way and to turn to the same information sources when problem-solving. When we share our conclusions with others in the sticky rice cluster we receive further support regarding our conclusions because everyone else has reached a similar conclusion. If everyone is in agreement, then the idea must be good, right? Receiving support from others in the sticky rice cluster can trigger a cognitive lock-in[35] that further isolates us from new or contradictory information. Living in sticky rice networks means that we are likely to miss out on the opportunity to consider new ideas and conflicting points of view.

The echo chamber effect might explain what happened on Nut Island. Nut Islanders never challenged the idea that their job was to keep the plant running—at all costs!—and, because they believed that they couldn't count on headquarters to help them out, that they had to do everything themselves. Living inside this echo chamber led them to undertake a number of actions that don't make sense from an outsider's perspective.

For example, because of a flaw in the plant's design, the Nut Island aeration tanks often became choked with grit—the sand, dirt, and assorted muck that inevitably finds its way into wastewater—especially if the inflow of sewage exceeded a certain volume. Too much grit and the tanks would stop working. The plant operators didn't even consider reporting the problem to headquarters. Instead, they dealt with the problem by limiting inflow to what they considered a reasonable level and diverting the excess—raw, untreated sewage!—directly into the harbor.

When inflows were particularly heavy, even the sewage that streamed through the plant could not be fully treated by the aging equipment. Again—instead of reporting the problem or looking at root causes—Nut Island plant operators did whatever they had to do to keep the plant running. They dealt with this particular issue by adding massive amounts of chlorine to some of the wastewater before piping it out to sea. While the chlorine eliminated some pathogens in the wastewater, it is also a known environmental contaminant that kills marine life, depletes marine oxygen supplies, and harms fragile shore ecosystems.

Among the plant's many increasingly outdated pieces of machinery equipment were the pumps that pulled fecal matter and other solids into digester tanks. Inside the tanks, bacteria were added to eliminate pathogens, reduce volume, and render the resulting sludge safe for release into the harbor. Years of patchwork maintenance had degraded the pumps but instead of asking headquarters to replace them, the Nut Islanders took matters into their own hands. Their fix: lubricating the machinery with large amounts of oil. A large percentage of this oil worked its way into the digester tanks and, from there, was released directly into the harbor. Many scientists believe that the disproportionately high concentration of oil in Boston Harbor sediments is a likely result of this practice.[36]

The Nut Islanders did not set out to pollute the harbor. Indeed, by all accounts, they were highly committed to the plant and its mission. But the same network structure that promoted camaraderie, workplace efficiency, and a deep trust in each other also promoted a way of looking at problems from the same perspective. When everyone in a sticky rice cluster "knows" that keeping the plant running is top priority—because that's what keeps the harbor clean!—no one even thinks to question if keeping the plant running—at all costs—might have a downside, such as polluting the very water the plant is meant to make clean.

Another disadvantage of being embedded in a sticky rice cluster is that the group norms that facilitate healthy or positive behavior can also reinforce *un*healthy or negative behaviors. Research on condom use, for instance, has found that individuals in more tightly connected networks are *less* likely to have sexual partners willing to use condoms.[37] Similarly, a large-scale study of villagers in rural India—where the custom of open defecation is the cause of many diseases—found that individuals in more connected networks were *less* likely to change their defecation habits by becoming latrine owners than were individuals in less constrained networks.[38] Even sticky rice teams can adopt negative behavioral norms, such as working such consistently long hours that members become ill as a result of sleep deprivation.

The stickiness of sticky rice clusters also encourages social exclusion, the dark side of stickiness. Because, of course, belonging to a group of people like us means excluding people who are *not* like us.

The more tightly knit the group, the more fiercely it defines and defends its borders. Although it might be tempting to think that social exclusion is something that is only practiced by the sticky rice cluster of mean girls in high school, the truth is that most groups—including work groups—protect their shared identity and structural integrity by excluding outsiders. According to a nationwide 2013 survey of 3000 full-time U.S. workers, 43% of workers say their office includes sticky rice clusters of co-workers who socialize during and after work, and often exclude others from participating.[39] Separate studies have found that as many as two-thirds of employees report experiencing some form of social exclusion at work.[40]

These startling statistics are problematic because social exclusion is not only a painful emotional experience, it has real and costly consequences for both individuals and organizations. For example, believing oneself to be excluded from forming certain relationships at work impairs time management skills and ability to delay gratification.[41] Social exclusion is also associated with greater levels of organizational deviance, lower job performance, greater intention to quit, and greater turnover.[42] A February 2014 survey by BambooHR of roughly 300 people who had quit their job within six months of starting it, found that 17% said "a friendly smile or helpful co-worker would have made all the difference," 12% wanted to be "recognized for [their] unique contributions," and 9% wanted more attention from the "manager and co-workers."[43]

And the effects of exclusion are contagious. A study led by University of Chicago professor John T. Cacioppo explored how exclusion and loneliness ripple through a network.

> We detected an extraordinary pattern at the edge of the social network. On the periphery, people have fewer friends, which makes them lonely, but it also drives them to cut the few ties that they have left. But before they do, they tend to transmit the same feeling of loneliness to their remaining friends, starting the cycle anew. These reinforcing effects mean that our social fabric and fray at the edges, like a thread that comes loose at the end of a crocheted sweater.[44]

Because sticky rice bonds strengthen group boundaries, they can intensify the amount and level of social exclusion in the workplace. In the case of the Nut Islanders, this meant excluding anyone from headquarters.

Finally, sticky rice encourages *relational inertia* because sticky rice bonds are, well, *sticky*. Like a spider's web, they can keep us bound far longer than we should be. The fact that sticky rice networks feel so good reduces the motivation to reach out to new individuals. Relationships stagnate. Social bonds—and especially those embedded in common third parties—create feelings of familiarity and comfort that can prevent us from expanding our networks. The ease of cooperation with familiar partners, and the uncertainty associated with the formation of new relationships, makes us less likely to initiate and consolidate new relationships. This is true even when we've outgrown our relationships. Relational inertia can leave us trapped like flies in our own net.[45]

To Recap...

Sticky rice clusters can help us achieve certain professional and personal goals. Teams that have sticky rice characteristics generally outperform teams that do not. Physically and mentally, we also seem to benefit if our family or core affinity groups are sticky rice clusters. The Nut Island plant workers loved their work "family." But if you want to increase your individual performance at work, and especially if you want to innovate, you may have to step out of some of your sticky rice clusters and into a different network position. In the next chapter, we'll take a closer look at the most important network position that you can occupy in your professional network.

Reflection Questions

Are there any sticky rice clusters in your professional network?

Are the sticky rice clusters in your professional network furthering your professional goals or are they holding you back?

4

Building Bridges

SELF-ASSESSMENT SNAPSHOT

Complete the *Professional Support Network Exercise* in the Toolbox at the end of this book. Look at the people in your professional support network and answer the following questions.

1. Do most of the people in your professional support network know each other reasonably well?
2. Are most of the people with whom you are close, also close with each other?
3. Do you have clusters of people in your professional network who know each other reasonably well but who don't know members of other clusters?
4. How many sticky rice clusters are in your professional support network?

Museum Tour[1]

Meet Suzanna Taverne. In April of 1999, "whiz-kid" Taverne became the managing director of the British Museum (BM). When the call came from the headhunters, Taverne knew she wanted the job. She was delighted to become managing director but was well aware of the task ahead: "I knew what I was getting myself into. There was a fair amount of apprehension as well as excitement."[2]

Taverne's hire was an effort by the board of trustees to halt the dramatic decline of the BM, which was in debt and out of fashion. Founded with a mandate to admit "all studious and curious persons both native and foreign born," the BM is the first publicly funded institution of its kind in the world. By the time Taverne took over, its original collection of 70,000 objects had grown to nearly seven million artifacts, rivaling that of other top museums in New York, Paris, and St. Petersburg. But unlike these other museums, which focused their collections on paintings—especially European paintings—the BM's holdings included a broad range of artifacts, such as coins, statues, pottery, and other treasures. Moreover, only a small part of the collection was British because many items had been obtained during Britain's imperial days, often under dubious circumstances.

In 1999, the BM was in big trouble. Despite being the world's second biggest museum publisher, the BM was broke. In 1996-97 alone, it ran up a deficit of £48,000. A damning report, commissioned by the board, criticized the BM's management, the lack of accountability, and the pressing need to balance the books. Perhaps worst of all, it was widely described as one of the least user-friendly museums in the world.

> It is a national shame that the British Museum, the repository of countless treasures accumulated from everywhere on earth, is still regarded by many as dusty, irrelevant and dull.[3]

Suzanna Taverne was an executive with high-level experience in finance, marketing, and managing change. Her no-nonsense approach to management seemed to be exactly what was needed to save the 177-year-old museum. While her co-director, Robert Anderson—a former curator at the BM—assumed responsibility for all curatorial issues, Taverne's mandate was to make the BM financially viable.

Once in office at the BM, Taverne moved swiftly. She announced plans to reorganize jobs, and created new restaurant facilities and information centers. She introduced a system of personal development, training, appraisal, and rewards. Warders, who in the past were forbidden by their contracts to speak to visitors, were given new uniforms and told to act friendlier. She boosted revenues by introducing charges for special exhibitions, extending opening hours ten hours, and instituting other revenue sources such as shops.

By all accounts, Taverne made significant progress in the very areas that the board of trustees had identified as critical to the BM's success. She was widely credited with turning around the museum's finances and overseeing a 50% rise in visitors. She oversaw the completion—on time and on budget!—of the spectacular Great Court conversion, the largest covered public square in Europe. Taverne attracted several high-end sponsors who contributed generously to the BM. Under her directorship, the BM was no longer the worst-run museum in Britain.

At the end of her first year, and buoyed by her success, Taverne confidently approached the board of trustees and suggested that the museum appoint a single director with control over both management and curatorial matters. She submitted herself to be that person. The board agreed that the museum needed a single director. But they stipulated that the director had to be a curator and a scholar, a requirement that essentially forced Taverne—who was neither a curator nor a scholar—to resign.

Taverne was stunned.

Taverne had demonstrated remarkable achievements in her short time at the BM, despite facing significant challenges. She was bright, hard-working, and highly accomplished. Taverne fully expected that these qualities, which had served her so well earlier in her career, would continue to serve her well in her new position at the BM.

What happened?

To understand what happened to Taverne, let's fast-forward two years to 2002 and compare her tenure at the BM with that of the new incoming Director, Neil MacGregor. In 2002, despite the efforts of Taverne and the subsequent interim director, the BM was still in dire financial straits. The revenue boost provided by the spectacular Great Court conversion was being wiped out by a catastrophic drop in foreign visitors because of the outbreak of foot and mouth disease, and the September 11 attack. BM's staff, including curators, needed to be cut by nearly 15%. Staff morale was low. Even worse, public approval was at an all-time low. Some felt that the museum's exhibits had become too crassly commercial. One newspaper went so far as to say that the museum was "in danger of selling its soul."[4] As one senior museum insider noted, the directorship would be "sheer hell for whoever gets it."[5]

Enter Neil MacGregor. Unlike Taverne, MacGregor did not come from a commercial background. He had little experience or expertise with the financial aspects of museums. Like Taverne, MacGregor did not have the "high level of curatorial knowledge and scholarly interest" that many felt were necessary for someone who was going to head the curatorial aspects of the museum.[6]

Yet, within six years—and during a period of enormous financial upheaval—visitor numbers reached record highs, the financial strains that the BM had been under had been nearly lifted, a BBC radio show about BM artifacts was a wild success, and the BM was rated the most desirable tourist attraction in the United Kingdom.[7]

Why did MacGregor succeed and Taverne did not?

The answer lies in the structure of their networks.

Positioned for Success

The professional networks of MacGregor and Taverne were structured very differently, and those structures introduced crucial differences in social capital. Here is a simplified graphic depiction of their networks. The connections represent strong positive working relationships.

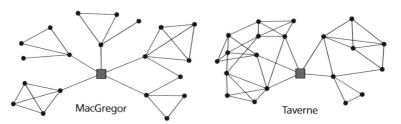

As you can see, both MacGregor and Taverne know the same number of people (5) and *their* connections know the same number of people (15). But look at how those people are connected to each other. Most of the people in Taverne's network fall more or less into two sticky rice clusters. In contrast, MacGregors's network has five distinct sticky rice clusters, almost of all which needed to go "through" MacGregor to get to one another. In other words, although the number of people in MacGregor's network was the same as the number of people in Taverne's network, the network structure was completely different.

And this is the answer to the puzzle of MacGregor's success and Taverne's dead end. MacGregor was a bridge between sticky rice clusters and Taverne was not.

Recall that the BM had an unusually large and diverse collection. The collection was segmented into different departments including, for example, Greek and Roman antiquities. Over time, the different collections and their associated staff had become clustered into tight-knit groups, each focusing on their department only. One curator described the clusters as "12 different Tuscan hill towns" with their own allegiances and ambitions.[8] The heads of these sticky rice departments were called the Keepers. Collaboration within clusters was common but collaboration between clusters was infrequent. In some cases, departments openly competed against each other for resources. In other words, like most organizations, the internal network of the BM was characterized by sticky rice clusters.

Taverne's social capital among the academic staff was weak. Although Taverne interacted occasionally with the Keepers in the course of her work, she wasn't benefitting from those connections. As far as the curators were concerned, Taverne's commercial background was already a strike against her. They were horrified by her brisk management style and Armani suits. She alienated the curators on her first day by admitting "art and antiquities have not been a particular passion."[9] Before she left, she made plain the animosity between herself and the Keepers, saying,

> There is this priesthood of curators, who look after the relics. There's this notion that only they can be the intermediaries between the relics and the public.... Anybody on the curatorial side was wary of me. If you are not a creative person, you're a philistine.[10]

Taverne's reputation was likely further damaged by her immediary with the curators, Robert Anderson. In 1999, Taverne shared the Directorship with Anderson, who was responsible for BM's curatorial matters. Anderson had been a Keeper, too, and was comfortable with the way the organization had traditionally operated. Taverne's relationship with Anderson was an unprecedented and uncomfortable arrangement. A reporter for *The Guardian* described a joint interview with the co-Directors:

> Sitting beside each other, Anderson and Taverne certainly seem to embody the culture clash. She: a 39-year-old veteran of the corporate arena and former "beautiful person" of Oxford, decked in navy-blue suit and a whizzy hair do. He: a 54-year-old curator with a portly figure and fly-away hair, who looks as if he might at any moment pronounce that "happiness is a cigar called Hamlet."[11]

For the most part, Taverne was content to let Anderson deal directly with the Keepers while she maintained an indirect connection to them. But Anderson was hardly Taverne's biggest fan. In fact, he went so far as to openly advocate for a scholar to fill the Director position, a decision which would—and did!—block Taverne's eligibility for the position.[12] It is easy to imagine he shared his unfavorable opinions about Taverne in his interactions with the other Keepers

In contrast, right from the beginning, MacGregor built relationships with the curatorial staff. He openly expressed his lifelong love with civilization's most exquisite objects. As he said, "I do love the things. They are so fascinating and so vulnerable."[13] In 2007, a journalist who followed MacGregor for a few months shared the following story:

> One morning I join MacGregor for his early morning walk around the museum. He does this every day, to talk to staff about their work before the public swarm in. . . . As well as the early morning walkthroughs, he hosts a breakfast open to all staff every Tuesday where the work of the museum is discussed.[14]

In addition to forming personal relationships with at least a few members in each of the curatorial fiefdoms, by highlighting their shared interest in historical art and objects, MacGregor fused the 12 departments into nine. Despite some initial grumbling, the curators became more comfortable working with each other. They even started referring to the BM as "the Collection" in the singular.[15] This was all the more remarkable in that during this time MacGregor eliminated nearly 10% of the curatorial staff.

But it was in his external network that MacGregor really defined his tenure at BM and distinguished it from Taverne's. Almost immediately upon assuming the Directorship role, MacGregor began globe-trotting, spending roughly 20% of his time traveling. In addition to making the usual visits to museums in Paris, Amsterdam, and Berlin, he formed personal relationships with curators and political figures in countries that did not always enjoy warm relationships with the west, such as Iran, China, Kenya, and Chile. Some of them were encouraged to loan objects to BM exhibits, such as *Museum of the Mind: Art and Memory in World Cultures*. In turn, the BM contributed to exhibitions in other countries. In 2005, for example, the BM loaned Nairobi 150 African objects for an exhibition on Kenya in the context of its surrounding cultures.

In contrast, Taverne focused her efforts on BM's internal matters. She streamlined departments and instituted internal policies to cut down waste. She worked closely with the board of trustees and traveled frequently to

Parliament to address legislation on critical museum matters, including the debate over museum fees and government funding. Instead of building or strengthening her relationships with the Keepers, she promoted exhibitions that she thought would appeal to the public. She viewed her role as "whip."

MacGregor saw his role as that of cultural ambassador and bridge-builder. His network included decision-makers who represented a wide range of cultures, occupations, and political leanings. It was MacGregor who took action when looters broke into the unguarded Baghdad Museum in 2003. A reporter described what MacGregor did when he heard the news.

> He flew back the following day, a Sunday, and drove straight from Heathrow airport to Bloomsbury. He rang the Prime Minister and got tanks—American ones—deployed in front of the Baghdad Museum, and secured an anonymous benefactor to fund a rescue mission. John Curtis, the museum's Near East curator, rang friends in Iraq for detailed information, and MacGregor used his reports to mobilise French, German, Italian, Russian and American scholars and get United Nations support.[16]

Bridge-Builders Do Better

People with a network structured like MacGregor usually outperform people with a network structured like Taverne. In fact, if you've ever wondered why some people seem to get ahead faster than others—even though they're no smarter or better at their jobs than other people—it may be because they—like MacGregor—are *bridge-builders*. *Bridge-builders* create bridges between sticky rice clusters. Not only do they create the bridge, they *are* the bridge.

Decades of research have established the enormous professional advantages gained by bridge-builders. To paraphrase University of Chicago sociologist Ron Burt, "Simply put, bridge-builders do better."[17] Compared to people embedded in sticky rice clusters, bridge-builders get hired sooner, receive more favorable performance ratings, get promoted faster, make more money, are more likely to be identified as top talent by the organizations in which they work, and are more likely to influence others in their organization with their opinions.[18] In one study of bridge-builders in a financial institution, bridge-builders—with the same level of education and experience—were 40% more likely than non-bridge-builders to be promoted![19] More than half of the predicted differences in career success were explained by the extent to which a person was a bridge-builder, far exceeding the impact of any other predictor.

Bridge-builders are also more likely to come up with new ideas, less likely to have their ideas rejected by others, and more likely to have their ideas evaluated as valuable.[20] Even when they don't come up with the idea, they are more likely to influence others toward taking strategic action. One study of change initiatives by researchers Julie Battilana and Tiziana Casciaro found that managers responsible for initiating and attempting to implement change initiatives were significantly more likely to successfully implement major change initiatives when they were bridge-builders.[21]

Okay, so now we know that bridge-builders do better and that they connect sticky rice clusters to each other. But *why* is being that connection between sticky rice clusters an advantage for bridge-builders?

Bridge-builders do better because they are *positioned* to do better. The bridging position is powerful for four reasons. Compared to other people, bridge-builders:

1. Get *new* information faster.
2. Get more *diverse* information.
3. Have more *control* over how information gets shared.
4. Can build new bridges more easily.

Bridge-builders get new information faster. Because the bridge-builder is connected to multiple sticky rice clusters who are not otherwise connected to each other, if something new and interesting happens in any one of the clusters, the bridge-builder will hear about it before someone in another cluster does.

Receiving new information before other people can be very useful. If you have the latest information at your fingertips, you have an edge in innovation because you are more likely to be aware of recent and relevant advances in technology, consumer tastes, and available markets. Bridge-builders can also use new information to more quickly solve problems or make higher quality decisions.

But one of the biggest benefits of getting new information first is that, by definition, other people don't have that information. And what we don't have, we want. As the Scottish philosopher and economist Adam Smith noted nearly 150 years ago "...the merit of an object, which is in any degree either useful or beautiful, is greatly enhanced by its scarcity."[22]

Scarcity increases value. People who possess things of value have power over people who want them. Bridge-builders increase their power by having the opportunity to introduce the new information to other sticky rice clusters. Having new information can give bridge-builders higher status. If you are a bridge-builder, having new information can also make you rich because other people—including employers!—will pay a lot to get access to what you know.

Having access to new information may explain the high status of river boat captains along the Mekong river. College of William & Mary Professor of Marketing Don Rahtz studies quality of life in southeast Asia, especially among the rural villages that populate the banks of the Mekong river in Laos. In a country with few roads and few people who can afford cars, the river functions as the major highway. Slow boats, often beautifully constructed of teak with bows colorfully painted with eyes to ward off river devils, traverse the brown waters of the Mekong, carrying passengers and goods from village to village. Each boat has a captain who navigates the waterways. Rahtz explained why these river boat captains have such high prestige in these communities.

> Every day, river boat captains travel up and down the Mekong river, stopping at villages along the way. At each place, river boat captains are welcomed and fed, even if the villagers themselves have to go without. The captain sits down with the men of the village who offer him food and beer, maybe a smoke. As they sit, the captain tells the men gossip and news from the previous village. Maybe this one is getting married or that one lost his boat. He might also bring news from the bigger towns about political developments or opportunities for work. Before he leaves, the men tell the river boat captain the news from their village. Everybody knows the river captains. If anyone wants to know what's happening on the Mekong, their best source of information is the local river boat captain.[23]

Bridge-builders get more diverse information. They receive more diverse information than other people because of another property of sticky rice clusters and that is *redundancy*. By definition, members of a sticky rice cluster are connected to each other. That means whatever one of them knows is likely to be known by most of them. Chances are that tapping the knowledge base of any one person in the cluster will give you the same information as tapping the knowledge base of any another person in the cluster. They are—in a purely theoretical way, of course—*redundant* information sources.

Redundancy doesn't just mean knowing the same facts, such as a particular baseball player's statistics or a particular job opportunity. It also means sharing the same worldview.

Members of sticky rice clusters see the world the same way because they share similar values, preferences, and interests. Not only do they speak the same "language," they also reference the same cultural symbols and rely upon the same sources for information.

Redundancy might explain the deepening bipartisan political rift in the United States. A 2015 Pew Research Center study found that 61% of online Millenials report getting political news on Facebook in a given week and only 37% get their news from local television news programs. In contrast, 60% of online Baby Boomers say that they get their political news from local television and only 39% get their political news from Facebook.[24] Within a sticky rice cluster the news sources might be even more narrowly determined by Facebook likes, tweets and retweets, and emailed articles/videos on the one hand, and by in-person conversations, local newspaper articles, and radio shows on the other. In the world of "alternative facts," it should come as no surprise that what we believe depends heavily upon where we get our information.

This is why, if you sit down with one member of a sticky rice cluster to talk about recent events and then sit down with another member from the same cluster, you are likely to hear a lot of the same news stories. The people you talk with probably don't realize that they're accessing the same information. They might not even realize that they see things similarly because they're using the same lens through which to see the world.

And this is another reason why bridge-builders have greater access to diverse information.

Within each sticky rice cluster, everyone is more similar to each other than they are to people not in the cluster. So, although members of the *same* cluster may be redundant in terms of accessing that cluster's information, each member will have very different information than members of *other* sticky rice networks. If you have access to different sticky rice clusters, you have access to more diverse information and more diverse ways of viewing the world.

Why is having access to information from different sticky rice clusters an advantage? After all, accessing divergent information is sure to be unsettling. You could never be completely sure about anything. How would you know if you were approaching a problem the *right* way if you also know that people in different clusters approach similar problems differently? Besides, why bother to approach an accounting problem using the perspective of your colleagues in marketing? Surely, accountants know more about how to fix their problems than marketers?

It turns out, the advantages are many. Let's look closer at problem-solving.

Because of their position in a network, bridge-builders are in a better position to apply an approach or solution developed in one cluster to a problem confronting another cluster. Being able to apply knowledge from one cluster to a problem confronting another may explain the findings of an intriguing study on open and distributed innovation.[25] Researchers analyzed 166 online science challenges involving over 12,000 scientists. In the challenges, individual scientists competed against one another to solve science problems for cash prizes. The problems were posted by companies from a wide range of industries including aerospace, agrochemicals, biotechnology, chemicals, consumer products, and pharmaceuticals. Most of the scientists who competed in the contests had considerable training in their field of expertise. However, the study found that the people who submitted *winning* solutions were much more likely than people who submitted non-winning solutions to have a very *different* field of expertise than the focal field of the problem.

Most pointedly, the study found that nearly three-quarters of winning problem-solvers stated that their submissions were partially or fully based on solutions developed previously by themselves or people in *their* field of expertise. In other words, they looked at the problem from the perspective of their field and then successfully applied what they knew from their field to a problem in a different field. In one instance, an aerospace physicist, a small agribusiness owner, a transdermal drug delivery specialist, and an industrial scientist all submitted winning solutions to the same scientific challenge of identifying a food-grade polymer delivery system. All four submissions successfully met the required challenge by using very different approaches to the problem—approaches that were well-known within the problem-solvers field of expertise but were unknown by the firms seeking help with their scientific challenges.

Bridge-builders can also synthesize information from multiple clusters to develop new solutions. Many top chefs, for example, are bridge-builders across different sticky rice cultures and their cuisines. They take ideas from each cluster and combine them in new and innovative ways. "I'm just doing what is natural to me," said Preeti Mistry of Juhu Beach Club in Oakland, California. Mistry is Indian by heritage but spent her childhood in Ohio before moving to San Francisco in her late teens. Her specialties include a ghee-grilled Bombay sandwich—filled with Jack cheese, chaat masala, pickled onions, Chiogga beets and Yukon Gold potatoes—that is a mix of modern Mumbai, California cuisine, and Midwestern comfort food.[26]

Bridge-builders have more control over how information gets shared. The third advantage of a bridge-builder is the ability to control how, when, and even if information that is circulating in one cluster gets shared with people in another cluster. Because the bridge-builder is connected to people who aren't connected to each other, any information that is shared between the two clusters must go through the bridge-builder, like water goes through one pipe to reach another. By virtue of the ability to open or close pipes between clusters, if you're a bridge-builder, you control the flow of information.

Imagine this scenario. Two sticky-rice villages, live on opposite sides of a river and, you, the bridge-builder control the bridge that traverses the river. In order for anyone in Village A to share information with someone in Village B, the information must go through you.

The first choice that you have is whether or not to carry or transfer the information across at all. Perhaps it is to your benefit not to transfer the information. For example, Village A might have a surplus of corn in a year that Village B has a deficit. Village A might be willing to sell their corn at a very cheap price but if you don't share that information with Village B, Village B might be willing to purchase corn at a very high price. So, now you have the option to purchase corn from Village A at a low price and sell it at high price to Village B, thereby turning a handsome profit.

You can also use your position to benefit from competition between the two villages. Perhaps you make it known that you are willing to sell your boat to one of the villages. The villages might compete to get the boat. Village A might offer 100 florins for the boat. But because their communication must go through you, you are in a position to distort or even lie about the bidding price of the other village. You may tell Village B that the other village is offering 500 florins for the boat, hoping to encourage Village B to increase their offer.

By the same token, it could be that each village would like to create a shared marketplace, with each village exchanging goods directly with the other. They may each communicate that desire to you. But you don't want to lose your role as powerful middleman. So to prevent the villagers from talking directly to each other, you keep that information to yourself. By hoarding information, you come out on top. If you really want to be devious, you could go so far as to distort information to protect your position—*Yeah, they were hopping mad but I was able to talk them out of attacking your village.* Many rising stars who benefit from occupying bridge-building roles in organizations are reluctant to give them up, sometimes purposefully causing bottlenecks and rupturing collaboration efforts in order to maintain their advantage.

The previous examples depict the bridge-builder as a greedy, self-interested negotiator who engages in networking behavior for personal benefit to the detriment of other people. This is certainly one way that the bridge-builder role can be enacted. In truth, it can be a very profitable short-term networking strategy. But it is a lousy long-term networking strategy. Sooner or later, someone in one of the villages will find out what you are doing and you may find, to your dismay, that you have burnt your bridges.

Further, because people communicate through the bridge-builder, bridge-builders have the opportunity to adjust their image with each contact. A bridge-builder can, for example, demonstrate her problem-solving skills to her colleague in marketing, her creativity to her colleague in advertising, her loyalty to the firm to her colleague in production, and her awareness of technical specifications to her colleague in R & D. Exposing a diverse set of people to a variety of personal and professional strengths explains why having more diverse contacts leads others to seek you out when new opportunities arise.[27]

Bridge-builders can build bridges more easily. There's a final way in which bridge-builders can benefit from their position and that is by connecting people *when it adds value to both parties to do so.* If you are a bridge-builder, you are in a position to understand the wants, needs, and resources available in different sticky rice clusters. From your vantage point, you might realize that there may be value in introducing a person from cluster A to a person from cluster B. Perhaps you know that a farmer in Village A—we'll call him Farmer A—has a pig farm that is overrun with a type of insect that chickens love to eat. You also know that a farmer in cluster B—we'll call her Farmer B—raises chickens but is unable to realize a profit because chicken feed is so costly. By introducing the two farmers to each other, you help Farmer A find an easy way to get rid of his pest problem and Farmer B find a low-cost way to feed her chickens. Moreover, by providing value to both farmers, you increase your own prestige and perceived value, not only in the eyes of the two farmers but also among the other people in their sticky rice clusters who will learn about the interaction. By acting as a catalyst for meaningful connection, you gain value *and* create value for others.

Note that bridge-builders only gain when making an introduction that adds value to *both* people. When the introduction brings value to only one person, the bridge-builder is essentially asking one person for a favor. When James asks Kate to interview his friend's job-seeking husband, Bill, for an open position, the introduction adds value to both parties when Bill is well-qualified for the job and a good fit for Kate's company. But the situation is quite different if Bill is either technically unqualified for the job or is a poor fit for the company. While getting Bill an interview may temporarily increase James's value to Bill (and, indirectly, Bill's spouse), it is unlikely to increase his value to Kate and—given that a hire is unlikely—it is also likely to decrease his value to Bill and his spouse in the long run. Most likely, it will result in wasted time for both parties and a *decreased* perception of the bridge-builder's value.

By the way, bridge-builders that connect two people to each other are not necessarily throwing away their bridging advantage. In truth, there's room for more than one person on the bridge. For the most part, sticky rice clusters are so focused on their own activities that they have little time—or inclination—to attend to the activities in other clusters. As long as the bridge is used by only a relatively small proportion of others, bridge-builders retain the benefits of their bridging position and can enhance personal prestige and value by inviting others into the bridge. Moreover, because the bridge-builder has strengthened her relationship with each person by adding value, the bridge-builder may gain even greater access to information available in each of the sticky rice clusters.

Building Bridges Is Hard Work

Despite the many benefits of bridge-builder networks, they are rare. In his book, *The Tipping Point*, Malcolm Gladwell estimates that true bridge-builders—he calls them *superconnectors*—number about one person in several thousand. Why? Why doesn't everyone become a bridge-builder? The answer: Because it isn't easy.

It's *hard* to be a bridge-builder.

The very qualities that make it easier for us to stay embedded in sticky rice clusters also make it harder for us to connect with people who are *not* in our sticky rice clusters. Meeting someone in another cluster can feel a little like being the new kid on the first day of school. Without a shared history or micro-culture, it is hard to know how to act. What if you're wearing the "wrong" clothes? What if you use the "wrong" word or phrase? It doesn't help to know that sooner or later you almost certainly <u>will</u> say the wrong thing. It's just not possible to understand all the quirks and nuances of a sticky rice culture as well as someone embedded in it.

And even as we are afraid of saying or doing the wrong thing, the people in the sticky rice cluster also view us with trepidation and uncertainty. Who is this stranger in our midst? Will the stranger harm us? Will they say and do things that reinforce their differences from us?

Even bridge-builders who have no problem forming relationships with people in different sticky rice clusters can run into trouble. If members of one cluster believe that they are very different from members of other clusters, they may view the bridge-builder suspiciously. *How could she be one of Us if she's also one of Them?* Sometimes they will pressure the bridge-builder—directly or indirectly—to behave more like members of their cluster or even to reject friendships with members in the other cluster. Caught in the middle this way, bridge-builders may feel conflicted about their loyalties and even their core identity. This tension can be very stressful. For example, in studies conducted among teenagers, bridge-builders had higher levels of social stress and lower self-esteem compared to teens embedded in sticky rice groups. This was true even when the bridge-builders were generally well-liked.[28]

Being a bridge-builder is further complicated by the path we took to get there. For many of us, being a bridge-builder is not something we *chose* to do. Instead, it is something that simply *happened to* us. Some of us become bridge-builders because of our race or gender, or because of what we do or like. Our preferences—while natural enough to us—can connect us to very different groups. Often without even realizing it, people develop a unique combination of relationships with people in different sticky rice clusters. Accidental bridge-builders might include bicyclists who love fine cars, female software engineers, and people who are multi-racial. Unintentionally, these people may find themselves occupying a bridge-building role between two or more sticky rice clusters.

Some people become bridge-builders as a function of unusual career trajectories. They might, for example, start out as an IT specialist and then take a position as a market analyst before moving into supply chain management. Dartmouth's Tuck School of Business professor, Adam Kleinbaum, called these individuals "organizational misfits."[29] His research showed that they were much more likely to be bridge-builders than were people with more traditional career paths because at each step of their career, they formed relationships with people in different sticky rice clusters. "Atypical career transitions may undermine perceived legitimacy, but they also create opportunities for forging rare and valuable bridges."[30]

The Politics of Bridge-Building

One strategy for building bridges between sticky rice clusters is to present the parts of yourself that fit best with each cluster. MacGregor, in the opening example, was a master at this. In 2007, MacGregor arranged a meeting with Dr. Zhao Rong, the head of cultural relics in the Chinese provincial city of Xi'an to convince him to take the unusual step of loaning the BM the famous terracotta warriors that were entombed there. Upon learning that his Chinese host was a fan of the movie *Braveheart*, MacGregor emphasized his Scottishness by holding forth eloquently on Mel Gibson's depiction of William Wallace. Although normally he made sure to share a bottle of 15-year-old Bowmore, an Islay single malt, and offered to arrange a tour of

Scottish distilleries for the British Museum's Chinese guests after the recent opening of the exhibition. Within the year, 46 crates of priceless Chinese artefacts were winging their way to London to be installed in what became one of the BM's most successful exhibitions.[31]

Adjusting self-presentation appropriately can make you seem more like the others, thereby easing *their* fear of you. Not surprisingly, one of the predictors of having a bridging network is the tendency to monitor different social situations and adapt your self-presentation accordingly. [To find out your tendency to adjust your self-presentation, complete the *Self-Monitoring* scale at https://openpsychometrics.org/tests/SMS/.]

For many of us, adjusting how you present yourself in different situations is not so easy. It's not easy to figure out the norms of behavior in a particular sticky rice cluster, let alone the several different ones. Norms are learned over time and reinforced through subtle social cues such as surprised expressions, smiles, and silence. Through action and social response, we learn which behaviors are acceptable and which are not. Is it okay to contradict others or will you be shunned for disagreeing? Are personal questions considered polite or invasive? Understanding the unspoken—and often unconscious—social rules of a sticky rice cluster can be challenging.

Even if we know what to say or do, presenting different selves to different people, can be stressful, especially if it means ignoring or repressing emotions or core parts of our identity. Imagine, for example, the seething resentment that boils beneath the calm facade of the flight attendant who is forced to put on a fake smile while interacting with sometimes rude and belligerent customers. People who engage in this type of "surface acting" with customers sometimes find the experience so stressful that they become more abusive to the people they supervise.[32]

Behaving differently with different people can make some of us feel inauthentic. If you feel this way, you probably believe that who you are is fixed and unchanging, and that it is *wrong* to act differently with different people. You are who you are and acting differently is the same as acting like someone you are not.

Presenting different aspects of our true self to different people needn't feel phony. It can even be empowering if you view bridge-building as a way to selectively release facets of your authentic self. As senior fellow at Harvard Business School, former chair and CEO of Medtronic, and author of the book, *Discover Your True North*, Bill George wrote:

> Authentic leaders match their behavior to their context, an essential part of emotional intelligence (EQ). They do not burst out with whatever they

may be thinking or feeling. Rather, they exhibit self-monitoring, understand how they are being perceived, and use emotional intelligence (EQ) to communicate effectively.[33]

As a bridge-builder, you have the opportunity to express your true self through selective sharing. With some people, we can show our creativity; with others, our analytical strengths. Humans are enormously complex and complicated beings. If we reach deep down, we are sure to find a part of ourselves that makes it easier for us to connect to each other.

To Recap...

Bridge-building comes with enormous advantages related to professional success. If you want to get ahead in your career, if you want to be involved in innovation, if you want to solve complex problems, if you want to influence others in your field, you have to become a bridge-builder. Despite all of the advantages, being a bridge-builder can be challenging.

Earlier chapters outlined a number of advantages associated with being embedded in a sticky rice cluster, including improved health, well-being, and job satisfaction. The current chapter seems to suggest that we have to give up the rewards of sticky rice clusters in order to instead build and benefit from building bridges between clusters. The question naturally arises: Is it possible to have the benefits of being in a sticky rice cluster AND be a bridge-builder?

The answer is *Yes*—but with an important caveat: The main benefits of sticky rice clusters are in your *purely social* relationships and the main benefits of bridging are in your *professional* networks. In the next chapter, we'll look at who should be in your professional network.

Reflection Questions

What does the shape of your network tell you about your network strategy? Do you have a bridge-building or a sticky rice strategy?

If you are a bridge-builder between at least two sticky rice clusters, are you reaping the advantages of being a bridge-builder? Why or why not?

Do you enjoy being a bridge-builder or do you find it stressful?

SECTION **II**

5

At Home on the Range

The Big Splash

In the spring of 2017, soft drink giant Pepsi launched a new and expensive global advertising campaign called "Live for Now Moments." In a press release announcing the campaign—the day before the first commercial was first aired—Pepsi noted that the campaign, "takes a more progressive approach to truly reflect today's generation and what living for now looks like."[1]

The flagship ad called "Jump In" had been created by PepsiCo's in-house content creation arm, Creators League Studio. Creators League Studio was overseen by Brad Jakeman, president of PepsiCo's global beverage group, and Kristin Patrick, senior VP-global brand development. Shortly after the ad was released, Jakeman tweeted that he was "super proud of the @PepsiCo #CreatorsLeague for producing this."[2]

In the commercial, a series of quick shots establishes that a protest march is taking place. Attractive, happy, young people—representing many different ethnicities and cultural minorities—file through the streets, chanting and holding signs that read "Join the conversation" and "Love." The protesters walk by model Kendall Jenner who is in the middle of a photo shoot. She watches the protesters longingly and then—impetuously—rips off her blonde wig to reveal her dark hair and joins in the march. Jenner strides to the front of the protest march and hands a Pepsi to a handsome but stern-looking riot police officer. The officer accepts the Pepsi. As he takes a sip, the crowd breaks into jubilant applause. The officer grins. The tag line, *Live Bolder, Live Louder, Live for Now* appears on the screen.

The backlash to the ad was swift and brutal. The ad was widely condemned as inappropriately referencing the Black Lives Matter protests. The *Independent* called it "possibly the worst commercial of all time."[3] Some people noted that the closing shot of Jenner offering the Pepsi to the police officer was strikingly similar to the iconic photograph of Ieshia Evans standing her ground against authorities during a Black Lives Matter protest. Bernice A. King, daughter of Martin Luther King Jr., referenced the final scene in the commercial in a sarcastic tweet—"If only Daddy would have known about the power of #Pepsi."[4]

Protesters on social media were quick to point out the incongruity of "corporate America co-opting the resistance movement and featuring a privileged white supermodel who uses a can of soda as a peacemaker between civil rights activists and police."[5] Mentions of Pepsi surged more than 7000% on social media following the first airing of the ad but nearly all of it was negative, dominated by the term *tone-deaf*.[6] Veteran commercials and music video director Joseph Kahn tweeted, "I've been studying commercials for 30 years. Kendall's Pepsi ad is legitimately the worst one I've seen."[7] The ad even served as fodder for late night talk show hosts:

> So far we don't know what has caused all of America's hot extras to take the streets. But I'm guessing it's a protest for Attractive Lives Matter.
>
> —Stephen Colbert, *The Late Show*[8]

> I saw that today North Korea conducted a missile test, which escalated tensions in the region. But don't worry. Things settled down when Kendall Jenner stepped in and handed them a Pepsi.
>
> —Jimmy Fallon, *The Tonight Show*[9]

For a few hours after the ad aired, Pepsi defended it, claiming, "This is a global ad that reflects people from different walks of life coming together in a spirit of harmony, and we think that's an important message to convey." In a statement provided to *Teen Vogue*, an official spokesperson for Pepsi explained:

> The creative showcases a moment of unity, and a point where multiple storylines converge in the final advert. It depicts various groups of people embracing a spontaneous moment, and showcasing Pepsi's brand rallying cry to "Live For Now," in an exploration of what that truly means to live life unbounded, unfiltered and uninhibited.[10]

However—less than a day after making these statements and under intense pressure—Pepsi announced it was pulling the ad. In an official statement, the company said,

> Pepsi was trying to project a global a message of unity, peace and understanding. Clearly, we missed the mark, and we apologize. We did not intend to make light of any serious issue. We are removing the content and halting any further rollout. We also apologize for putting Kendall Jenner in this position.[11]

Some have speculated that Pepsi was trying to provoke negative publicity in the belief that all publicity is good publicity. If so, they badly miscalculated. Experts say that Pepsi probably spent about $5 million to create the commercial and another $100 million to purchase advertising space and time.[12] The negative sales impact was short-lived but the image of a company that is out of touch with consumers lingers.

How did Pepsi get it so wrong? One thing to note is that this commercial was not created by a single person, nor was it approved by a single person. Lots of people contributed to the design and production of the commercial, from the creative team to the board. As late night host Jimmy Kimmel noted,

> The fact that this somehow made it through—I can't imagine how many meetings, and edits, and pitches, and then got the thumbs-up from who knows how many people, is absolutely mind-boggling.[13]

One explanation for what went wrong lies in the nature of the people involved in the making of the commercial. In this case, it was not the *structure* of the team or organizational network that was responsible for Pepsi's public relation debacle. Instead, the problem lies in the *range* of individuals in the networks connected to the making of the ad.

Lone Rangers

Effective networks include a *range* of individuals. Range refers to the extent to which the people in your network are *un*like each other. People who have a lot of range in their networks are connected to people who represent a variety of functions, industries, ethnicities, geographic areas, and other categories.

There seemed to be very little range in terms of ethnicity at PepsiCo's Creators League Studio. This is true of most creative businesses. More than three quarters of "creative" jobs in America are held by Whites, whereas less than 9% are held by Blacks. That compares to a population which is around 64% White and 12% Black. More than 40% of White workers hold creative jobs, while less than 30% percent of Black workers do.[14] These statistics seem to be reflected at Creators League Studio. Indeed, *all* the people on the creative team that produced the "Jump In" Jenner commercial were White.[15]

Range offers a number of advantages. Range triggers creativity and innovation, reduces conflict, improves the quality of decision-making and increases knowledge-sharing. Greater range may even offer some health advantages. Studies on social relationships found that having a more diverse social network is associated with better health outcomes such as less cognitive decline with aging and less dementia,[16] and a decreased risk for the reoccurrence of cancer.[17]

But *why* does range generate these advantages?

Rangers See More

People who include a range of people in their networks develop something psychologists call *integrative complexity*.[18] Integrative complexity is the recognition and integration of various perspectives and their interrelated possibilities. A person with integrative complexity is less likely to see the world in binary, black and white terms. Instead, their world is a tapestry, with strands of actions and reactions interacting with other strands of actions and reactions so that they can see connections between seemly distant events and a local problem. Compared to people with less range, people who have more range also have more integrative complexity. They are more likely to perceive issues as having multiple root causes.

Integrative complexity is one reason why individuals with wide-ranging networks are more likely to develop thoughtful and innovative solutions to problems. Innovation and creativity require seeing familiar problems and objects in new ways. Integrative complexity is a direct result of constantly being exposed to different and even contradictory ideas. If you have range in your network, you are more likely to develop new ways of thinking and perceiving the world.

In contrast, people who have relationships with mainly like-minded people tend to have a restricted view of the world. That's because like-minded people have similar backgrounds and histories. They turn to similar sources for information, entertainment, and personal fulfillment. Their daily life is filled with similar experiences. All of these similarities shape the way they perceive the world. The all-White creative team at PepsiCo likely had similar experiences with race and ethnicity which shaped their worldview.

Networks with greater range connect you to people who see the world differently. By seeing the world through their eyes, you see it from their unique perspective. We are often encouraged to think "outside of the box" when approaching a new problem. But, as University of Chicago professor Ron Burt suggests, there is greater value in approaching problems as if you were "inside a different box."[19] In the case of PepsiCo, perceiving the advertising campaign from the viewpoint of someone who is not White might have caused someone to reconsider the appropriateness of selling a soft drink by having a pseudo-famous white, rich celebrity pretend to be in a protest march that rather unsubtly referenced the Black Lives Matter protests.

Remember the scientists who successfully solved problems in the online challenge in the last chapter? They were successful precisely because they applied knowledge gained from deep immersion in one field to a problem needing a solution in another. The same study found that the more similar the field of the scientist was to the field of the problem, the *less* likely he or she was to develop a winning solution. Value comes from exposure to differences. The greater the difference, the greater the value.

Rangers Keep the Peace

Range reduces conflict and increase integration because it helps break down stereotypes. When most of our relationships are with people like us, we have plenty of opportunities to see how each person differs slightly from the stereotype of our group. Millennials know that not every Millennial is an entitled, social media-engrossed slacker because they know plenty of counter-examples. But someone who doesn't have any Millennials in her network may be less sure.

When we define some people as belonging to the Other group—that is, people who are not like "Us"—we start to see them as more alike than different from each other, especially when we don't have any countervailing evidence. People like us are not all the same but *They* are one homogenous mass. Having a simplistic view of others makes it easier to treat people as interchangeable members of a group rather than as individuals. It also makes it hard to find points of connection.

Range increases the complexity of our understanding of other people. It helps widen the gap between seeing and interpreting so that we get a chance to come up with alternative explanations. Range makes it more likely, for example, that when we see a rich White model rip off her blonde wig and literally throw it at her Black assistant—instead of leaping immediately to the interpretation that she is a carefree and socially conscious hippy-rebel—we consider instead the possibility that she might be insulting people who genuinely experience and protest against social injustice.

Rangers Are Better Deciders

Range also encourages higher quality decision-making. Oddly enough, just knowing that someone approaches a problem differently makes us re-examine the problem more closely as we try to understand how someone could possibly approach the problem *that* way. More thoughtful consideration of the information related to the problem leads to a more thorough and considered decision.

I see this principle in action every day in the classroom. I often ask my MBA students to read and prepare business cases for classroom discussion. Cases are real-life stories about real managers who need to make decisions about, say, how to handle a low-performing employee or a failed change initiative. The value of the assignment isn't so much that the students come to their own conclusions about the case, it's in listening to their colleagues see the same problems very differently. A typical MBA class includes students representing a wide range of industries, countries, and backgrounds. They always disagree about some aspects of the case and their debates spark insight and encourage deep thinking. I've seen students go from believing that an employee should be fired immediately to believing that his *manager* needed training in how to give effective performance feedback.

You don't even have to know people all that well for network range to improve your decision-making. An interesting series of experiments conducted in Asia and in the United States demonstrates the value of merely being *exposed* to diverse perspectives.[20]

The researchers placed participants in groups with varying levels of ethnic and racial diversity and asked them to calculate accurate prices for simulated stocks. Each individual first estimated the price of the stock privately and then bought and sold those stocks—using real money and keeping any profits they made—in the presence of other group members. When trading, individuals could observe the behavior of others in their group. As the researchers predicted, those observations turned out to be highly influential. If a person thought that a stock was worth $100, but observed that others bid $120 for it, he or she was much more likely to value the stock higher and bid higher. They seemed to have figured that there is safety in numbers and if more people thought that the bid should be higher, than it should probably be higher. Some people ignored what the others did and held onto their original estimate. Perhaps they felt more confident relying upon their own calculations. The researchers wanted to know, did the diversity of the group influence the *accuracy* of the stock estimate?

The answer is yes. When participants were in groups with more racial and ethnic diversity, their answers were 58% more accurate. The prices they chose were much closer to the true values of the stocks, whether or not they held onto their original estimate or recalculated it. In groups with little ethnic or racial diversity—whether in the United States or in Asia—the opposite happened. When surrounded by others of the same ethnicity or race, participants were more likely to copy others, often in the wrong direction. Mistakes spread as participants seemingly put undue trust in others' estimates, mindlessly imitating them. In contrast, being surrounded by greater diversity led to a more realistic appraisal of the stock. As the researchers noted,

> When surrounded by people "like ourselves," we are easily influenced, more likely to fall for wrong ideas. Diversity prompts better, critical thinking. It contributes to error detection. It keeps us from drifting toward miscalculation.[21]

Network range helps us make better decisions. Perhaps if the people involved in the "Jump In" Jenner ad had had more range in their networks, they would have considered their decisions more thoughtfully.

Rangers Learn More New Tricks

Range also increases our ability to learn something new. Instead of seeing people who are different from us as being exactly like everyone else that shares their difference, we begin to accept that people can be different in multiple ways and that each person's experience and background is unique. If all my professional contacts are in public relations, it is easy to stereotype accountants as being, for example, nitpicking bean counters. But if I have some accountants among my professional contacts, I can easily see that while some may be nitpicking bean counters, others are not. Some, in fact, may be wildly creative. Would you be surprised to learn that Rolling Stone lead singer Mick Jagger and saxophonist Kenny G. both studied accounting before turning their creative talents toward music?[22]

When we start to recognize that different people see the world differently, we start to see *everyone* differently because everyone is shaped by many different constellations of experiences. Sure, those experiences include things like coming from another culture or socio-economic background, but they also include having a family member die young or growing up with ten siblings or losing 200 pounds or any number of things. We are all different in unique ways.

Perceiving people as individuals makes it harder to believe that we know what's in their head. And that makes it more likely that we will learn from them. Because the first step in learning from another person is believing that the other person might know something we don't.

But Life Is Hard on the Range

Despite all the advantages, incorporating a range of people in our networks is hard. It's hard because interacting with people who are like us is a lot easier than interacting with people who are *not* like us. We like being around people who are like us. When we're with people who are like us, there are fewer opportunities for misunderstandings and conflict. We all agree on what is "appropriate" behavior, as well as how to distinguish right from wrong and good from bad. When we're with people who are like us, we don't have to worry about doing or saying the wrong thing. We don't have to explain our jokes because we share a similar sense of humor. We're more likely to "get" where people like us are coming from and they are more likely to understand where we're coming from. All in all, it just plain feels good to be with people who are like us.

Our natural tendency to form relationships with people like us—referred to by social scientists as the *homophily* or, the *birds of a feather*, principle—explains why we tend to form professional and personal relationships with people who are similar to us in race and ethnicity, age, religion, education, occupation, and gender, in roughly that order.[23] Homophily influences who we marry, who we choose as friends, and who we prefer as co-workers.

We can see the influence of homophily in where we choose to live. We tend to like towns and neighborhoods populated by people like us. That's why people with similar tastes and preferences can be located by zip code, a fact not missed by marketers. One marketing firm, Claritas, has gone so far as to split the U.S. population into more than sixty psycho-demographic clusters, based on such factors as income, reading and television habits, and which products they've bought in the past. For example, the *suburban sprawl* cluster is composed of young families making about $41,000 a year and living in fast-growing places such as Burnsville, Minnesota, and Bensalem, Pennsylvania. Members of the suburban sprawl cluster are more than twice as likely as other Americans to buy Light n' Lively Kid Yogurt. People in the *towns & gowns* cluster are recent college graduates living in places such as Berkeley, California, and Gainesville, Florida. Towns & gowns members drive small foreign automobiles and eat DoveBars. They watch *Saturday Night Live*, and read *Rolling Stone* and *Scientific American* magazines.[24] Knowing the tendencies of the clusters makes it easier for businesses to locate potential customers. An executive seeking a location for a new Baby Gap store, for example, is much more likely to select a suburban sprawl zip code than a towns & gowns zip code.

The net result of our homophilous tendencies is that even our professional networks tend to be composed of people who share many of the same demographic, behavioral, and even personality characteristics. Without conscious efforts to fight against it, homophily will dominate *all* of our relationships.

Bridge-Builders and Rangers

At this point, you may be thinking that incorporating range sounds a lot like bridge-building. After all, both range and bridge-building connects you to different types of people. But, although related, range is *not* the same as bridge-building. Range refers to the *types* of people in your professional network; bridge-building refers to the *structure* of your direct and—equally important—*in*direct relationships in a larger network. You can have a wide range and few bridges; you can also have limited range and many bridges.

Having a network with a wide range and few bridges is fairly common. If you are in a sticky rice network, you already know that the people to whom you are connected to are mostly similar in some way, although they might be different in other ways. For example, perhaps your sticky rice network was built during an internship. You and the other interns bonded over your experience and now that you are all hired into the same organization, you remain tightly connected. You still socialize with each other and call each other up for advice, even though your intern days are long behind you. On the one hand, you are all very similar in terms of your training, your organizational perspective, and probably your age. On the other hand, you may represent a range of ethnicities, come from different parts of the country, and be a mix of political conservatives and liberals. So your network has range even though it is structured like a sticky rice cluster.

Although less common, people in bridging networks can also have limited range. For example, suppose you have ten people in your professional network and none of them know each other directly. You've definitely got a bridging network. Do you also have range in your network?

Well, maybe not.

Even though you are technically a bridge-builder, the sticky rice clusters that you access might look pretty similar. You may have a friend at an accounting firm, one at a marketing company, and one in high tech but if they're all senior managers like you, then you still have limited range because, in many ways, senior managers have more in common with each other than any one of them do with an entry-level employee. While it's true that your network includes people in unconnected sticky rice clusters, the people in those clusters are still very similar. You have a bridging network structure but very little *range*.

While there has been a back-and-forth debate in the academic community about which matters more—the bridging structure or range—the truth is that both matter. To truly have access to diverse perspectives, you have to form relationships with people who are very different from each other, and also with people who connect to very different sticky rice cultures.

Broadening Your Range

Even though a network with range offers you some of the same advantages as a bridging network, it has very different implications for *networking*. To create a bridging network, you need to understand the structure of a larger network—such as your organization's network—and seek out gaps or "holes" in the structure. That requires a little work on your part because understanding how people or departments are related to each other is not intuitive. When seeking to build bridges, it's okay to reach out to people who are like you. [We'll talk more about specific strategies to "see" networks accurately in later chapters.]

But to increase *range*, we need to connect with people who are *not* like us. By expanding the range of our networks—even just a little bit—you can limit your exposure to homophily traps. To do that, you will need to *confront implicit bias, learn about your friends' friends, embrace weirdness*, and *cast a wide net.*

Confront implicit bias. To confront implicit bias, you first have to acknowledge that it exists. Implicit bias refers to the attitudes or stereotypes that affect our understanding, actions, and decisions in an unconscious manner. These implicit biases can make it hard for us to form relationships with people who are not like us because they sometimes lead us to say and do things that match our preconceived notions. This can happen even when our intentions are positive. For example, in a scene in the film *Get Out*, a White man—eager to show his acceptance of a biracial couple—asks the couple how long they had been dating by saying, "How long has this *thang* been going on?" The term *thang*, of course, is a slang word for *thing* and is part of so-called urban dialogue which is itself stereotypically associated with people who are Black. When we do or say things that indicate we hold a stereotype, it tells the other person that we see him or her first—or only!—as a member of their group and only secondarily as an individual.

But relationships form between individuals, not stereotypes.

Some of you may be thinking that you don't have any stereotypes floating around in your head and influencing your perceptions. You are almost certainly wrong. One of the most tragic examples of implicit bias plays out in our cities and towns every day. A police officer sees a sudden movement during a routine interaction with a citizen and has only a split-second to assess hostile intent. Is the person reaching for a gun or for an identification card? As we all know from the nightly news, the same physical movement may be interpreted quite differently if the citizen is Black than if he or she is White. Interpretive leaps made in milliseconds can be the difference between life and death.

We all make dozens of interpretative leaps every day. We leap so quickly to our interpretation of the other person's actions that we don't even know we're making an interpretation. We believe what we "see." The problem is that that these leaps influence what we do and say, and it can be very hard to find out if we are wrong. Unlike the police officer who can search for a gun, most of us rely upon the way people react to our actions. All too often, we see their reactions as confirmation of our original beliefs. We never get a chance to correct our initial interpretative leap.

Implicit biases have consequences, not the least of which is to make it harder to develop range in our networks. Fortunately, a number of steps have shown promise in confronting implicit biases and reducing their strength.[25] By taking some of these steps, you will make it easier to have positive interactions with people who are not like you.

1. *Expose yourself to counter-stereotypic examples of group members.* You can do this through movies, books, and other media. In one experiment, people showed less implicit bias toward Asian Americans after they watched *The Joy Luck Club,* a movie about Asian immigrants to the United States.[26]

2. *Consciously contrast negative stereotypes with specific counter-examples.* For example, suppose you hear or think of a negative stereotype about people who are Black. You can compare that stereotype to what you know about a friend or famous person such as Oprah Winfrey or Neil deGrasse Tyson.

3. *Force yourself to interact with people who are different from you.* Sometimes we get so overwhelmed with fear that we'll say or do the wrong thing that we simply avoid interacting with people who are not like us. But the research shows us that the more we interact, the more likely we are to have positive interactions.[27] So, give it a try. Even something as simple as making small talk before a meeting can be a start.

4. *Use your perspective-taking skills.* When interacting with other people, try to take their perspective. Remember that perspective-taking is not the same as empathy. Empathy is identifying with someone because you've had a similar experience. Perspective-taking is trying to understand how the other person views the world. Ask yourself, "How would I feel *if I was that person* and I was in that situation?"

The key to confronting implicit biases is to simply do it. It may not be comfortable, it may not be easy, but you can be sure that it will open you up to meeting new people and new ways of thinking.

Learn about your friends' friends. Interestingly, we can gain some of the advantages of network range by having a relationship with someone like us who has a relationship with someone who is *not* like us. In other words, we benefit if our *friends* have networks with range, even if we don't. Information about other types of people travel through our friends so that we get some insight into how other people see the world without having to actually interact with people who are not like us.

This can be especially important when interacting with someone who is not like us makes us uncomfortable. For example, some White people worry that they will unintentionally say something racist or provoking when interacting with a Black person. Anticipating problematic interactions can generate so much anxiety that some White people deal with it by simply avoiding direct interactions with Black people. By doing so, they limit the range of their networks.

But these anxious White people can get some of the benefits of ethnic/racial diversity without the anxiety and discomfort of direct interaction IF they have some White friends whose networks include Black friends. That's because without the cognitive overload of anxiety and other associated emotions, it is easier to digest information about people who are not "like us." Considering this information builds empathy and reduces anxiety even further.

Moreover, observing or simply knowing about our friends' connections also nudges us to consider—usually subconsciously—that it is "normal" for people like us to be friends with people who are not like us. You start to think, *If my White friend can have a positive relationship with someone who is Black, maybe I can, too.* The combination of reduced anxiety and changing ideas about what is normal, makes it easier for us to develop new relationships with people who are not like us. The power of indirect range is not limited to White people, by the way. If you're Black, having a Black friend who has a White friend also makes it easier for you to have more—and more positive—interactions with people who are White.

As we've seen before, we are influenced by the actions of others, even when we don't observe those actions directly. By the same token, our network choices influence others. The more *our* networks demonstrate range, the more we make it possible for our friends to develop networks with range.

Embrace weirdness. Weirdness is how we describe thoughts and behaviors that don't make sense to us. Sometimes people who don't look like us in terms of gender, race/ethnicity, or other demographic characteristics will appear "weird" but the idea of weirdness goes beyond differences associated with visible traits or personal experiences. Instead, weirdness reflects different ways of being and thinking.

University of Virginia Professor of Management Martin Davidson and author of *The End of Diversity as We Know It* notes that weirdness manifests itself in two ways.[28] The first involves people who act weird just for the fun of opposing the normal rules of conduct. These weirdos are self-proclaimed "rebels." Weirdness of this type is commonly found in creative industries, where being different makes one stand out—in a good way. (Think: the pop star Sia who always performs with a face-covering wig.) But it's also common in other industries, although the weirdness might be more subtle. (Think: the guy in marketing who wears monogrammed handkerchiefs and a Trilby on casual Fridays.) This kind of weirdness can be refreshing or annoying, but it doesn't really contribute anything new to you or your organization.

The second kind of weirdness comes from people who think differently. These "big W" weird people often go against conventional norms but they don't do it for the sake of standing out. Rather, they are trying to envision a particular future or achieve a larger goal, and they recognize that following a conventional path won't get them there. As Davidson notes, "[T]hey are just focused on getting a great result."[29]

Expand your network's range by learning how to embrace weirdness. Embrace weirdness by welcoming opportunities to learn about a different way that the world might work. Welcoming weirdness goes beyond staying open to new and perhaps startling ways of understanding the world you live in. It also goes beyond mere acceptance of differences. Instead, welcoming weirdness requires an openness to change, sometimes profound change, in one's *own* beliefs about how the world works.

Frankly, suspending our deeply held beliefs about what constitutes a fact and how things relate to each other is very difficult—if not impossible—to do. Not believing what you truly believe is practically an oxymoron. If I know something is true how can I possibly believe that it isn't when my eyes and everyday experience tells me that it is?

The key is to embracing weirdness is to act *as if* you what you know to be true might not actually be true. I don't mean that you should try to trick others into thinking you are more open than you are. I mean try to *behave* as if you were open to considering a different way. You might not be able to control your thoughts but you can control your actions. People who are open to considering a different way don't start conversations by attacking ideas. They don't demean, bully, belittle, cajole, or otherwise try to convince a weird person to see the world "normally."

Instead, people who act *as if* they might believe, *listen*. They ask questions, especially *how* and *why*. They do this not to find a way to trip the person up but to give them a chance to explain what they think in their own way and in their own time. They ask clarifying questions to make sure that they understand what the other person is saying. The reason that acting like this works is that it forces you to really think about the idea and to consider it in a new way. Scientists call this *effortful thinking* and it is associated with a more complex understanding of the issue at hand. Listening to someone—really listening—is also a great way to build a positive relationship.

In other words, if you act *as if* you *might* be open to accepting another person's weirdness, you leave open the possibility of not only learning something new but also building a new relationship in the process.

And sometimes—not every time, but sometimes—that's exactly what will happen.

Cast a wide net. One last way to incorporate more range in your professional network is to look beyond your current organization when identifying people in your professional network. Cast a wide net. Extend your thinking beyond even your industry or profession. Connecting with people outside of the predominantly White creative industry might have made it easier for the creative team that created the "Jump In" Jenner commercial to connect with people who are not White.

Many people focus their networking efforts solely within their current organization. This is a big mistake. For one thing, with today's dynamic careers, you are unlikely to remain in one organization for your entire career. In 2017, the typical 60 year-old has held an average of about 12 jobs.[30] And that number is only going to go up. A study by LinkedIn found that people who graduated from college between 2006 and 2010 averaged nearly 2.85 jobs in their first 5 years in the workplace.[31] Limiting your connections to one organization limits your options. Build your professional network long before you even contemplate moving to another organization. If you do, your network will be ready when you need it most.

Even if you feel 100% certain that you will spend the rest of your professional life in one organization—a dubious assumption for most people!—you still benefit by developing a professional network outside of your organization. Your organization, as different as some people might seem from each other, is still a sticky rice cluster compared to other organizations in your industry or profession. Within your organization, people have learned some rules about how "things are done around here." By maintaining a professional development network that includes people outside of your organization, you can bring new ideas and insights into your organization.

If you don't include people outside your organization, you will miss opportunities to be exposed to new ideas and new ways of looking at problems. Including outsiders in your network is particularly important as you progress in your career because people in leadership positions are expected to develop strategies for the future of the organization. If you can't see from inside another box, then you can't see any other future than the one that everyone else you know sees.

Bad Connections

In the next chapter, we'll explore the strength of relationships in your network. But before we do, let's take a look at the *types* of relationships in your network. All the benefits of networks that we've discussed to this point are a function of having *positive* relationships. Negative relationships, on the other hand, have many disadvantages.

Negative relationships range from low levels of dislike or tension to intense animosity and even outright hatred. While it is certainly possible to have both positive and negative feelings toward someone—the so-called frenemy!—most of us can clearly distinguish between mostly positive and mostly negative relationships. Even among teenagers, frenemies are rare. A few years ago, I surveyed more than a thousand high school students and only *one* described a relationship as both positive <u>and</u> negative.

If your professional network has a lot—or even a few—people who you don't really like, you're in trouble. Because while it can be tempting to assert that how you *feel* about a work relationship doesn't matter, the truth is, it does. We know, for example, that engaged employees work harder, are more productive, and are more likely to stay at their organizations.[32] What drives engagement?

Positive relationships.

Eighty percent of respondents in a recent U.S. survey indicated that the number one reason that they felt engaged at work was the quality of their relationships with co-workers.[33] An ongoing Gallup poll consistently finds that one of the top indicators of employee engagement is agreeing with the statement, "I have a friend at work." While negative relationships are relatively rare—typically no more than 8% of all social relationships in an organization—their presence can have an outsized effect on your work performance and your personal well-being.[34]

We Don't Like to Work With People We Don't Like

Negative relationships hurt us at work. Individuals who have a relatively large number of negative relationships typically receive lower individual performance evaluations and bring down the performance of their teams.[35] Perhaps this is because they are less likely to be trusted or to receive help from others.[36] In fact, they are less likely to interact in *any* way with their co-workers. People may go to great lengths to avoid interacting with people they dislike. One person told me that she wouldn't leave the office until her nemesis had gone home for the night solely because she had to walk past his office to get out of the building! She left that job as soon as she could.

Researchers Tiziana Casciaro and Miguel Sousa Lobo argued that we so strongly prefer working with people we like that we'll even choose to work with someone *less* competent if we like them better than a more competent a co-worker.[37] To test their ideas, they asked employees at several large organizations to indicate how positively they felt toward other people and how competent they thought their co-workers were. They then looked at company records to see, when given an option, with whom the engineers chose to collaborate. Surprisingly, although people believed that they were choosing teams based on competence, the data showed that that was *not* what they actually did.

Everyone wanted to have on their team the well-liked person who was also rated as highly competent. Similarly, no one wanted to work with an unliked person who was also relatively *in*competent. But most people fall somewhere in-between the *stars* and the *incompetent jerks*. When Casciaro and Lobo explored how we made decisions about the in-betweeners, they found that employees preferred to work with liked but *less* competent co-workers rather than _un_liked but *more* competent co-workers. These *lovable fools*, as the researchers called them, were more desirable as work partners than *competent jerks*.

In a related study I conducted with Connie Yuan and Kate Ehrlich, we asked members of 53 sales teams to tell us who they tapped for expertise and who they thought was competent.[38] We also asked them to rate their co-workers in terms of how much they liked them and how much they *dis*-liked them. We thought that people might prefer to get information from competent people who they also liked. But our data told a slightly different story. Unexpectedly, we found was that people didn't seek out people that they liked as much as they avoided people who they disliked. This was true even when they rated the person the person as highly competent. We simply don't like to work with people we don't like.

Bad Relationships Make Us Feel Bad

Not only do we dislike working with people who are widely disliked, the negative effect of these relationships extends beyond work-related tasks to our personal well-being. In conducting research for their book *Toxic Coworkers: How to Deal with Dysfunctional People on the Job*, psychologists Alan Cavaiola and Neil Lavender surveyed more than 1,100 employees. They discovered that roughly 80% reported moderate to severe stress as a result of working with a difficult coworker, boss, or subordinate. Being in a negative relationship reduces our personal satisfaction, life satisfaction and psychological well-being.[39] At the same time, it increases psychological distress and stress.[40]

Not surprisingly, knowing what we know about network effects, the negative impact of one negative relationship can have ripple effects throughout a department or organization.[41] As Wharton Professor and best-selling author Adam Grant wryly noted,

> [T]he negative impact of a taker on a culture is usually double to triple the positive impact of a giver. Think about it this way: one bad apple can spoil a barrel, but one good egg just does not make a dozen.[42]

My advice regarding negative relationships is simple: Get rid of them. Address, eliminate, or otherwise reduce the number of negative relationships in your network. Maintaining a relationship with someone you dislike—even a supervisor—is likely to do much more harm than good. Either repair the relationship or get out of it.

To Recap...

Effective networks include a range of people who are unlike each other. Networks with range increase creativity and innovation, reduce conflict, improve the quality of decision-making and increase knowledge-sharing. As we saw in the case of the "Jump In" Jenner commercial, limiting the range of your network can have a direct impact on the quality of your work.

Although a network with range offers you some of the same advantages as a bridging network, it has very different implications for *networking*. One type of relationship that should never be in your network is a *negative* relationship.

In the next chapter, we'll look at the strength of your different relationships and why nearly forgotten—or dormant—relationships are the secret powerhouse in your network.

Reflection Questions

What types of people are *over*-represented in your network?

What types of people are *under*-represented?

What are you doing to address your implicit biases?

Are you in a negative relationship? Is there a way to either repair the relationship or get out of it?

6

Circles and Sleepers

SELF-ASSESSMENT SNAPSHOT

Complete the *Professional Support Network Exercise* in the Toolbox at the end of this book. Consider each person that you listed as *close*, and answer *Yes* or *No* to the following questions:

- Does this person have direct or indirect access to resources that have the potential to assist me in my career?
- Does this person have a perspective, expertise, ability, or knowledge that I lack and can't find elsewhere in my network?
- Does this person want me to succeed as much as I want him or her to succeed?
- Can I talk to this person about private matters?
- Does this person often provide me with new insights and ideas?

Social Circles

George Jones is the CEO of Tritus,[1] a multinational company based in Boston serving the combined industries of health information technologies

Connect the Dots, pages 93–116
Copyright © 2019 by Information Age Publishing
All rights of reproduction in any form reserved.

and clinical research. Tritus provides biopharmaceutical development and commercial outsourcing services to countries around the world. The company does pretty well for a small business with only fifty employees. In 2016, company revenues topped $10 million.

George is known to be a shrewd negotiator. Over the years, he has overseen multiple large acquisitions, each of which boosted the company's profits. One deal in particular earned him the nickname "Golden Boy" George, for his deft handling of a complicated merger that involved several partner companies operating in different parts of the world under different regulatory environments.

Although Golden Boy George can be tough, he can also be charming. As the public face of his company, he is often seen in the company of some of the most famous men and women in the world. By all accounts, he is a well-read and engaging conversationalist. After meeting him at a dinner party, Catherine Deneuve, one of the icons of French cinema was said to have remarked, "Quel homme charmant!" (Translation: *What a charming man!*)

George doesn't only socialize with the rich and famous. He is equally likely to have lunch with one of his mailroom attendants as he is with his VPs. One story that is well-known among Tritus employees is that of a visiting CEO's account of arriving unexpectedly at the company headquarters with the intent of dropping in on George. But George was not in his office. His personal assistant said that George was "on his daily constitutional"— code for his tendency to stroll around the building and chat with employees at all levels. After nearly an hour, the visiting CEO finally located him in the company cafeteria, sharing a cup of coffee with a man who had worked in the mailroom for years.

As CEO, George is responsible for the direction and strategy of his company. An adept Ranger, he is constantly asking people for their opinions and ideas. *What would you do?*, is a familiar question. He famously got the idea for one of the company's best-selling product by visiting a dialysis center and asking the workers there what would make their job easier.

But George doesn't turn to everyone for his questions. When the questions are personal—when the decisions are big—he turns to a small group of people he calls his "inner circle." George's inner circle includes his wife and sister, his father, his business partner of fifteen years, a childhood friend and now patent lawyer, his high school coach, a college roommate who now runs his own business, a former business school professor, and his first boss. George says he won't take any major step before turning to this group.

"They are always there for me," he said. "No matter how much I think I know what I'm doing, I always check with them before taking a major step."

A few years ago, George asked his inner circle about his plans to expand the company by acquiring a West coast bio-technology firm. "We'd done our due diligence and the numbers looked good," he said.

But his inner circle questioned his plan. One person asked him how the move aligned with his commitment to maintaining a family-like organizational culture. The other organization was nearly twice as big as Tritus. Would acquiring a new company with more employees change Tritus's culture beyond repair? Was the potential cost to the present culture one he was willing to pay?

Another reminded him that the deal would require his presence at many meetings on the West Coast over the next three years. George placed a high value on his family relationships. His children were in elementary school and his parents were in poor health. Would frequent travel create pressure and worry that might harm his family life?

Another member of his inner circle remarked upon the changing regulatory climate. The Food and Drug Administration had just announced a series of additional health and safety regulations that would make it harder to test new technologies through clinical trials. While Tritus could manage a slower time to market on existing products, the same could not be said about the new company.

Finally, still another inner circle member who had a strong relationship with several members of Silicon Valley's elite noted that she had heard rumors that the West Coast company was about to be slapped with a multi-million dollar lawsuit for failing to pay contractors. Did Tritus have the money to deal with the legal issues? Did it want to be involved with a company that was widely believed to renege on contracts?

In the end, George decided to forgo the purchase. The following year, an opportunity arose to acquire a slightly smaller but equally profitable biotech firm on the East Coast. George reviewed the financials and—after checking with his inner circle—made the purchase.

The acquisition was a success. The other company's culture became more like Tritus's family-like culture, and George was able to stay connected to his family in the way that felt right to him. At the same time, Tritus continued to post profits and expand market share. "My inner circle feeds me," said George. "They know me so well and I value their opinions. If I'm facing a major challenge or dilemma, I turn to my inner circle first."

Yes **Relationships**

In the previous chapters, we explored the impact of individual position in a larger network structure—embedded in sticky rice clusters or bridge-builder between sticky rice clusters—on personal and professional effectiveness. Now we consider whether or not the people who are in your professional network *should* be in your network. The main criteria for inclusion in your network? Value. Every single relationship in your professional network should add *value*.

To determine a person's network value to you, ask yourself the following two questions:

- ▪ Does this person have direct or indirect access to resources that have the potential to assist me in my career?
- ▪ Is this person *interesting*? Does this person have a perspective, expertise, ability, or knowledge that I lack and can't find elsewhere in my network?

For every one of your professional contacts, you should be able to answer the first question with a resounding, *Yes*. Each person should at least have the *potential* to contribute to your professional well-being.

Be careful that you don't define *resources* too narrowly. The single biggest mistake that would-be networkers make is to "network" only with so-called "important" people who they *know* have stuff that they want. This is blinkered thinking. Just like a race horse wears blinkers to limit its scope of sight, assuming that you know everything about who a person is or will be limits what you can see in them. It is a mistake to assess someone's value based only on their control over *tangible* resources such as staff, budget, jobs, or material goods. Too often, we think that only high-status people offer value. That's simply not true. In a knowledge economy, the truly powerful people are those who offer less tangible resources, such as wisdom, expertise, alternative perspectives, social connections, and personal influence.

To assess a person's ability to provide you with *intangible* resources, ask the second question. Is the person interesting? If the answer is *Yes*, then the person adds value to your network. People who are interesting may not have much tangible to offer, although they may have more to offer later in their careers. Connect with them now because once they gain more status and prestige, it will be much harder to find opportunities to interact with them, let alone form an authentic relationship. Get to know interesting people now.

Of course, your assessment of who is interesting may change over time. Someone who seems interesting today may seem less so if they fail to develop and grow. A person may also become less interesting to you as others with the same perspective, expertise, ability, or knowledge join your network. When multiple people offer the same resources, your network has either decreased in range or begun to more closely resemble a sticky rice cluster. Either way, you've reduced your network's potential.

People who don't add value to your network should never be among your active professional contacts. The right place for them is either among your dormant relationships—more on this later!—or outside of your network altogether. To the extent that you must interact with them, keep your interactions positive in tone but do not invest time or energy into maintaining the relationship.

If you have relationships with people who support you personally but do not add value in terms of fulfilling your professional or work-related goals, call them friends. While many of your friends will also add value in terms of your career, some of them will not and that's okay. Friends nourish us and provide value in other ways, and they are no less important to us as a result.

How Strong Are You?

Professional networks include relationships of varying strength. While all of your professional relationships should be positive, you will naturally feel closer to some people than to others. The *strong* relationships in your professional network are with people that you regularly rely upon to give you professional advice and support. Like George's inner circle, these are the people you turn to time after time.

People vary in how they define a *strong* relationship. Some people only consider a relationship strong if they've known each other—and each others' families!—for many years. These people are likely to say that they have very few strong relationships. If this describes you, you're not alone. A nationwide survey of more than 2000 U.S. citizens found that, on average, most talk about "important matters" to no more than two people![2]

Others call a relationship strong if interactions with the other person make them feel validated, understood, and cared for, even if they only met the person recently or only interact a few times a year. People who identify strong relationships in this way may say they have twenty or more strong relationships.

In addition to your strong relationships, you probably also have a number of positive but not particularly strong relationships. These relationships are often mistakenly called *weak* relationships but a better term for them is *collegial* relationships. Because there's nothing weak about them. Collegial relationships differ from strong relationships only to the extent that they matter to you personally. Like strong relationships, collegial relationships are positive but, unlike strong relationships, they are not particularly close. That's okay. As you'll see, collegial relationships can be very rewarding, as long as your interactions with the other person include some level of mutuality, trust, and learning.

You also probably have relationships with people that you haven't interacted with in a while. Maybe you worked on a project together a year or more ago. You enjoyed the connection while you were working together but haven't been in touch since. Relationships like these are called *dormant.* They may not be currently active but you know that you could connect again with these people if you needed to.

Effective networks have more dormant relationships than collegial relationships, and more collegial relationships than strong relationships. To achieve the right balance among these different types of relationships, you'll need to continuously and purposefully make choices about when—and when not!—to add, remove, and strengthen relationships.

The Beauty of Being Strong

Let's consider first *strong* relationships. Strong relationships have significant career advantages. The research tells us that people with whom you have strong relationships are more likely to share insider-only business knowledge and strategies, publicly vouch for you, introduce you to others, and provide emotional support. Individuals in strong relationships look for opportunities to benefit each other.[3] And, when opportunities arise, individuals in strong relationships are likely to think of each other first. As we saw in previous chapters, there are also many health and well-being benefits associated with strong relationships, including lower workplace stress, higher life satisfaction, and greater resilience to disease. Perhaps because they feel so rewarding, strong relationships also make us happy.

Strong relationships make it easier to share knowledge because they are more likely to provide a common vocabulary for sharing information, have faith that a challenging communication process will result in learning, and also trust that the information will not be misused or shared in a way that hurts the giver. People that you feel close to will work harder to make sure you understand what they're trying to tell you. And you are more likely to go the extra mile to make sure that they really understand what you're trying to tell them. Instead of giving up at the first blank look, you'll draw on greater reserves of patience to repeat, explain, and repeat again.

Strong relationships are also uniquely able to facilitate the sharing of wisdom. Wisdom, unlike information, comes out of experience and includes strategic and political insights, such as the unwritten rules that govern your organization or industry. Wisdom of this kind can be learned by working within the organization or industry. For example, it takes wisdom to know how budget and staffing decisions are made and which people are most influential in the process. Moreover, wisdom is built up over time and through repeated interactions. It may take many meetings and budget reports and observed promotions to understand that the Finance department really determines who gets budget and staff, that the VP of Finance relies heavily upon the opinion of her executive assistant when making staffing decisions, and that her executive assistant loves talking about her grandchildren. Because organizational wisdom is based on experience and can be difficult to articulate, it is particularly valuable.

Wouldn't it be great to know about job opportunities weeks or even months in advance? Strong relationships make it more likely that you will learn about career and job opportunities.

> Obviously you'd still have the formal process, but it would be good to know of potential opportunities a few months in advance. It would give you the chance to have a think about it and maybe do some research.
>
> —Senior civil servant[4]

Strong relationships are a gateway for opportunity.

You also learn more about the other person when you have a strong relationship. You may have begun your relationship in a narrow task-focused context, like a work project. Interacting regularly over work-related matters makes it more likely that your interactions will extend into other areas. Maybe you'll start talking about your weekend activities or your hobbies or your family. As you start to get to share this type of information with each other, you get a richer, more complex understanding of the other person.

A complex understanding of the other person can make a big difference when trying to promote someone's interests and abilities. A marketing colleague that I talk with frequently may share with me her love of white-water rafting and mountain-climbing. Knowing that she likes risk-taking and outdoor adventures may make it more likely for me to bring her name up when a particular job opportunity arises, such as an opening on the account team serving a client that specializes in athletic wear for hikers.

Three Crucial Characteristics

Not all strong relationships offer career advantages. Effective strong professional relationships have high levels of three crucial characteristics: *mutuality,* *trust,* and *learning,* each of which offers distinct career advantages. Together, these three crucial characteristics make the people with whom you have strong relationships powerful players in your professional network. Strong relationships require a significant investment of one of your most limited resources—time and energy. Build and nurture strong professional relationships *selectively.* If your strong professional relationships do *not* demonstrate high levels of all three crucial characteristics, they may actually be *reducing* your effectiveness. Let's consider each of these characteristics in turn.

Crucial Characteristic 1: Mutuality

> I like to define networking as cultivating mutually beneficial, give-and-take, win–win relationships...The end result may be to develop a large and diverse group of people who will gladly and continually refer a lot of business to us, while we do the same for them.
>
> —Bob Burg
> Author of *Endless Referrals* and *The Go Giver*

Powerful strong relationships are *mutual.* Mutuality refers to the supportive attitude and intent of each person in the relationship. All of the people in George's inner circle were fully committed to supporting him—and he was fully committed to supporting them. When his former high school coach was considering starting his own business, he asked George for his advice.

Don't confuse mutuality with payback. Mutuality does *not* mean constantly engaging in relational arithmetic to make sure that you are getting as much as you are giving. Instead, mutuality occurs when each person in the relationship believes that the other person cares about the other and is looking out for their best interests. Mutuality may not translate into immediate rewards. For many people, being in a relationship characterized by mutuality is rewarding in and of itself. It's good to know that someone has your back.

Warren Buffet calls Charlie Monger—the vice chairman of Berkshire Hathaway, and his close associate for more than fifty years—his "abominable no-man" because he helps one of the most successful investors in the world avoid mistakes and see his own blind spots.[5] After decades of nurturing their relationship, the two men know each other so well that they are able to critique each other's choices honestly and without fear.

Are your strongest professional relationships characterized by mutuality?

One thing to look out for is when the so-called "reward" you receive for staying in a particular strong professional relationship is dysfunctional. We all tend to seek out people who reinforce and validate our self-image. The congruence between how we see ourselves and how other people see us is reassuring because it confirms our social reality. People who have a positive self-image tend to form strong professional relationships with others who respect, appreciate, and value them. People who have a negative self-image tend to seek out relationships that reinforce a self-concept of being powerless, unappreciated, or otherwise not valued. If you find yourself in one of these relationships, get out. Who can forget the scene in the movie *The Devil Wears Prada* in which the beleaguered assistant played by Anne Hathaway turns her back on her job, tosses her cell phone into a fountain, and smiles beatifically as she walks away from her toxic boss?

Your strong relationships won't support your professional development unless you build them with people who empower, appreciate, and value you.

Crucial Characteristic 2: Trust

Effective strong relationships are also characterized by high levels of *trust*. Trust is the belief that another person is both well-intentioned and able when it comes to taking actions that affect you. Strong relationships build mutual trust through opportunities to provide support, demonstrate trustworthiness, and fulfill commitments. As we come to know each other better, we are more willing to give each other the benefit of the doubt. We develop confidence in the other person's competence and character. This makes it easier for us to speak frankly about organizational events and to share bad news when bad news needs to be shared.

Who do *you* trust to give you useful and honest feedback? That person probably belongs in your inner circle.

Strong professional relationships that aren't characterized by high levels of trust receive disproportionately fewer rewards. According to a 2015 survey by The Creative Group, nearly a third of advertising and marketing executives interviewed said a coworker has tried to make them look bad on the job.[6] That's a poor return on a significant investment of time and energy. If you find yourself watching your back, anticipating the next twist of the knife, the relationship definitely isn't worth investing in.

Reduce your investment in strong relationships that aren't characterized by high levels of trust. Start to think of the other person as more of a colleague than a close confidante. Paradoxically, the relationship may become more rewarding when your returns match your investment.

Crucial Characteristic 3: Learning

Lastly, powerful strong relationships are characterized by *learning*. Learning relationships occur when each person shares and seeks a different perspective on the world in order to discover different ways of thinking. In contrast, non-learning or *confirming* relationships occur when the relationship reinforces and validates the same world view. Confirming relationships are enjoyable and comforting. Healthy, supportive friendship groups are often characterized by confirming relationships. Of course friends share information with each other. But people in confirming relationships usually don't offer dramatically different world views. In the polarized U.S. election year of 2016, for example, most friendship groups converged on a single candidate, such Clinton, Trump, or Sanders. While individual members certainly shared political information with each other, they almost always shared information that supported their "shared" candidate.

Be prepared to be challenged. People in learning relationships encourage each other to wrestle with new ways of thinking and working. They push each other to build new skills and try new things rather than stay focused on safe existing competencies. This isn't always easy. Sometimes learning conversations can be uncomfortable, even disquieting. But learning is always accompanied by some level of struggle. Learning relationships will—and should!—challenge you. Accept that you will experience some discomfort. It's worth it.

Conservative Supreme Court Justice Antonin Scalia and liberal Supreme Court Justice Ruth Bader Ginsburg had a learning relationship. Scalia was a staunch conservative—hand-picked by Reagan—who loved to make extreme and audacious statements. Ginsburg, in contrast was a Clinton appointee and well-known for her strong liberal leanings and reserved manner. Yet, they were close friends, despite their strong political differences. Beginning in the 1980s, the two developed a strong relationship over their shared love of opera, their upbringing in outer-borough NYC, and their fondness for souvenir-hunting. Their odd couple friendship was even the subject of a comic opera, *Scalia/Ginsburg*. Instead of driving them apart, their sometime ferocious differences were a source of learning. As Scalia remarked before his death in 2016, "If you can't disagree ardently with your colleagues about some issues of law and yet personally still be friends, get another job, for Pete's sake." For her part, Ginsburg noted that "my opinion is ever so much better because of his stinging dissent."[7]

If you find yourself in a strong professional relationship that isn't characterized by mutuality, trust, and learning, you may be reducing your effectiveness. Ask yourself the following questions:

- Do you believe that the other person wants you to succeed as much as you want that person to succeed? If the answer is *Yes*, then you are in a relationship characterized by *mutuality*.
- Do you feel that you could talk to the other person about private matters? If the answer is *Yes*, then you are in a *trusting* relationship.
- Do you often leave conversations with additional insights and ideas to mull over? If the answer is *Yes*, then you are in a *learning* relationship.

In the past, you may have seen opportunities for strengthening these relationships but have shied away. Think again. Strengthening key relationships is a great way to maximize your network's potential.

Five Strategies for Building the Right Strong Relationships

Effective networking requires building, nurturing, and leveraging relationships. The first step to developing an effective network is to *build* relationships. When it comes to building strong relationships, I have *five* pieces of advice:

1. Seek quality, not quantity
2. Build strong bridges
3. Seek out complementary skills/experience
4. Include mentors
5. Include sponsors

One, seek quality, not quantity. Don't get hung up on numbers. Despite the typical networking coach's advice to get "as many business cards and LinkedIn contacts as possible," the truth is that quantity doesn't matter. The absolute number of relationships in your professional network isn't as important as the *quality* of those relationships. This is particularly true when it comes to strong relationships.

One study of top leaders found that most thrived when their networks included 12 to 18 strong relationships.[8] However, the number that's right for you may be much higher or much lower. George, for example, only had nine people in his inner circle. We all have a personalized quotient of relational energy, the energy that we have available to expend toward our relationships.[9] Some people have more relational energy, some have less.

The decision whether or not to build a relationship can be captured by a mathematical equation that balances your relational energy with your relationship needs. Spending energy on one person means you have less available to spend on other people. Get to know your personalized quotient of relational energy and work with what works for you. If you're trying to make everyone your close friend, you're going to have a tough time creating an effective network.

Don't confuse the *frequency* of interaction alone or the power level of your colleague with the *quality* of the relationship. You may interact on a daily basis with your boss or a direct report without having a particularly strong relationship. If you are spending a lot of time and effort on relationships that aren't characterized by mutuality, trust, and learning, you are wasting your relational energy. Find ways to reduce the frequency with which you interact with these people. Your strong relationships are your inner circle. Be selective about who you include in this group.

Two, build a few strong bridges. Because we tend to introduce the members of our inner circle to each other, strong relationships are less likely to be bridges. Because of their rarity, you may benefit particularly by having a few strong bridging relationships. Having a strong bridging relationship means that you'll gain more cluster-specific information—and, especially, valuable wisdom—because the trust and learning benefits of powerful relationships extend into sticky rice clusters. Your strong relationship partners will vouch for you to other sticky rice cluster members, even when those other sticky cluster members don't know you directly. This makes it easier for you to build trust with different parts of the larger network without having to also build more relationships.

So, when developing your professional networks, include at least some bridging among your strong relationships. This is usually not hard to do for mid-career or higher professionals who may have already formed bridging relationships as a function of working in multiple departments or organizations but it can be an issue for early-career professionals who are more likely to be embedded in sticky rice clusters. Frequent interaction occurs naturally among people in a sticky rice cluster but may need to be more purposeful with people outside the cluster. To build strong bridging relationships, create opportunities to interact more frequently with people in other clusters.

But don't worry if only some of your strong professional relationships are bridging. Having too many bridging strong relationships is not important and may even reduce your general well-being. Low emotional stability, for example, has been argued to be both a cause and an effect of bridge-building among strong relationships.[10] Some of the benefits of having strong relationships come from the ability of the people who know you to communicate with each other to support you. As a rule of thumb, aim for roughly 20 to 25% of your strong relationships to also be bridging relationships.

Three, build strong relationships with people who offer complementary skills and strengths. These types of relationships are more likely to be characterized by mutuality *and* to provide opportunities for learning. For example, you may be a great public speaker while your colleague is a master event organizer. Apple's Steve Jobs and Tim Cook had complementary skills. Jobs was an innovative designer, a master marketer, and a passionate stickler for details. He could also be narcissistic, difficult to work with, and spiteful. Cook, on the other hand, was known for his ability to build relationships and to stay out of the day-to-day details of the product development process. The two formed a strong relationship. Cook helped then-CEO Jobs soften his rough edges and Jobs prepared Cook to demonstrate the passion and confidence that he would need as Jobs's replacement. As Cook noted when reflecting upon what he learned from Jobs, "I learned that focus is key. You can only do so many things well, and you should cast aside everything else."[11]

One of the benefits of surrounding yourself with people who offer complementary skills and strengths is that you build your own human capital. Learning from people in your network can help you develop your technical and managerial skills, gain deeper expertise in your area, and increase your ability to handle the challenges you will face in the workplace. In this way, social capital builds human capital.

But the social-to-human capital cycle doesn't end there. As you leverage your social capital to build your human capital, you increase your value in the marketplace. More people—and more powerful people—will want to connect with you to get access to the resources that you "own."[12] You become more attractive as a professional contact. Others want access to *what* you know or can do, as well as *who* you know. In this way, human capital creates even more social capital which—if you choose your contacts wisely!—creates even more human capital.

Once this virtuous cycle is set in motion, the benefits grow rapidly. In a phenomenon known as *the Matthew effect*,[13] after the parable of the servants in the biblical Gospel of Matthew, those rich in social capital attract more people and, as result, become even richer in social capital. In other words, the rich get richer and the poor get poorer! It's worth noting that you are not the only one who benefits from this virtuous cycle because, as *your* social capital grows, so does the social capital of everyone in your network. Everybody wins!

Four, build strong relationships with one or more mentors. One special type of learning relationship is the one you have with a *mentor*. Mentors provide career advice and coaching. Formally or informally, they offer regular support and suggestions to help you develop as a person and as a professional. A good mentor gives you professional guidance and honest feedback. He or she helps you set professional goals and monitor your progress toward reaching those goals. The mentor-protégé relationship is ideally warm and friendly. Mentors create a safe space in which to discuss personal challenges and barriers.

Sometimes your immediate supervisor will also be your mentor. But this is not always the case. Mentors focus on developing competencies, an approach that can be a challenge for those supervisors who see their job primarily as one of evaluating performance. Your mentor(s) may not even belong to your industry or profession. Their role is not to get you a job or a promotion but to help you develop yourself as a professional.

If you don't have a mentor in your professional network, find one. In fact, find more than one because having multiple mentors among work, family, friends, and other industry and community members enriches both career and life satisfaction.[14] It is likely that there is already someone in your life who has the ability and desire to be your mentor. Perhaps it is a former teacher or coach or even someone you haven't seen for years. Whoever it is or was, don't be afraid to approach them again just because you no longer interact regularly. Chances are, they'll be happy to see you again.

> You don't have to hang your hat on just one critical mentor. A mentor could be someone you have coffee with once. And that's okay – and they help you through one thing that you're curious about. And maybe something else occurs to you 5 years down the road, and you want to call them out for coffee again. Or maybe you have multiple people that you mean throughout your life that have mentored you in different ways. I think what's critical is that you don't need one magical person or magic bullet. It can be many mentoring moments, as opposed to a person. And think about it in the evolution of your career.[15]
>
> —Jane Allen, Chief Diversity Officer, Partner,
> Global Renewable Energy Leader, Deloitte

Although many people have relationships with mentors that—while rewarding—are not particularly strong, you will get more out of the relationship if it is a strong one. We'll talk more about how to strengthen relationships in later chapters.

Who in your professional development network is—or could be—a mentor?

Five, include one or more sponsors among your strong relationships. Sponsors are people who wield power within your organization, industry, or profession. Sponsors may be mentors but often aren't. Mentors tend to care deeply about you as a whole person and stick with you through the ups and downs of your career. Sponsors, on the other hand, are interested primarily in promoting talent. Sponsors may continue to support you through a couple of personal or professional failures but will move onto other protégées if you fail to rebound from your failures or if your performance otherwise fails to live up to their expectations.

Sponsors promote your career by offering you visibility and access to other powerful people. In the mid-seventies, David Bowie became a sponsor for the then-unknown musician Iggy Pop. Pop would go on to become an internationally recognized rock star. Many years later, Pop described his relationship with Bowie this way,

> He was more of a benefactor than a friend in a way most people think of friendship...I met the Beatles and the Stones, and this one and that one, and this actress and this actor and all these powerful people through him.
>
> —Iggy Pop[16]

Sponsors have the power to significantly raise your visibility to senior management. Sponsors have power and/or an influential position within your organization and industry, and use it to advocate for you and help you get projects and assignments that can enhance your position and visibility. Sponsors open doors.

Having a powerful sponsor elevates your worth in the eyes of others. As a comparatively junior person or relative unknown, you pose a puzzle for others in more senior positions who need to evaluate you. You are a question mark in their eyes. Even when your performance is good, it can still be ascribed to circumstance, luck, or the effort of others. The support of a powerful sponsor is like a stamp of approval.[17] You become less of a question mark and more of an exclamation mark. In a sense, your sponsor's status rubs off on you.

When once asked to invest in a friend's new venture, Baron de Rothschild is said to have replied that he would not invest, but would walk arm-in-arm with his friend across the exchange floor. In short order there would be investors to spare. People observing the pair would infer that Rothschild had thrown into the venture, which would ensure the venture's success.[18]

A sponsor can have a profound impact on virtually every aspect of your career, boosting your ability to ask for and get raises and promotions and find satisfaction at work. More than any other type of relationship, sponsors can dramatically and positively influence your career outcomes. Yet relatively few employees—19% of men and 13% of women in one survey—report having a sponsor.[19]

If you don't have a sponsor, find one. Scan the horizon for leaders who either embody your values or are likely to value your strengths.[20] Look for organizational and industry leaders with whom you could build a relationship characterized by mutuality and learning. To whom could you offer complementary skills and expertise? For example, if you have strong tactical follow-through skills, perhaps you could offer those to a charismatic leader who may lack the skills or interest required to execute on a vision.[21] Successful protégés build trust and increase mutuality by advancing their sponsors' passion and helping build their legacies outside the organization.[22]

The Ups and Downs of Weakness

Collegial relationships differ from strong relationships only to the extent that they matter to you personally. They should still demonstrate mutuality, trust, and learning albeit at lower levels. Like strong relationships, collegial relationships are positive but, unlike strong relationships, they are not particularly close. You may have a good relationship with Pat in accounting but you don't consider her a member of your inner circle.

Collegial relationships offer at least two enormous advantages over strong relationships. One, they are a lot less time-consuming to maintain than strong relationships. Often, they can be maintained with relatively effortless actions, such as occasional hallway conversations, Facebook likes, and LinkedIn updates. In other instances, maintaining the relationship may require regularly scheduled meetings or get-togethers, even if those meetings only occur once every few months.

The other advantage that collegial relationships offer is that they are much more likely than strong relationships to include dissimilar people, helping you to increase your network's range. Our tendencies toward homophily make it hard to include people who are not like us among our strongest relationships. But for those of you who purposefully and thoughtfully push yourselves out of your comfort zone, it is far easier to form positive and authentic relationships with different types of people if the relationships are collegial rather than strong.

Of course, collegial relationships do have several disadvantages. Because collegial relationships are easier to build and maintain, it's easy to grow your network beyond your ability to handle it. As more and more people get added to your network, you may experience either *relational overload* or *network rigidity. Relational overload* occurs when you find yourself facing so many relational demands that you feel overwhelmed and exhausted. You may even start to feel vaguely guilty for spending time on yourself and your inner circle. *Network rigidity* occurs when you maintain the same set of collegial relationships. Over time, the information, perspectives, and insights you gain from your network become more predictable and therefore less useful.

Five Strategies for Building the Right Collegial Relationships

To leverage the advantages of collegial professional relationships and minimize the disadvantages, I have five pieces of general advice.

1. Quantity is good when it comes to collegial relationships, but only up to a point.
2. Collegial relationships should include all the important stakeholders in current projects.
3. Include lots of bridging relationships
4. Include relationships with people who extend your network range.
5. Keep churning.

One, quantity is good when it comes to collegial relationships, but only up to a point. At any one time, most people can maintain collegial relationships with roughly 150 people. This number comes out of research conducted in the early 1990s by Robin Dunbar, a professor of evolutionary anthropology at Oxford University. Dunbar compared brain size to social group size. He reasoned that knowledge of complex relationships requires a more complex brain structure. Based on his research, he argued that the human brain is only capable of maintaining active relationships with an average of about 150 people, a number that has come to be called Dunbar's Number.[23]

Dunbar's Number has been found in several types of networks, including online Facebook friendships. A study of more than three thousand U.K Facebook users between the ages of 18 and 65, conducted by Dunbar, found that—just as in off-line life—users had an average of about 150 individuals with whom they kept in regular contact. "The interesting thing is that you can have 1,500 friends, but when you actually look at traffic on sites, you see people maintain the same inner circle of around 150 people that we observe in the real world," Dunbar noted.[24] Subsequent researchers have found the average number to be slightly higher, but the general principle remains. We can handle many more collegial relationships than strong relationships but the number is not infinite.

Maintaining a useful set of collegial relationships is as much about time management as it is about understanding your relational energy. If individuals are not necessary to the achievement of your short- or mid-term professional goals, they probably shouldn't be in your set of active professional relationships.

One easy test you can do to determine if someone should be among your collegial relationships is to imagine scheduling a meeting with that person and then having it cancelled at the last minute. Would you feel elated or sad? Your answer will tell you if that person should be among your collegial—or strong!—relationships or if that relationship is not one in which you should invest. As Dan Ariely noted in his interview with psychologist Ron Friedman as part of the Peak Work Performance Summit, "If you feel elation, you don't want to do it. You're doing it out of obligation or discomfort with saying no. If you're sad, then you should accept the invitation—it's something you want to do."[25]

Important exceptions to the imaginary cancellation test are your stakeholders. While you may not look forward to meeting with a particular stakeholder, stakeholders are an important part of your network of collegial relationships. Be sure to allocate some of your time and relational energy to them.

Two, collegial relationships should include all the important stakeholders in your current projects. Whenever you join a new organization, take on a new position, or start a new project, your first step should be to determine which people, roles, and departments have the power to help or prevent you from achieving your project or career goals. Whose support or assistance do you need? Whose non-compliance could make your project or career grind to a halt? To achieve your professional goals, you must have collegial relationships with all of these stakeholders. To make sure you don't miss an important person, map out exactly what you need to get done and whose help you need to do it. Don't overlook people occupying lower level administrative roles. They can be surprisingly powerful. You don't want to miss an important deadline because no one was willing to prioritize your order fulfillment request!

To identify important stakeholders, complete the *Professional Stakeholder Network Exercise* in your Toolbox. Which stakeholders are missing from *your* network?

Three, collegial relationships should include lots of bridging relationships. Collegial relationships are easier than strong relationships to maintain across bridges. One influential network researcher, Mark Granovetter, even went so far as to claim that *only* collegial relationships form bridges.[26] While we now know that isn't true, it is far more likely that a collegial relationship will connect you to a unique sticky rice cluster. To increase the amount of bridging in your network, seek opportunities to make purposeful connections with people from different sticky rice clusters. The relationships you form as a result are likely to be collegial relationships.

Four, collegial relationships should include relationships with people who extend your network range. Don't fall into the trap of only maintaining friendships with similar people. For example, according to a 2014 Public Religion Research Institute poll, more than three quarters of White people report that the network of people with whom they discuss close matters is entirely White.[27] If you're White and this describes you, then it is high time to develop at least a few collegial relationships with people from other ethnicities.

Five, keep churning. Unlike strong relationships, which tend to be stable over time, collegial relationships should be in a constant state of churn. Churn refers to the extent to which people move in and out of your network. Having adequate churn in your network can reduce the likelihood of relational overload and network rigidity. Churn helps you maintain only as many relationships as you can handle without feeling overloaded. At the same time, churn helps you avoid network rigidity by keeping a steady stream of new and diverse information flowing into your network. Churn can also help you keep your network current with your professional needs. It is highly unlikely that the people who should be in your professional network this year are the same people who should be there even a few years later.

Churn is not only good for you, it's good for your organization. The churn in *your* network reduces the likelihood that your organization's network will get locked into clumps of sticky rice clusters. That's because churn is particularly important when it comes to your bridging relationships. By churning your bridges, you free yourself up to build new bridges.

It works like this: Imagine that your organization is like most networks and has become populated with sticky rice clusters, some of which are connected to you and almost none of which are connected to each other. You try to help the organization—and yourself!—by facilitating the flow of information and wisdom across bridges. But that's a pretty big task, especially if your organization doesn't have many bridges. People may turn to you so often to help with translating and transferring information that you become backlogged with requests, effectively becoming a bottleneck. You start to divert the bulk of your energy and time toward managing the relationships between the clusters.

In this scenario, not only are you overwhelmed—and overworked—but you're blocking the flow of knowledge and other resources throughout your organization. Too, without more connection and opportunities to promote mutual understanding, those clusters may grow hostile to each other, thrusting you into the role of mediator. While there are benefits to taking on the mediator role, you need to weigh them against the off-task time it takes to translate and mediate, as well as the disadvantages to the organization as a whole.

To maintain your valuable bridge-building position without becoming a bottleneck—and without burning out!—introduce people in different sticky rice clusters to each other. By doing so, you shift some of the burden of bridging to others. Maintain your relationships with the two people you just connected in a way that doesn't increase your time (e.g., arrange group meetings or activities). Alternatively, you can choose to weaken one or both relationships still further so that you remain collegial with one person but maintain only indirect access to the other. This last strategy effectively lets one or both relationships fade into dormancy. That's not necessarily a bad thing. In fact, it can be a very good thing because dormant relationships are the major drivers of power in your network.

Sleeping Beauties

> One of the challenges in networking is that everyone thinks that it's making cold calls to strangers. Actually, it's the people who already have strong trust relationships with you who know your dedicated, smart, a team player, who can help you. Even college students have professors, family friends, alumni of their college. Your network is the people who want to help you, and you want to help them, and that's really powerful.[28]
>
> —Reid Hoffman, co-founder of LinkedIn

Without proactive effort, collegial and even strong relationships fade away over time and become inactive or *dormant*. Dormant relationships are those strong or weak relationships which are no longer part of your active network. These sleeping beauties could be colleagues from a previous job, a teammate on a now-defunct team, or college roommates that you haven't seen for ten years. Dormant relationships are the secret powerhouse in your network.

Dormant relationships have two powerful advantages. One, because they require no time, effort, or emotional investment, you can handle an infinite number of dormant relationships. This is great news! Letting relationships become—or remain—dormant frees you up to focus on your strong relationships and to create new collegial relationships through churn. The second advantage is related to the first. Dormant relationships can be re-activated! As long as the initial relationship was positive, dormant relationships can be re-awakened at any point. Although they will naturally fade away over time, they are likely to retain some echoes of the initial relationship. Relationships that were once extremely strong—such as that between college roommates—may remain strong, even after lying dormant for many years.

Even a short interaction can retain traces of positivity for a long time. I still remember an exchange I had nearly twenty years ago when I was a doctoral student. I was feeling overwhelmed with the workload and questioning my ability to succeed. One of my professors—perhaps recognizing my feelings—reached out to me with a few kind words. It was a small gesture on the professor's part but it had a big impact on me. I have never forgotten it. In the years since then, that professor has occasionally asked me for small favors, such as reviewing an academic paper or talking with a prospective student. No matter how busy I am, I never refuse.

Despite their enormous advantages, dormant relationships also come with two big disadvantages. One, dormant relationships are useless if you completely forget about them. Two, even when you do remember them, they are useless if you are reluctant to activate them. To remember and leverage dormant relationships, you will need to create a memory system that works for you and turn to it regularly.

Dormant relationships are useless if you completely forget about them. Creating a memory system needn't be complicated. If you're like me, you probably don't remember everyone you meet. I've always admired people who can meet someone once and never forget his or her name. But that's not me. I often forget the names of people I've worked with for more than ten years! Luckily, there are many simple ways to "expand" your memory and remember your connections.

The biggest one is obvious: Social media. In the old days, people would put notes on their rolodex. Today, we use Facebook, LinkedIn, Twitter and other social media accounts. For some of us, relational management software applications, such as SalesforceIQ and Contactually, are a godsend. They can help you segment your contacts into manageable segments.

Patrick Ewers, one of Silicon Valley's top relationship management coaches, advises networkers to limit themselves to no more than five segments.

> Before you go out and tag every single person with every single interest, narrow it down. Otherwise, it becomes a real brute force effort. You constantly have to add and remove people and tags. It's one of those things that gets stale really fast. It's like your address book that you never use. The key idea is simplicity.[29]

Even email works. Heidi Roizen, one of Silicon Valley's power players, says that she makes a point of following up every meaningful interaction with an email the next day. Doing so helps her follow through *and* get the person's contact information into her database. "It's my quick and dirty way of keeping track of every interesting person I've ever met."[30] Find a system that works for you and use it regularly to capture your interactions with others.

Dormant relationships are useless if you fail to activate them. Of course, the best system in the world won't help you if you don't use it regularly. In my experience, the biggest reason why people fail to leverage dormant relationships is fear. Some fear that reaching out to someone else will be perceived as overly intrusive. We don't want to "bother" anyone. Others fear the embarrassment of having the other person look at us blankly or—worse—indicate by word or expression that they don't feel as positively toward us as we obviously felt toward them.

If fear stops you from re-connecting with dormant relationships, it may be because you associate re-connecting with trying to get something from the other person. While this may indeed be the case, it doesn't have to be the only time you re-activate your dormant relationships. If you get in the habit of re-connecting in order to give, I guarantee you that your qualms about reaching out to request will reduce.

If you have already developed the habit of giving to your network and yet you still feel hesitant to re-activate a connection, ask yourself one question: Would I like it if this person had contacted me? If the answer is Yes, then go ahead. Chances are, they feel the same way.

It's perfectly okay to let relationships lie dormant. In fact, it can be more than okay—it can be the absolutely *right* thing to do. Just because you haven't talked with someone in two years, it doesn't mean that your relationship is dead: it's just not growing (right now!). Instead of forcing yourself to keep relationships active—sometimes through the dreaded *just checking in* phone call—think of dormant relationships as seeds you have planted. When your reason for connecting with someone is real and reasonable, do it. Don't avoid re-connection.

Getting Out of a Bad Relationship

There are many reasons why you might remain in a value-less or even a negative relationship. Perhaps you stay in it because you fear the other person's disapproval or disregard. Perhaps the person has high status—or is connected to someone who has high status—and you fear the repercussions of severing ties. Or, you worry that you'll hurt the other person's feelings. Some relationships continue because of physical proximity—as when you find yourself constantly interacting with the guy in the cubicle next to you, even though he drives you crazy!

Perhaps the relationship was nourishing in the past but the person, relationship or circumstances are now different. You might find yourself regularly spending time with people you knew in college, even though you don't really enjoy spending time with them anymore. And, of course, some relationships continue purely as a function of *relational inertia*. Relational inertia occurs when you continue to maintain the relationship simply because you always have. You go for lunch every Thursday with the same group of engineers, even though you're tired of listening to them gripe about work. These are all common reasons why value-less or negative relationships continue but they aren't *good* reasons.

Your time and relational energy are limited resources. People who regularly tax your mental, physical, or emotional resources without adding value make it harder for you to give to your work—and non-work!—tasks and relationships. You only have one life to live. Do you really want to spend it with people who take the life out of you? Jennifer Lawrence, the *Hunger Games* actress and Academy Award winner, keeps a very small circle of close friends and is very particular who she lets in that circle. "The moment I feel like someone is using me or is in it for the wrong reasons, I have zero guilt about just cutting them the f--- out of my life."[31]

Cutting back resource-draining relationships is like pruning a grapevine. Unpruned, a grapevine expends all of its energy on vine growth instead of grapes. In contrast, a pruned grapevine flourishes, yielding more and higher-quality grapes. Pruning your network can release relational energy that you can use to invigorate other relationships.

Cut back on the time and energy you spend on value-less or negative relationships. Some strong relationships may be more nourishing as collegial relationships, and some collegial relationships be more powerful if they become dormant. Only in the most extreme cases do you need to disconnect yourself completely from someone in your network.

You don't have to ghost people to reduce the strength of your relationship. Investing less in a particular relationship might be as simple as turning down a few luncheon requests or responding more slowly to phone calls, emails, or texts. If necessary, make small behavioral changes, such as eating lunch at a different time or walking down a different hallway on your way to the copier.

Stop saying *Yes*—or start saying *No!*—to unnecessary projects that keep you connected to certain people. Get comfortable saying things like, "I have some work I need to do right now. Can we talk another time?" and "I won't be able to do that, sorry." Surround yourself with nourishing relationships and you will flourish.

To Recap...

A balanced and effective network requires a few strong relationships, a larger number of active relationships, and a constantly growing supply of dormant relationships. Creating the right balance of relationships requires that you purposefully build and nurture connections that add value. It also requires that you purposefully *dis*connect or, prune relationships that no longer add value.

In the next chapter, we'll look at concrete strategies and specific steps that you can take to build and nurture the right professional relationships for *you*.

Reflection Questions

Do you have any strong or collegial relationships that aren't *Yes* relationships? Why are they still in your professional network?

Do all of your strong relationships demonstrate high levels of the three crucial characteristics?

Think of someone who used to be in your network and with whom you wish you could now reconnect. What's preventing you from reaching out to that person?

7

Casting Your Net

SELF-ASSESSMENT SNAPSHOT

To answer these questions, please complete the *Professional Support Network Exercise* and the *Professional Stakeholder Network Exercise* in the Toolbox at the end of this book.

1. List three *types* of people who are not in your *supporters* network but should be (i.e., which *whats* are missing?)

   a. _____

   b. _____

   c. _____

2. Name three *individuals* (or work roles) in your *stakeholder* network whose collaboration or compliance you need but do not have.

   a. _____

   b. _____

   c. _____

Not Content to Stay in Park[1]

Elizabeth Parker was very excited about her new position as undersecretary of Environmental Affairs, Water Division, for the State of Delaware. The Water Division engineered and constructed dams, maintained the pipeline that transported fresh water, oversaw sewage disposal and marine transportation, and collected all of the water revenues from the many cities and towns throughout the state. Parker had spent many years as a volunteer for the Women's League of Voters, researching environmental issues and influencing the state's environmental legislation. The mission of the Environmental Affairs was very important to her personally and she was highly motivated to have a positive impact on the state's environment.

The problem started on her first day. Parker arrived at her office early, eager to begin her new job. The first thing that struck her as strange was there were no files from her predecessor. But, before she could think too long about what that meant, James Benson—the secretary of Environmental Affairs and her boss—stopped by her office to invite her to a 9:15 am meeting with the rest of the agency.

In the meeting, she was introduced to the other 25 members of the agency. One by one, the men—they were all men—stood up and stated his name, job title, and how much he looked forward to working with Parker. Parker returned the well-wishes and then, at 9:30, the meeting was adjourned. She returned to her office and ordered some office supplies. At noon, she went out for lunch and to run some errands. When she returned, she asked each of the five directors to come in and meet her. Dutifully, each one did. She said hello, they said hello, and then each one scurried back to his office as soon as he could politely do so.

Parker called up Rhonda Baker—one of her League of Women Voters contacts and someone who had done work with the Water Division—to ask about the department and Benson, in particular. "Benson is the quintessential government employee," said Baker. She added, "He's survived as long as he has because he doesn't rock the boat. The person who had the undersecretary job before you was transferred because he was pushing Benson to do something he didn't want to do. Frankly, he'd love it if you just twiddled your thumbs. I mean, after all, you're a political appointee. It's no skin off his back if you sit in your office and do crossword puzzles all day."

Parker hung up the phone, disturbed by what Baker had told her. Parker hadn't taken the undersecretary position because she wanted to sit around and do nothing. She wanted to make a difference. It became clear that she needed to figure out what needed to be done and then put herself forward as the person to do it. Of course, she was a newcomer to the organization and she didn't know what she didn't know.

She thought about going to Benson but then thought again. Benson didn't seem forthcoming about possible projects. In fact, he did seem perfectly content to let her park herself in her office and do nothing. Parker figured that she needed to talk with some of the career government workers in the Water Division. Surely, they would have thoughts on what needed to be done. But, although Parker had considerable experience with the Environmental Affairs department from her League of Women Voter's days, almost everyone she knew either served in an outward-facing role or was a political appointee. She didn't know any career government workers.

How was Parker going to figure out what needed to be done?

By developing a networking strategy.

Networking Your Way

By now it should be clear that effective networking is not about attending networking events, collecting business cards, and getting a lot of LinkedIn followers. It's also not about crafting a memorable elevator speech, dressing to impress, working a room, or projecting your "personal brand" in-person and on-line. Sure, these activities will help you make a more favorable impression—and impression management *does* matter when you first meet someone—but effective networking is not *just* about managing impressions. Effective networking is about managing *relationships*—real relationships built on genuine connection—using your own personalized networking strategy.

Before reading further, I encourage you to complete the exercises in Appendices A, B, and C. These exercises are designed to help you assess your current network using established research-based methods. They are based on years of working with executives, managers, and students. They will provide you with a realistic assessment of your current set of professional relationships. Much like starting any journey, it's difficult to get to where you want to go if you don't know where you are.

If you haven't yet completed these exercises, please do so before continuing to read.

What is a networking strategy? A networking strategy is a purposeful plan to build, nurture, and leverage a set of valuable and positive professional relationships that are structured to maximize the flow of resources to you, to all the people connected to your network, and to the organizations and communities in which you reside. Your personal networking strategy will be unique because *you* are unique.

You have a unique constellation of interests, goals, likes, dislikes, time, energy, and resources. You already have a set of professional relationships that no one else has. Networking according to some cookie cutter formula or business guru's generic advice won't work. Effective networkers build, nurture and leverage their professional networks in their own way. The purpose of this chapter is to help you take that first step by developing a *personalized* networking strategy for *building* your professional networks.

Stepping Out

At this point, you've identified your professional contacts. You've assessed the extent to which each relationship is nourishing and adds value. You've identified opportunities to build *bridges*, the *types* of people who should be in your network but aren't, and the *stakeholders* that you need to seek out.

Parker began developing her network strategy by mapping out her organizational network. She took out a piece of paper and a pencil. She hadn't been in the organization long but she had the organization chart and that was a start. Too, Baker had given her some insight into how the department worked. All she had to do was figure out who wasn't in her network but *should* be.

She started with the basics. The entire Water Division consisted of five departments and more than fifty employees. In addition to Benson, there were three people in top management positions—herself and two other undersecretaries. Only three of the employees in the division were political appointees like herself. The rest were career government workers. Parker figured that since the staff in the five departments were the closest to the day-to-day implementation of Division policy, they would know what projects were worth doing. Every department had a director and an assistant director. Parker decided to start with them.

Parker also suspected that if she wanted to take on a project of any major scope, she'd have to get one of the other undersecretaries, Scott Walters, into her stakeholder network. Baker had told her that Walters was a close associate of Benson's and served as his top advisor. Benson was afraid of rocking the boat. If Parker wanted to make waves, she'd need to get someone like Walters on board her ship. Baker had worked closely with Walters. Perhaps she had some insights to share with Parker.

Parker put down her pencil, satisfied with her efforts. She had identified the types of people who should be in her network but weren't and a specific stakeholder that she needed to seek out. Now, she was ready to start building new relationships.

Building a network strategically means forming positive relationships strategically. To do this in your own network, you will need to:

1. Optimize the context for relationship-building,
2. Prepare to engage, and
3. Engage in meaningful and positive interactions.

Step 1: Optimize the Context

The science regarding relationship-formation suggests that serendipity plays a relatively minor role. We do *not* form relationships by chance. Instead, relationship formation is heavily influenced by the context in which we meet people, as well as our innate biases. Effective networkers know this and create the conditions that make so-called "spontaneous" relationship formation more likely. Many budding entrepreneurs, for example, join co-workspaces as a way of meeting new people.

> The owners [of Cambridge Business Lounge, a communal workspace in Cambridge, England] are incredibly supportive and made a big effort to get to know me and why I was using the centre. Every time I worked there, they were able to introduce me to new people that they thought I'd get on well with, and potentially could work with too… I've met amazing people, gained new clients, raised my profile in the city, been a judge for the Cambridge Food & Drink awards, been interviewed on BBC radio and made fab new friends.
>
> —Kelly Molson, web designer[2]

It has long been known in the social sciences that relationships are much more likely to form between people who take part in the same activities.[3] This happens for a couple of reasons. First, our interests draw us together which makes it more likely that we have a reason for interacting. Then, as a result of interacting over our shared interests, we tend to become more alike, triggering our homophilous impulses and making it more likely that our interactions will develop into a mutually rewarding relationship. Finally, just seeing each other regularly makes a relationship likely to form. We tend to like the familiar and, when you see the same person time and again, you become familiar to each other, making it more likely you'll want to connect.

So, to optimize the context for relationship-building, you'll need to find an activity that is likely to bring you in contact with the people who are not in your network but should be. Parker decided to optimize her relationship-building context by visiting every one of the directors and assistant directors in the Water Division. She sent each one an email, making an offer of lunch and requesting a tour of their department.

Finding an activity with which to connect with *stakeholders* is straightforward. By definition, they have some stake in a project, work, or task activity that you are engaged in; your work is the shared activity. But to extend your network *range* or to *build bridges* to other clusters, you may have to try new activities or, at least, go about your old activities in a new way.

Choose your activities carefully. Some activities are better for relationship-building than others. Starting or joining a book club, for example, is a much better activity for relationship-building than attending the book signing of a local writer. Similarly, training for a marathon event with other runners is a better activity for relationship building than just running in the event. That's because genuine relationships are more likely to form around activities or experiences that have three critical components: *passion, interdependence*, and a shared identity or, *we-ness*. Activities that have these three components increase your odds of forming valuable professional relationships.

Choose activities for which you have a passion. When an activity means something to you, your engagement in it will reflect authenticity. (It'll also be a lot more enjoyable for you!) Being authentic—that is, feeling like your real self—is an essential foundation for building genuine connections. Select an activity in which you have an inherent interest, expertise, or experience.

What activities come to mind?

To meet new people, you may have to explore your interests and current activities—your passions—in a new way, one that is likely to build bridges, extend your range, and attract your stakeholders. For example, let's say you realized that everyone in your professional network works at your current organization and you'd like to include people who work in other organizations in your network. You also like to run 5Ks. Well, instead of always running alone, push yourself to join a local running club. If you can't find one, start one by contacting your local YMCA or library. Thinking about new ways to engage your passions will help you step outside of your comfort zone to embrace the familiar in an unfamiliar context.

Choose activities that require interdependence. Just being in the same room as another person is not enough. If there is no interdependence in your interactions with potential relationship partners, you have no opportunity to observe each other, learn about each other, and develop trust. This is why conference sessions and report-out meetings are not great ways to build relationships but serving on panels, committees, boards of directors, project teams, and task forces are. These activities force you to interact collaboratively with others.

> Trade associations are a lot of work and you don't get paid to do them, but participating in them can amplify your presence in your industry beyond the scope of your company. Not only will you meet other leaders, but you'll also have a shared endeavor. And of the best ways to build relationships is through a shared endeavor.
>
> —Heidi Roizen[4]

So, instead of just starting or joining a running club, build interdependence by proposing that members help each other train for and complete a 5K, half-marathon, or full marathon. Likewise, instead of just volunteering your time for the local charity, make the activity interdependent by offering to serve on the board of directors or work on a committee project. You can really exploit this aspect of relationship-building with your stakeholders because, by definition, you're already interdependent when it comes to achieving your project or work goals. Highlighting that interdependence in your interactions will strengthen your relationships.

The lack of passion and interdependence is why most "networking" events are not a good use of your limited time. In fact, they are one of the most difficult environments for making connections because there is no opportunity for working together interdependently. There's nothing to focus on except the awkward task of so-called "networking." They can be particularly torturous for network purists and introverts, both of whom hate meaningless chatter, self-promotion, and requesting contact information.

> Too many introverts take their identity as an excuse to ignore networking altogether: *it doesn't feel comfortable for me, so I won't do it.* But you're missing huge opportunities in the process. What's critical to recognize is that there's not just one way to network; it's not all about going to 500-person cocktail parties and trading business cards. You can network in small groups; you could invite a colleague out for lunch, or host a small dinner party, or get curious about other things you all have in common... play to your strengths.
>
> —Dorie Clark, adjunct professor
> Duke University's Fuqua School of Business[5]

Instead of going to "networking" events, engage in activities that engage your passions and offer opportunities to collaborate.

Lastly, choose activities that build a shared identity or we-ness. We-ness is the feeling that you get when you believe that you and the other people in the activity are part of something greater than yourselves. You start to see the other people in the activity as the same as you in some way, even if you are very different on the surface. One of the easiest ways to develop *we-ness* is to share a goal, preferably one that requires you to collaborate in order to achieve it. A shared goal might be to beat the average run time of a rival running group or to collectively lose 300 pounds or to make a local charity self-sustainable. Do you have any personal or professional goals that could be furthered through collaboration?

Another strategy for building we-ness is to emphasize an identity that is already shared by all activity members. Wearing or otherwise displaying shared symbols (e.g., t-shirts, logos, badges), sharing a group name (e.g., *Tough Mudder Legionnaires*), and constantly using the term *we* to refer to activity participants will enhance we-ness.

One final thing to consider as you select your networking activities: Make sure you find an activity that works for you and your lifestyle. Ideally, the activity will fit seamlessly into your life without adding time or draining other resources. You can ensure this by thinking about all of your current activities as possible networking opportunities. For example, consider your networking strategy when you form project teams or agree to collaborations at work. With whom do you want to form a stronger or more multi-faceted relationship? Could this collaboration be an opportunity to build a bridge with another function or cluster in your organization? Might it put you in touch with potential sponsors or mentors?

> Recently I met a man who was recruited as a wealth manager in a new city and quickly needed to build a book of business to assure his professional success. He did it. How? He joined the symphony.[6]
>
> —Judy Robinett
> Author of *How to Be a Power Connector: The 5-50-150 rule*

Professional networking activities do not have to take place solely over work-related activities. For example, even though he was a stakeholder, Parker decided that she wanted to connect with Walters outside of work. Baker had let her know that Walters loved yoga. Parker was a yoga enthusiast, too, so she asked Walters if she could try out the studio he frequented after work. Walters was delighted by her interest and mentioned an upcoming yoga event that they could both attend.

Think about your networking strategy when you engage in your non-work activities. Is there a way to do your current activities in a new context? Ask people who share your interests how, where, and when they do what you like to do. Talk about your non-work activities when you interact with other people and be open to learning about new ways of pursuing them. If you're just starting out, consider serving on a political campaign.

One of the most productive networking activities I did as a junior professor was to participate in a faculty playgroup that included faculty from many different departments, all of whom had young children. Participating in the playgroup introduced me to individuals that I would never have met otherwise while still spending time with my kids (my passion!). As we played with our children, we worked together to keep diapers changed, sticky fingers contained, objects out of mouths, and toy tug-of-wars resolved with a minimum of tears (interdependence!). We talked about what it was like to be academics and parents (*we-ness!*), sharing the insider tips we had learned about managing time, navigating campus politics, and increasing productivity. We began to invite each other to make academic presentations to our departments, work on cross-departmental projects, and serve on campus-wide committees. Several of the faculty I met in that playgroup remain among the core group of people to whom I regularly turn for professional and career advice.

Once you determine the activities that will connect you with people you'd like to include in your professional network, you're ready to go to step two of building relationships: Prepare to engage.

Step 2: Prepare to Engage

Okay, now you know who you'd like to meet and have selected an activity that includes the three critical components. You've optimized the relationship-building context and are ready to start building relationships. But, before you do, stop a moment, and *prepare to engage.* You've put a lot of thought into selecting your activities. Your time and energy is limited and you certainly don't want to waste them. To maximize these opportunities to build nourishing, valuable, and genuine relationships, you need to prepare yourself to be someone with whom others *want* to connect. I am *not* advocating that you act disingenuously. Instead, I am suggesting that you bring your best self to every encounter.

Here's where some of the advice you've heard about first impressions really does matter. Interacting with others in a way that leaves a positive first impression increases the likelihood that you will form a positive relationship. We gain overall impressions of people very quickly. One analysis of dozens of scientific studies found that we determine whether we feel positively or negatively toward someone within *thirty seconds* of our first interaction![7] Not only that, but those initial first impressions quickly become hardened and often persist for as long as we know the other person. First impressions *do* matter.

There have been many books written on managing first impressions so I won't cover topics here that others have covered well elsewhere.[8] But I will note three facts from the science of interpersonal attraction that you can leverage:

1. We are attracted to people like us.
2. We are attracted to people *who like* us.
3. We are attracted to positivity.

We are attracted to people like us. As suggested earlier by the *homophily* principle, we're more likely to form relationships with people who we see as similar to us in some way.

The easiest and most obvious first signal of similarity is visual appearance. Looking the part is important. Unlike a job interview or a typical networking event, the idea is not to "dress to impress" but to dress in a way that makes it easier for others to think, "*This person is just like me!*" If you're joining a running club, don't show up for the first run in cut-off jeans. If you're joining a board of directors, don't show up for the first meeting in sweatpants. A little while ago, I spoke with someone who is teaching for the first time at a university I know well. His first question?: *What do the other professors wear at work?* This is a man who knows the importance of looking the part. Wear appropriate clothing.

Another way to encourage someone to see you as similar is to talk about things you have in common. This is the purpose of small talk. Small talk is talking about things we are likely to all have in common, like the weather, a recent sporting event, or a popular show. Talking about something held in common makes us feel more similar to each other. Use this tendency to your advantage. Given that you've chosen a particular activity over which to connect, you can be pretty sure that discussing aspects of that activity are likely to be good conversation topics. Be prepared to discuss some current events, too. Before going to the activity, skim relevant websites and journals, and formulate an opinion on some of the top stories. Before visiting the various departments in the Water Division, Parker made a point of reading the local paper to make sure that at the very least she knew if the local sports team had won or lost the night before.

Your strategy should be a little different if you picked the activity for the purpose of putting you in contact with a *specific* person—such as a potential mentor, sponsor, or stakeholder. In this case, you want to do your homework. Learn something about the person. Their company's website is a good starting point but it will be worth your while to spend a few minutes going beyond the website. In the time of LinkedIn, Facebook, Google, Twitter, and dozens of specialist social networking sites, such as AccountingWeb, it is easy to gather some basic facts about what someone does and what they value. See if you have friends or colleagues in common, or if you belong to some of the same associations, clubs, or online communities. Mentioning that you have a friend or colleague in common increases the likelihood that you will be perceived as "like me" because it indicates that you are already connected in the same network. Parker leveraged this principle when she mentioned Baker to Walters and discussed their shared love of yoga.

We are attracted to people who like us. Our tendency to be attracted to people who like us reflects two important principles: *reciprocity* and *balance.* If someone smiles and acts positively toward us—perhaps by offering to do us a favor or giving us a compliment—we tend to reciprocate by acting positively back. When someone "gives" us positive attention, we tend to reciprocate by giving it back. It's hard to dislike a colleague who likes you. When visiting the various departments in the Water Division, Parker made a point of chatting with people about the pictures of their children on their desks, asking friendly questions and smiling to show interest.

The following are a few examples of possible conversation starters. [Please remember that they will only be effective if they are *true!*]

- *Great presentation! I really liked how the graphics underscored your main points.*
- *You made a terrific comment in today's meeting.*
- *You sound like you have experience in this area.*
- *I'd really like to hear your thoughts on the talk we just heard.*
- *I heard that you made a knock-out pitch to our new client. How did you do it?*

A few chapters ago, we learned that we seek balance in our relationships to people. It turns out that we also seek balance in our beliefs. For most of us, it is unsettling to think negatively about someone who seems to think positively about us. It just feels wrong and while we sometimes find ourselves in that situation, more often we start to feel more positively toward the other person.

If I believe that I'm basically a good person and you seem to believe the same, then we both share the same belief about me. To maintain cognitive balance, I will come to feel more positively towards you. Astonishingly, the reverse is also true. If I have low self-esteem and you seem to believe that

I'm a good person, then we don't share the same belief about me. In that case, to maintain cognitive balance, I am *less* likely to feel positively toward you. Luckily, not only do most of us have positive self-esteem, the reciprocity principle helps nudge us toward liking the people who like us.

We are attracted to positivity. We all want to associate with upbeat, energizing people. We respond positively to people who act positively toward us, either by giving us a compliment, agreeing with us, or simply smiling at us. We avoid people who seem distant, cold, or uncaring. Michael Paterniti, a writer for *GQ* magazine, travelled more than seven thousand miles to interview the man that scientists called "the happiest man in the world" on account of MRI brain scans that noted his huge level of "positive emotions" in his left pre-frontal cortex. Paterniti wrote:

> Being in his presence was to be infected by a floating kind of joy, an unthreatened eagerness to see the world, in its dark time, as capable of change, as a place containing infectious joy and happiness as well.[9]

While you and I might not generate *that* level of positivity, we can try to bring our best selves to every encounter. To spark positivity, think about using words and phrases that make other people feel better about themselves. (Hint: They're often the same words that make you feel better about yourself!) Find something that you can genuinely compliment about the other person. Above all, withhold negative comments when you first meet people.

You will be perceived as upbeat and energizing if you act in a way that communicates openness and interest in others, and if you avoid looking stressed, anxious, and tired. Look and act, not only as if you have all the time in the world—even when you don't!—to listen to what others have to say, but that you welcome the opportunity to listen. It takes less than a second to smile and make eye contact.

Learning to project positivity may require you to pay attention to your usual body language and make targeted changes. Some people will find this more challenging than others. Introverts, for example, may be unaware that they often have a "resting face" expression that others interpret as unhappy, even angry. To project positivity, they will have to make a concerted effort to change their "usual" expression by turning up the corners of their mouths.

Some other body language tips:

- Smile when you meet people, smile when you listen to them speak.
- Make eye contact with other people when they talk to you.

- Orient your body toward the person who is speaking to you—and not toward your computer, phone, or a stack of papers!
- Lean in slightly toward the person talking.
- Nod when people are talking to indicate listening without interrupting.
- Avoid speaking in a flat monotone. Modulate your voice.
- If you speak softly, speak slowly.
- Avoid hunching forward or crossing your arms across your chest.
- Avoid indicating impatience by tapping, checking your phone, or picking at something.

To the extent that it feels natural, project *energy*. Babson College Professor of Management Rob Cross finds that people identified as energizing create what he calls *pull*. "People want to be around energizing people. Energizing people replenish rather than drain resources," says Cross.[10] Energizers are four times more likely to be high-performers than people identified as low-energy or de-energizing.[11]

> The best networkers attract people towards them, and they are the sort of people you enjoy spending time with. I found that the great networkers I spoke to in my research tended to be upbeat, positive and generally enthusiastic about the future and what it held for them... The flipside is that negative, apathetic and critical people tend to act like a drain on our emotions and energy, which leads to a reduction in their social capital. Who would you like to spend your time with, someone you feel good with or someone who drains the positive energy out of you?"
>
> —Heather Townsend, author
> *FT Guide to Business Networking*[12]

Adopt an energizing mindset. Energizing people encourage new ideas. They get excited about possibilities. Some people believe that they won't look smart unless they pick apart an idea to find all of the ways and reasons why it won't work. Elizabeth Parker adopted an energizing mindset by eagerly seeking ideas from everyone she met when visiting the various departments and never criticizing a response. "When you look around the Division," she'd say. "What do you see that is not getting done but *should* be getting done?"

No one wants to bring new ideas to someone they think will shoot them down. Never make *No* your first response to a new idea or proposition. Even if you do end up rejecting an idea, separate out your rejection of the idea from the person who presented it. Often, there's no need to reject anything because—through the course of your energizing conversation—a half-baked idea will develop into an exciting new possibility!

Step 3: Engage

Okay, so now you've found an activity and you've prepared yourself to engage with others. To optimize the likelihood of building positive relationships with other people, you have one last step: *Engage in meaningful and positive interactions.* Engaging with others means initiating some conversations and responding appropriately when someone else initiates a conversation with you. If you've found an activity and are prepared to engage, starting a conversation will be no problem. You will have things in common to discuss and a shared interest in talking more about what you're doing together.

But just starting a conversation is not enough. You want the interaction to continue to be positive, maybe so positive that you start to feel a genuine connection. Luckily, there are three things you can do to make a positive connection more likely. I call them the *Three A's*:

- ▪ **A**ctivate reciprocity.
- ▪ **A**ctively listen.
- ▪ **A**sk good questions.

Engage using the *Three A's* and you will easily and naturally form positive connections.

Activate reciprocity. Reciprocity is one of the most powerful relationship-building principles. Activate the power of reciprocity by acting kindly and generously in your interactions with others. Never underestimate the value of asking, "How can I help you?"

> Most people think there's no way to help someone as famous and wealthy as Reid or Bill Gates. Let's run the thought experiment. How could *you* help Bill Gates? Donating to his favorite charity won't help. There's no one you could introduce him to who he can't already meet. Buying a Microsoft product won't make a difference in the grand scheme. But the truth is, what Gates craves, and what you might have, is *information.* A unique perspective. An insight on something that's happening in your corner of the universe. He can't buy that off a shelf. If you can connect information you know to something Gates *needs*—suppose your 10 year-old cousin is obsessed with a new app that may reveal a new trend in computing—he'll find it valuable, and you're more likely to be able to build a relationship with him. At the least, it's a powerful first gesture that's the opposite of "gimme."[13]

At a minimum, give the gift of your appreciation. When someone helps you in your work or career or even in the activity you are engaged in, thank him or her. Do this either in person or, after the fact, by sending a hand-written thank you note or gift. When you can, give someone else a sense of accomplishment in your success by thanking them for their contribution.[14] For example, you might thank the person who ran alongside you for giving you the strength to make it to the finish line.

Actively listen. Active listening means listening to understand the facts and emotions that a person is communicating both verbally and non-verbally, paraphrasing your understanding of the entire message, and checking for understanding. Active listening is powerful, partly because so few people do it. We rarely really listen to what someone is trying to tell us. Instead, we rehearse what we're going to say in our heads while the other person speaks. We can't wait until it is "our" turn to say something brilliant. Or, we miss the thread of the conversation completely because we are distracted by something else—a noise, a feeling, or random thoughts about the stain on our jacket, the movie we watched the night before, or the machinations of the universe.

It may seem that active listening is a passive process because it puts your attention on what the other person is saying. But it's actually a very active process. Rather than waiting for an opportunity to say what is on your mind, active listening requires you to *really* listen to what the other person is communicating both verbally and non-verbally. The point of paraphrasing is to communicate your understanding of what the other person is trying to tell you. It requires you to listen to what the person is saying and feeling, and then to repeat it, but in your *own* words.

> Employee, exasperated: *What does the boss expect us to do about these broken-down machines?*

> Manager, demonstrating active listening: *You're tired of working with worn-out equipment, aren't you?*

Active listening is deceptively difficult to do well. It's hard not to jump into the conversation with an opinion or suggestion. Sometimes we can't wait to share a similar experience we had. While we often do this with good intentions—to communicate our similarity, and to provide evidence of our empathy—it has the effect of taking the attention off of the other person and back on ourselves. *You don't need to tell me more,* is what we are really communicating, *because I can "listen" to myself.* We assume that having gone through a similar event is the same as having the same physical and emotional experience, but, of course, no one experiences the world in the exact same way.

It can be surprisingly difficult to listen to what is being said while simultaneously finding your own words in which to restate it. But it's worth trying. Active listening builds closeness and understanding faster than anything else. Practice it regularly and it will transform all of your relationships.

Active listening is a skill like any other. It has to be practiced to be performed well. Understand that as you begin to change your listening style to a more empathetic one, you may often feel inefficient. It takes time to truly hear someone and to replay the essence of their thoughts back to them so that both parties are clear on what was said. The payback is dramatic, but it comes over the long run.[15]

—Ram Charan, author
The Discipline of Listening

Active listening has another advantage when it comes to building relationships: it gives you a deeper understanding of the other person. Having a more complex understanding of another person makes it more likely that you will find a way in which you and the other person are similar. For instance, you might be an engineer and I might be a salesperson but by engaging in active listening, I might discover that we are both avid cyclists. Discovering a shared identity or *we-ness* makes it more likely that we will form a genuine connection.

I should note that active listening does *not* mean agreeing with the other person. You may strongly disagree with every word. But by stating out loud what you understand the other person to be saying, you make a discussion possible. So few people truly engage in active listening that when you do it, you stand out as someone who *really* listens.

You can make more friends in two months by becoming interested in other people than you can in two years by trying to get other people interested in you.[16]

—Dale Carnegie, author
How to Make Friends and Influence People

Ask good questions. Active listening is important but so is asking good questions. Use the 80/20 rule and spend 80% of your time listening and 20% asking good questions. Listen first, then ask. A good question demonstrates that you've been listening to the other person, stays on topic, contributes your own perspective, is open-ended (requires more than a yes or no response), and encourages the other person to share his or her personal perspective or opinion. Examples of good questions include:

- *Why did you decide to come here today?*
- *What do you like about this activity?*
- *What are you hoping to achieve or do?*
- *How can I help you?*

Make a point of asking your stakeholders for their thoughts about your shared project, task, or work effort. When appropriate—and only if you are sincere!—ask questions to get advice. People who regularly seek advice and support from their colleagues are rated more favorably by others—including supervisors—than those who never seek advice and support.[17] Like Elizabeth Parker, ask your stakeholders:

- *What seems to be going well?*
- *What are some challenges that you see?*
- *How might you do things differently?*

If you can, ask questions in person so that you can take full advantage of the richness of nonverbal cues when you listen to the answer your questions. If that's not possible, pick up the phone and make a call, preferably with video. Try never to use text-only communications, such as texts and email, when you are seeking to build relationships. These media lack the depth and nuance of richer media that can communicate thoughts and feelings through gestures, sounds, and expressions.

Avoid asking leading questions or questions that indicate you already know the answer. These kinds of questions will trigger resentment and defensiveness. Examples include:

- *What aren't you able to get this done?*
- *What kind of plan is that?*
- *Don't you think Ben knows that?*
- *Most experts believe that this isn't a legitimate problem. What about you?*

Be Yourself

It may seem hypocritical after all this to add, *Be yourself.* After all, you will be doing some things that are new to you. You may be in a situation that is entirely new to you. You will probably feel a little out of your comfort zone. You may not feel as self-confident as you usually do. What does it mean to "be yourself" when you are feeling unlike yourself?

One way is to think of your "self" a little differently.

Sometimes we imagine that who we are never changes, that we are the same exact same person in all situations. But the truth is that we are complex and complicated beings with many different aspects and layers. Like a prism—a solid crystal with multiple facets, each one reflecting light differently—your real self has different facets that you can choose to reflect in different situations.

I once had a student, Dave, who did everything possible to appear invisible. During class, Dave sat in the very last row with his head down over his notes, avoiding eye contact. It wasn't that he didn't know the material or was unprepared for class. When called on, he spoke softly and looked uncomfortable. However, his answers demonstrated a firm understanding of course content and assigned materials. Dave was just shy—or so I thought until I was talking to another student after class and mentioned Dave's shyness. *Him?* She said in disbelief. *We're in the same club and he is always the first person to make a comment or offer a suggestion. He's friends with everyone and he's not afraid to say what's on his mind.* It seems that classroom-Dave didn't behave the same as club-Dave. Dave was always himself, of course. It's just his self was different in different contexts.

Harvard professor Hermaine Ibarra suggests that each of us has multiple selves.[18] Our authentic self might include contradictory aspects, such as competing tendencies to make quick decisions and to exhaustively analyze options. It might even include an imagined self, one who is confident and self-assured.

Try on your different selves. Emphasize the one that works best for you in a given situation. If you are staying true to yourself, you will project a person who is complex but not contradictory. You can even tap into a *future* self by acting like the confident person that you'd like to become.[19] A future self is just a person that you aren't yet but that you will be one day. Sure, today you feel awkward and uncertain—*nothing I can say could possibly be of interest to anyone!*—but you know that one day, you *will* have lots to share and you *will* be able engage with people honestly, openly, and without fear. Why not try to be that person today?

Be careful not to present a false self. If you consciously present yourself as holding a value, supporting a goal, or taking an action that you don't truly hold, support, or intend to take—or if you support one goal, value, or action in one context and an opposing goal, value, or action in another context—people will rightly judge you to be a phony. No one respects a chameleon who says one thing to one person and then says the complete opposite to another. Instead, be your best self.

To Recap . . .

A networking strategy is a purposeful plan to build, nurture, and leverage a set of valuable and positive professional relationships that are structured to maximize the flow of resources to you, to all the people connected in your network, and to the organizations and communities in which you reside.

Like Parker, develop a strategy that helps you meet *your* professional goals. Because you are unique, your personal networking strategy will be unique.

For the most part, build relationships without regards to a person's specific resources. Value the people in your network for their potential. Instead of focusing on what individuals have (or don't have), focus on the quality of your relationships, the perspectives they give you on yourself and others, and the ability to learn. To build relationships, put yourself into places where you're likely to meet the kinds of people who are not in your networks—but should be—prepare yourself to make every interaction as positive as possible, and then engage using the *Three A's* to easily and naturally form genuine connections. Lastly, be yourself.

In the next chapter, we'll take a look at strategies for nurturing your professional network by maintaining and developing your relationships.

Reflection Questions

What three activities could you take part in over the next three months to build relationships with people who aren't in your network but should be?

Do you project positivity? Ask someone you trust and who knows you well if anything you typically say or do that might come across as negative (i.e., cold, uncaring, distant). Are there small changes you can make to your body language to communicate positivity?

The next time you meet someone for the first time, practice active listening. Notice how this conversation differs from your normal 'first' conversations.

8

Nurture and Nature

Connect the Dots, pages 137–151
Copyright © 2019 by Information Age Publishing
All rights of reproduction in any form reserved.

Bill and Rudy

Besides being the 42nd President of the United States, Bill Clinton is known for his ability to connect with people. Many people credit the enormous number of people who call him friend to his innate charm and listening skills. When in a conversation, Clinton always gives his full attention to the person with whom he is speaking. He makes direct eye contact, never allowing his focus to get distracted. He *really* listens to what others have to say. People feel that he is genuinely interested in getting to know them as individuals—what *they* do and what *they* are interested in. He makes them feel like the most important person in the room by projecting an authenticity and charm that makes people feel he truly cares about them.[1] "He hugs you," said Max Heller, the former mayor of Greenville said after meeting Clinton. "He hugs you not only physically, but with a whole attitude."[2]

What is not as well-known is the effort that Clinton puts into *nurturing* his relationships. In addition to maintaining a robust correspondence with hundreds of people, Clinton was legendary for calling people late at night and asking their opinion on various matters.

> My phone used to ring all the time late at night with calls from the White House and usually I would sit there in my pajamas talking with the President about anything from college basketball to our mothers.
>
> —Terry McAuliffe, former Governor of Virginia[3]

Clinton rarely forgets a name, a face, a conversation—or a promise. Christine Comaford-Lynch, five-time CEO and author of *Rules for Renegades*, recalls her first meeting with Clinton. As a result of donating many hours of her time to support TechNet, a bipartisan group of tech execs, she was invited to a party at the White House. For a while, she simply watched Clinton interacting with others. Then she approached him.

> Our interaction blew me away for 3 reasons: 1) he was incredibly charismatic, 2) he wouldn't let go of my hand, and gave me the "I'm-hanging-in-for-the-long-haul-shake," and 3) when I asked him for more government support for American entrepreneurs, he expected me to follow up. He sent me a note about a month later asking where the proposal was that I had offered to write![4]

Clinton's relationship with Rudiger (Rudy) Lowe is typical of the way he maintains relationships. The two first met in 1967 when Clinton was president of the Georgetown student body. Clinton had spent much of the fall preparing for the upcoming Conference on the Atlantic Community

(CONTAC), which brought together students from Europe, Canada, and the United States to examine issues facing the community through a series of seminars and lectures. As chairman of CONTAC's nine seminars, Clinton's job was to place the delegates, assign paper topics, and recruit experts for all eighty-one sessions. One of the participating students was Rudy Lowe, a Fulbright scholar from Germany.

Martin Walker, former U.S. bureau chief of Britain's the *Guardian* and Oxford classmate of Clinton described the story of the first meeting between Rudy and Bill this way:[5]

> "Since you're a Fulbright, how would you like to meet Sen. Fulbright?" Clinton asked, referring to the senator from his home state.
>
> "I'm just a young German student. I'm nobody," Loewe [sic] recalls saying. "Sen. Fulbright is one of the most powerful men in America, chairman of the Foreign Relations Committee. He wouldn't want to meet me."
>
> "Lunch or breakfast. Yes or no?" Clinton pressed. So Loewe stammered his thanks as Clinton went to a phone, spoke briefly, came back and said "Breakfast tomorrow, in his Senate office."

When Lowe returned to Germany after completing his Fulbright he received the first of many letters that he would receive from Clinton over the subsequent decades, each written in his exquisite script. They were "like works of art," recalled Lowe.[6]

And not only letters. Not long after sending the first of his letters, Clinton went to visit Lowe and his family in Germany. As he recorded in his autobiography, *My Life*, the trip was both uplifting and somber.[7]

> In Bamburg, Rudy's thousand-year-old hometown, he took me to see the East German border nearby, where there was an East German soldier standing guard in a high outpost behind barbed wire on the edge of the Bavarian Forest.

According to Lowe, Clinton was "very taken by the physical manifestation of repression and animosity" and made a point of stepping two meters across the border line to pose for a picture. "He said they wouldn't shoot an American," recalls Lowe.[8]

In years to come, Clinton would return several times to celebrate Faschingsfest—a Carnival Season festival similar to Mardis Gras—and good company with Lowe and his family. In between, of course, he sent many more letters, including thank-you letters to Lowe's mother. Clinton even learned a little German. Later, Lowe would send Clinton's daughter, Chelsea,

German children's books and short stories that had German written on one page and English translation on the next. Lowe encouraged her to learn the language, which she did, eventually spending six summers at Waldsee, a German immersion program.[9]

Through Lowe, Clinton stayed connected with developments in German politics and social policies. Many years after their first meeting, Lowe became a major figure in Bavarian broadcasting. As such, he helped set up the Bavarian government's invitation to Clinton in 1990. As Walker noted, Clinton's relationship with Lowe was not just good for both of them, it was good for the country.

> When the Arkansas press grumbled that Clinton was spending too much time out of state, Clinton had the perfect riposte. His German trip had resulted in a new Siemens factory coming to the state, with more than 300 high-tech jobs.[10]

It will come as no surprise that Clinton is often credited as being one of the best networkers in the world. Yes, he was charming in his initial interactions but the real secret to Clinton's networking success was his ability to *nurture* his relationships.

Nurture Relationships

You *nurture* a network by maintaining and developing relationships. Too often, we let relationships fade, even important relationships, because we're distracted by the day-to-day business of living our lives. Sometimes we recognize that a relationship is slipping away but don't have the skills or energy to maintain it. Other times, we meet someone that we think could be very important to us—perhaps as a mentor or sponsor, or as a way of staying in touch with some aspect of ourselves or the world that we rarely access—but we don't know how to nurture the relationship in a way that feels natural and authentic.

Nurturing a professional relationship means different things at different times in the relationship's trajectory. At the beginning, it might mean ensuring that a positive interaction occurs again. Later, it may mean strengthening feelings of trust and deepening awareness of the other person's tangible and intangible assets as well as sharing more of one's own professional strengths, interests, and goals.

You don't have to spend years developing relationships. As noted earlier, dormant relationships are powerful drivers of career success, especially when initial interactions are characterized by positivity and mutuality. Too, relationship-building doesn't necessarily call for grand gestures or even significant investments of time or effort. Sure, you can strengthen a relationship by having lunch or going out for coffee together, but there are many other less time-consuming ways to stay connected. When thinking about whether and how to strengthen relationships—especially new or bridging relationships—create networking strategies that work for *you* and your lifestyle, as well as for the different individuals with whom you'd like to connect on a deeper level.

There are at least eight ways to nurture professional relationships that range from straight-forward tactics for turning an initial interaction into a budding relationship to broader and more holistic strategies for deepening and strengthening existing bonds.

1. Follow up every meaningful interaction.
2. Maintain and update your professional online presence.
3. Do what you say you will.
4. Express gratitude.
5. Share more of yourself.
6. Seek out opportunities for collaboration.
7. Get in the habit of giving to your network every day.
8. Create time for networking.

These approaches work for most people but they are not hard and fast rules. Think of them instead as suggestions or recommendations. Use them to help you develop a personalized networking plan that includes relationship-nurturing strategies that work for *you*.

One, follow up every meaningful interaction. Use email, text, phone call, or handwritten note, as appropriate. I've mentioned this before but it bears repeating because it is surprising how often this simple action doesn't happen. Employ a default of email because it gives you a record of that person. Keep the email short but include in the body a reason that you found the interaction interesting (e.g., *I appreciated your tips on blogging!*). This confirms the link psychologically but it also gets the person in your email system, along with a piece of information about the person. Later, you can search on the person's name to refresh your memory about the interaction.

Clinton sent dozens of follow-up notes each month to people he had met in person. Long before he was in the White House, he recognized the power of sending handwritten personal notes, For Clinton, it wasn't just about "making contacts"—it was about nurturing genuine relationships with a wide range of people.

The flipside of following up, of course, is the impact it makes on the *other* person. Bill Stokes, founder and chairman of the Washington Network Group, one of the first networking groups in the D.C. area, says that people who follow up with him are the ones he remembers.

> I would say I meet 20 to 30 people at a networking reception and only about three or four will send me a message in the first week. I will get one or two a month later and I cannot remember who they are...[11]

In your follow-up, if you have not already done so, request an electronic connection to the person's online presences. Social media platforms such as Linked-In, Twitter, Facebook, Instagram, or Tumblr are not great ways to start relationships but they are good ways to nurture them. Social media can let you know when your contacts celebrate important milestones and events, such as birthdays, promotions, and new jobs. To nurture relationships, send a quick email, post a reply or comment, or simply post a like. "Cheering on your contacts on social media lets them know you stand behind them," says Dorie Clark, marketing strategy consultant and author of *Stand Out Networking: A Simple and Authentic Way to Meet People on Your Own Terms.*[12] By taking these relatively effortless actions, you reinforce your appreciation of people's presence in your network, and an awareness of things that are important to them.

Two, maintain and periodically update your professional online presence. You do not need to blog or tweet on a daily basis. Although those are certainly good ways to share your thoughts and goals, they require significant expenditure of time and effort. According to personal social media expert and Professor of Marketing at College of William & Mary Dawn Edmiston,

> Most individuals need to spend no more than 10 minutes a day managing their online presence, to include engaging with others and sharing content. And I would definitely encourage the use of free tools to support the management process to include Google Alerts, Mention.com and BrandYourself.com.[13]

Maintain one or two professional social media accounts. LinkedIn is likely to be one of them but you probably also want to have a presence on at least one other social media site such as FaceBook, Instagram, Pinterest, or one of the many specialized career-related sites such as ResearchGate, Mashable.com, or CareerBuilder.com. Initially, your online content might include a short video clip of you introducing yourself and what you do, as well as a brochure or brief description of your position, business, or organization. You may also want to share articles in which you have been quoted or cited, podcasts that you have given, papers that you have authored, and links to media featuring you or your work.

Maintain your online presence through periodic comments, updates on activities and events in your professional life, and replies to the comments of others. One tip: If you post links to recent articles or sites that you think others would find interesting, be sure to summarize the main points of interest in a sentence or two. "I hate when people send me emails with a link to an article," says Irene Gordon, CEO of Ingredion. "There's one guy whose emails I love to open because he takes the time to summarize the article. Now *that's* valuable."[14]

Depending upon your industry and interests, you may want to post pictures of beautiful, intriguing, or otherwise thought-provoking items and scenes as you come across them. All of these undertakings offer the members of your network—as well as anyone researching you!—an easy, effortless way to learn more about you and your interests.

Three, do what you say you will. People need to know that they can count on you to do what you say you will do. By keeping your promises, you signal to others that you value and care about their interests. You also reinforce their perception that *you* are a valuable person, one that has resources that you are willing and able to share. Feeling valued by someone who has value makes you a more desirable relationship partner. It also builds trust, which further nurtures the relationship.

Err on the side of under-promising and over-delivering. "It is easier to exceed expectations if those expectations are not completely over the top or in your face," write Pfeffer and Walker, authors of *People are the Name of the Game.*[15] If you think you can gather some requested information in two or three days, say that you can do it within a week. The image of you that will stick is the one that concludes your interaction. In other words, it is not the promise of a fast turn-around that your colleague will remember but the sooner-then-expected delivery of the request.

Be realistic about your schedule. One academic I know confided that whenever he is asked to give a talk he checks his schedule for the following week, even if the proposed talk isn't for months. By doing this, he avoids the wishful thinking that we all do when imagining our magically wide-open future schedules. His thinking is that if he doesn't have time *next week*, he probably won't have time six months in the future.

Be sure to track your commitments. If you're like me and have a tendency to forget conversations, get in the habit of carrying around a notepad (or your phone) on which to take notes. This can be particularly useful when you are talking with a number of people in quick succession or when you bump into someone unexpectedly. A colleague of mine utilizes wearable speech-to-text technologies—in her case, an Apple Watch—to quickly and seamlessly send herself reminders on just such occasions (e.g., *send link to Wall Street Journal article on wage report to Sabina*).

Once you've made a commitment, do whatever follow-up work needs to be done in order to meet it. A good rule of thumb is that if it takes less than five minutes, do it as soon as you can. If it takes longer, delegate it or schedule time to do it. Some executives purposefully block out "power hours" in their weekly schedule to deal with the many small commitments they know they will make.

Find a commitment strategy that works for you and stick to it. Not only will you strengthen your relationship with the person to whom you made the commitment, you will foster a reputation for trustworthiness that will be distributed throughout your network. "[F]ollowing through as promised builds a surprisingly rare reputation that can be leveraged in a number of ways as it builds the confidence of others," write Pfeffer and Walker.[16] According to one study of over 17,000 C-suite executives over a ten-year period, 94% of successful CEO candidates scored high on "consistently following through on their commitments."[17]

Do *you* do what you say you will do?

Four, express gratitude whenever you receive help or support. You can never tell someone *Thank you* too many times when you do so sincerely. Thanking someone generates positive feelings in the person being thanked as well as the person doing the thanking. In other words, thanking someone makes *you* feel good. And when you feel good, you give more. Servers who write *thank you* on a restaurant bill, for example, get higher tips than those who don't![18]

According to Sean Stephenson, former intern in Bill Clinton's White House, Clinton would go out of his way to express gratitude.

> On July 24, 1998, I was attending an event in the Rose Garden, when out of the blue the president said, "I'd also like to thank Sean Stephenson, [Boys Nation] class of 1996, now an intern in Cabinet Affairs. Thank you for what you are doing here." Then he nodded and smiled in my direction. Was he doing that because it was standard protocol, or because he really was truly grateful for my service at the White House? I'm going to choose to believe the latter. It felt great.[19]

Figure out a gratitude system that works for you. Stock up on cards and stamps; store them within arm's reach of your desk. When someone has helped or supported you, send or mail a thank-you note. You don't need to write much. A line or two will do. *Thank you for reaching out to Dave on my behalf. I appreciate it!* An email will work in a pinch but most people prefer a handwritten note. When appropriate, send a small gift. I happen to mention in passing that I like spiced nuts to a young researcher who was visiting our university. I was touched, when a week later, I received a thank you note along with a can of local spiced nuts from her home town.

The impact of expressing gratitude goes beyond your relationship with one person. Thanking someone increases the flow of helping and resource-sharing to *other* people, too. Being thanked reminds us that we helped someone and associates that memory with the warm glow of feeling appreciated. As a result, we are more inclined to pay it forward and help others. One study found that individuals who received sincere expressions of gratitude—when compared to individuals who had not received an expression of gratitude—were more likely to respond positively to a request for help made a day later *by someone else.*[20] Whenever you express gratitude for help that you have received, you make it more likely that someone else will also receive help.

The extended effects of gratitude are heightened by publicizing generous acts to others. Not only does receiving thanks publicly strengthen our individual inclination to give—and increase the positive reputation of both the giver and the thanker—it also encourages others to believe that helping and appreciating each other is the norm. There are many ways to express gratitude publicly. Here are four:

- Publicly thank someone (e.g., in a meeting, speech, etc.).
- Write a testimonial on LinkedIn, Yelp, or other appropriate places.
- Offer to serve as a reference.
- Nominate someone for an award or public recognition. To make your nomination known, ask others to support your vote.

Expressing gratitude makes us feel good, makes others feel good, strengthens relationships, encourages the person who helped you to help someone else, and makes it more likely that others will help, all which allows more resources to flow freely through the larger network of which you are a part. Make expressing gratitude a cornerstone of your relationship nurturing strategy.

Five, share more of yourself. Selectively share personal information about yourself. Personal information can run the gamut from relatively safe facts such as, *I've run three marathons,* to more intimate personal matters such as your hopes and fears, direct experiences of accomplishment or embarrassment, and even feelings of inadequacy. In general, expressing feelings is more personal than expressing opinions and expressing opinions is more personal than relaying facts. Sharing personal information has a greater impact on people and relationships when that information is not known by most people.

Sharing personal information strengthens relationships because it gives the other person more information about you, which deepens your ability to find points of connection. Because it can also leave you vulnerable to attack or damage, sharing personal information tells the other person that you trust them not to hurt you. Feeling trusted and being trusted further strengthen closeness. On top of all the good vibes generated by your self-disclosure, the reciprocity principle pushes the other person to respond by also sharing personal information and being vulnerable, further deepening the relationship.

But be careful! Self-disclosure can backfire if it's too much, too soon.

Many factors influence an individual's tolerance for self-disclosure, including personal experience, personality, and culture. To be safe, the nature of the information you share should be only a little more personal than the information that the other person has shared with you. Psychologist Arthur Aron of Stony Brook University suggests that you aim to be about 10% more personal than the other person.[21] More than that and you risk overwhelming the other person with expectations of self-disclosure that they feel unable to reciprocate.

An easy way to get more personal without getting *too* personal is to increase the number and variety of topics you discuss with the other person. Don't limit your interactions to just one or two topics, such as your department and your current project. Instead, branch out and introduce new topics into your interactions. Good starting points include current events, sports, your non-work activities, and anecdotes about past travel or vacation experiences.

One thing you should *always* share: Your career strengths and goals. Get in the habit of sharing these with everyone. I don't mean a canned elevator pitch. I mean clearly and proudly articulating what it is you're good at and how you want to grow professionally. Make it easy for people to support your career by letting them know how you define yourself professionally and where you hope to go in the future. If you're not clear on your strengths and goals, ask someone you trust what they think.

If sharing your strengths and goals feels too personal or makes you feel too vulnerable, lower the risk level by thinking of them as facts, not opinions or feelings. Oddly enough, making your professional facts well-known can make them easier to share them in casual interactions. Look for ways to publicize your career "facts." Display awards, degrees, professional certifications, and letters of commendation. If you accomplished an important goal, let others know. *I'm so pleased that my team brought in our latest project on time and under budget.* If you have a career objective, state it. *I'm always looking for projects that allow me to work directly with clients.*

Some people may feel that sharing their career strengths and goals is too *imp*ersonal for relationship-development. These people often feel the need to turn *up* the intimacy level by articulating their so-called professional "weaknesses" such as personal challenges and areas in need of improvement. If this describes you, watch out. If you mainly share weaknesses, then the *only* information other people will have about you is what you are *not* good at.

If you can't help sharing weaknesses, then at least seek balance. Whenever you feel the urge to share something about your professional weaknesses, find a way to also articulate your professional strengths. Reframe your weaknesses as growth opportunities that will allow you to support your strengths. For example, when you feel the desire to say, *I'm not very good at public speaking,* say instead something like, *My strengths are really in building engagement in one-on-one interactions; I've love to improve my ability to make that kind of connection through my public speaking.* Figure out a few phrases and then practice them until they become second nature.

Six, seek out opportunities for collaboration. We've already noted that activities that include elements of interdependence make positive relationships more likely because people work together to accomplish shared goals. For similar reasons, collaborations also renew and strengthen *existing* trust and liking bonds.

For your core relationships—or for relationships that you'd like to become core relationships—seek out additional opportunities to collaborate. Pick projects that allow you to work together in new ways. In academia, for example, it is common for two scholars to "find a project" to work on together because they'd like to work more together rather than because their research areas intersect perfectly. Similarly, many Hollywood actors forgo reading scripts and instead make choices based on directors. Christopher Plummer described his thinking when offered the opportunity to replace Kevin Spacey in *All the Money in the World*:

> I met Ridley in New York; he flew all the way from London. I've always been a fan of Ridley and wanted to work with him. I thought, "My God, here's an incredible chance." We talked for a few minutes. He obviously has an extraordinary sense of humor, and that endeared him to me immediately...

I kind of knew I was going to do it even if I hated the script. I had a feeling. It was almost insane, so I thought. "Great, let's try it!"[22]

One potential pitfall is *collaborative overload.* As any manager knows, the pressure to be involved in collaborative activities has never been greater and collaborative overload can be crushing. One study estimates that people spend as much as 95% of their time on the phone, on emails, in meetings, or in virtual spaces collaborating on projects.[23] According to Bonnie Flatt, an executive coach with MasterCoaches LLC in Toronto, one of her clients said that he's got so many things on his agenda, he now has to schedule bathroom breaks![24]

Some people tend to collaborate at higher rates than others. In fact, one study found that 20% to 35% of value-added collaborations come from only 3% to 5% of employees.[25] While these collaborations add value to the organization, the people who take part in them can suffer from the demands on their time and energy. No wonder more than 60% of all employees report feeling overworked and burnt out.[26]

Be careful that looking for opportunities to collaborate doesn't put you on collaborative overload. Choose your collaborative activities wisely.

Seven, get in the habit of giving to your network every day. Giving to others is the number one thing you can do to build and strengthen relationships. Don't just wait to be asked. Set aside a few minutes every morning to scan your professional networks and determine how you'll give today. There are many ways to give, many of which take little time or effort.

> The successful networkers I know, the ones receiving tons of referrals and feeling truly happy about themselves, continually put the other person's needs ahead of their own.
>
> —Bob Burg
> Author of *Endless Referrals* and *The Go Giver*

The number one rule of giving is to *only* give something that you think the other person would value. This rule is easiest to follow when someone contacts you directly and makes a request. But even if someone hasn't a specific request, you should only give if you have a good sense of what the other person finds valuable—something that is more likely if you have practiced active listening and asked good questions in your initial interactions.

When you come across something that you think the other person would value, share it. Keep your communication short and to the point. For example, if you think a foodie might welcome an insider tip about a new restaurant, you might send the following email: *Hi Kris, I recently went to Club Nouveau in Chicago and was bowled over by the filet mignon. I know you love a good steak and thought you might want to give it a try next time you're in town. Regards, Sam.* Make sure that the subject line in your message clearly conveys the content (e.g., *Just had a great steak at Club Nouveau in Chicago!*) so that a busy executive can decide when or if to open your email.

Consider giving time and effort. When someone in your network requests your time, be as responsive as you can. We don't always think about our time and effort as human capital but they absolutely are. If you're early in your career, time and effort may be your most valuable human capital assets. Younger people are likely to be relatively energetic, capable of working long hours and still functioning effectively. They may also have comparatively few family and other non-work obligations. At the same time, as budding professionals, they are still in the process of developing their knowledge and expertise, and establishing their reputations. This all adds up to making the early stage of your career a terrific time to be generous with your time and energy.

Later on in your career, as your time becomes an increasingly limited resource, you need to be much more strategic when considering to whom you give your time. Strike a balance between hoarding your time and squandering it. Think of your time as an investment. A well-placed investment at one point in time can pay off later in time-savings. For example, when launching project teams, spending time early in the process on relationship-building can save you considerable time later when you draw upon the time of others.

Giving time or effort might mean:

1. Writing an article or giving a talk.
2. Vouching or providing a testimonial for someone's expertise, character, or ability.
3. Talking with someone who is referred to you.
4. Mentoring or sponsoring others.
5. Helping someone complete a project or task, even when doing so is not part of your job requirements.
6. Listening to someone talk through job or career challenges

Although you don't need to go out of your way to make big gestures, big gestures will have a correspondingly big impact. While in office, Bill Clinton was known to clip out articles or even parts of a crossword puzzle that made him think of a particular person. He'd mail the clip to the person with a brief note scrawled in the margin.[27] While this is a small gesture in terms of the effort involved, the fact that the leader of the free world took a moment away from running the country to let someone know that he was thinking about them, made it a big gesture.

In addition to your human capital, of course, you have social capital to give. Giving social capital means providing access to your network. In addition to introducing two people in your network who would both benefit from knowing each other, there are a number of ways in which you can share your network with others. Here are five. I'm sure you can think of many more.

1. Post a link to someone's blog, website, Facebook, or twitter feed on your blog, website, Facebook, or Twitter feed. Mention their accomplishments and strengths on your social media accounts.
2. Invite someone to give a talk or presentation to people in another sticky rice cluster.
3. Pass on a referral.
4. Invite someone to an event or activity sponsored by your company or community organization.
5. Invite or sponsor someone to join a group of which you are a member

Giving does not mean depleting your own resources. Only give to the extent that you are able. As Warren Buffet noted, "Should you find yourself in a chronically leaking boat, energy devoted to changing vessels is likely to be more productive than energy devoted to patching leaks."[28] Give whatever help and support you can without depleting your own resources.

Eight, create time for networking. It takes time to build and nurture networks. To truly realize the power of networking, you will need to re-allocate your time. Instead of focusing entirely on task completion, aim to spend *at least* 20% of your work week nurturing relationships. Carla Harris, vice chairman, managing director and senior client advisor at Morgan Stanley, and author of *Strategize to Win* and *Expect to Win* argues that investing even smaller amounts of time can pay off in the long run.[29]

> How much time should you spend on this? Well, always execute on the deliverables, but I believe you can do both because at some point you are going to go and get a cup of coffee. If it has been a week and you have not had a light touch with someone where it was not directly assignment related, then that should be a red flag to you. Take a half hour out of your day to go out and be intentional about making those connections.

Setting aside as much as 20% of your professional life to manage your network is a hard pill to swallow for those of you who view networking as taking time away from your "real" work. But networking is critical, not just to your career but also to the success of the teams and organizations to which you belong or lead. As Ross Walker and Jeffrey Pfeffer note in *People Are the Name of the Game: How to Be More Successful in Your Career—And Life,* "Simply put, networking is not something that can, or should be outsourced."[30]

Structure your life to give you the time and energy to build important relationships. Start by setting aside a few minutes a day. Gradually increase your time commitment until you reach a level of relationship-building that works for you. As Sally Krawcheck, owner and Chair of Ellevate Network, notes, "Invest in your network the way you would spend money on a gym membership and time running on a treadmill."

Networking is a lifelong endeavor. Make it a daily habit.

To Recap . . .

Nurturing relationships is about finding simple ways to connect with others on a deeper level. Clinton was a natural at nurturing relationships but what worked for him might not work for you. Strengthen your connections to others in a way that feels right for *you.* I've listed eight ways to nurture relationships. Some will be right for you and some will not, because every person and every relationship is unique. For some people, nurturing relationships might mean being more active online and on social media. For others, it might mean handwriting more notes or sending out more invitations to events. Networking cannot be reduced to a simple formula. Pick the networking strategies that work for you and disregard the rest.

What will *you* do to nurture *your* professional relationships?

Reflection Questions

What is your preferred way to follow up meaningful interactions?

Is your professional online presence up to date?

Do you have a commitment strategy?

Who in your network can you thank today?

How will you create time for networking?

9

The Magnificent Seven

SELF-ASSESSMENT SNAPSHOT

1. Do you identify more as White or as a person of color? _____
2. Were you raised in a relatively affluent or relatively impoverished household? _____
3. In an average month, how often do you take part in networking activities? _____
4. Do you feel that you can be yourself at work? _____
5. Are you currently—or do you desire to be—in a core business role with profit and loss responsibility? _____

Changing Times

Four friends met for lunch at a bustling downtown eatery to celebrate Jasmine's recent promotion. Cheryl raised her glass of sparkling water in

Connect the Dots, pages 153–173
Copyright © 2019 by Information Age Publishing
All rights of reproduction in any form reserved.

salute, "Congratulations! It's been a long time coming and well-deserved." Erica and Kate smiled warmly while Jasmine rolled her eyes.

"Oh, please," she said. "Three other people in my department had the same hire date and they all got their promotion months ago. I've always been a bit slow, I guess." She smiled. "But I won't lie, it feels good." She checked her watch. "Where's Jena?"

"Jena really wanted to come but she had to use her lunch hour for a parent-teacher meeting," Cheryl replied. "You know, it's bad enough that there's no school on parent-teacher meeting day and we have to scramble for babysitters but then they make it even harder by making us come in for meetings during the work day. Like we don't have a million things already to do during lunch hour!"

Erica piped in. "And don't say that you're slow, Jasmine. Those three other people who got earlier promotions were men—and White. Of course, they got promoted first."

Jasmine looked down for a moment. "I don't think that's a fair thing to say. Those guys worked hard. They were always in the office late. Although I have to admit," she said reluctantly. "Kurt does spend a lot of time in the department head's office, talking about whatever game just happened or is about to happen. They're both huge sports nuts." She paused. "Sometimes I feel like all I do is keep my nose to the grindstone while he spends half his day shooting the breeze."

"Exactly," inserted Kate. "And when was the last time you were invited to go on sales calls with your supervisor? Or out to dinner with clients?"

"To be fair, Jack has asked me to join him on calls a couple of times. Of course," Jasmine added. "Every time I go, the client is Black so I know exactly why Jack brought me along." Cheryl nodded knowingly. "And, yes, I've been invited to a couple of client dinners but sometimes I couldn't go because I was working on a deadline or something else came up. I did go once, though, and frankly it was uncomfortable. Jack introduced me and then I just sat there like a lump while he and the other guy talked sports all night. I tried to start a conversation about an interesting article that I had just read and they looked at me like I had three heads."

"Well, at least you got asked," Kate snorted. "I found out through the grapevine that my boss's wife told him not to go out to dinners with me. As if I was interested in her fat old husband! He's so scared of her that he won't even invite me to lunch unless someone else is there."

Erica pursed her lips and dug her fork vigorously into her salad. "Client dinners are not all they are cracked up to be. I was supposed to have drinks and dinner with one of our top clients a few weeks ago. That's great news for me, right? A chance to show my stuff. So, first thing, he shifts the meet time from 5:30 pm to 7 pm. Okay, fine, I can accommodate. I'm flexible. We're meeting at the restaurant in his hotel but, when I get there, he texts that he's running late because he had to take a last minute call and that I should just come up to his hotel suite for a drink. Well, of course, I came up with some awkward excuse and said *No*. He came down a little while later, smiling, but conversation over dinner seemed a little forced. At one point, he got irritated with me for not knowing some figures—figures that I've been asking his administrative assistant to give me for weeks, I should add. I thought I handled it okay but, next day, my boss tells me that the client says he was disappointed with my 'follow-through.' So now I'm off the account. Do men have to deal with this kind of stuff? You tell me."

Cheryl shook her head. "I've had stuff like that happen to me before, too. You know what makes me mad? I just found out that Scott—the new guy in the office—has been going *skiing* with Connor—my manager's supervisor—on the weekends. I was pretty mad about the whole 'old boy network' thing. So the next time I bumped into Connor, I said—very casually—that I'd love to try skiing some time, where do you go skiing? And do you know what he says? He says, Where I ski is far too dangerous for beginners. Then he suggests I take some *lessons*. It turns out that both he and Scott have been skiing since they were five. When I was five, my mom was trying to scrape up the money to get me winter boots. Skiing was something only rich people did."

The four women fell silent for a minute as the waitress took away their dishes.

Finally, Jasmine spoke up. "Well, we've made it this far."

"Yeah, we've made it this far," sighed Erica. "But how much farther can we go? The deck is stacked against us and there's nothing we can do."

The four women paid their bill and left the restaurant. They were all well aware of the career obstacles they faced. But was Erica right? Wasn't there *anything* that they could do to get around some of those obstacles?

It turns out that there is.

The Networking Problem

Up until now, we've discussed the general benefits of particular network structures and specific networking behaviors. It is clear that networking works. What's not so clear is if it works equally well for *everyone*. There's a lot of evidence to suggest that people who are members of historically disadvantaged groups—such as women and people of color (POC)—have a harder time building, nurturing, and leveraging their networks effectively.

For women, exclusion from informal professional networks has been identified as one of the greatest barriers to career success.[1] One multinational study of over 240,000 men and women found that 81% of women report some form of exclusion at work even though 92% of men don't believe that they are excluding women at all.[2] Women often feel left out of the kind of informal get-togethers and casual social events the offer opportunities for people to build and nurture relationships with other professionals in a relaxed, fun environment.

The problems are similar for POC. Researchers looked at the careers of more 1,200 N.F.L. coaches from 1985 to 2012 and found that black coaches consistently moved more slowly up the ranks than their white counterparts, despite roughly equal performance, skill sets, experience, education, and age.[3] Herman Edwards, a former player who coached for nearly 20 years in the N.F.L., noted that many coaches are hired and promoted based on their relationships with other coaches. "When you're a coach, you're calling guys you know to fill those positions. As a minority coach, you fall behind the eight ball that way."[4]

Women of color are doubly disadvantaged. A survey of nearly 30,000 people revealed that only *half* of Black women say they have received senior-level support in advancing their career, compared with about two-thirds of White, Asian, and Hispanic women.[5] A follow-up survey[6] of 70,000 people found that only 28% of Black women report that their managers defend them or their work, compared to 40% of White women. Not surprisingly women of color are more skeptical about promotion opportunities. Whereas 59% of White women believe that that they have equal opportunity for growth as their peers, only 48% of Black women feel the same way.

Previously, we saw how more social capital is associated with better career outcomes. People who develop professional networks that are characterized by bridging, range, and a balance of weak and strong ties have access to more social capital than people who develop professional networks that don't have these qualities. In general, this is still good advice. But the *playbook* for building and nurturing networks isn't the same for women and POC as it is for White men.

Why?

Homophily (Again)

Remember *homophily*? (Yes, *that* word again!) Homophily is our natural tendency to form relationships with people who are like us. This hard-wired tendency means that we are far more likely to form a relationship with someone who is similar than we are to form one with someone who is *dissimilar*. Unfortunately for women and POC, homophilous professional networks aren't as effective as they are for White men. In fact, the homophilous professional networks of women and POC have one enormous disadvantage and that is that they *lack access to power*.

Power comes in many forms. But at its most basic level, a person has power when he or she can influence others either because they have *direct* access to resources that others want—such as money, jobs, a proven track record—or because they have *indirect* access to desirable resources through their personal connections. Powerful people can make things happen for people in their network. Harvey Weinstein, the now-disgraced but once powerful film and television executive, exercised his power to promote his wife's fashion brand.

> Now we have Harvey Weinstein married to the designer, who is able to put her dresses on … anybody in Hollywood. Yes, it is really that simple. Who is going to say no to the wife of Harvey Weinstein?"
>
> —Julia Samersova, casting director[7]

Although there have been some gains, the people who have the most power in nearly all U.S. organizations are White men. Women and POC have far less representation at senior management levels. For example, despite comprising 47% of the work force in 2016,[8] women represent little more than a quarter of executives and senior managers, hold only 4.2% of CEO jobs, and occupy fewer than one-fifth of board seats at S&P 500 companies.[9] Black workers represented 11.9% of the 2016 workforce, but only 3.4% of CEO jobs.[10]

Moreover, women and POC tend to occupy low wage or support functions. POC are far more likely than White workers to work in a low wage job. In 2010, for example, the median earnings of Black women were 90% of the median earnings of White women; and the median earnings of Black men were 68% of the median earnings of White men.[11] In 2016, Black workers made up nearly 17% of service occupations, which offer median weekly earnings of $523, but only a little more than 9% of management, professional, and related occupations, which offer median weekly earnings of $1,188.[12] Similarly, Hispanics—who make up roughly 15 percent of the workforce—account for roughly half of all farm workers and laborers, 44 percent of grounds maintenance workers, and 43 percent of maids and house cleaners.[13]

Where people work matters, too. More than half of all high-level women in large organizations work in support areas such as human resources, legal services, and information technology. These areas support the function of the organization but are not core to the organization's business. Women enter these support functions as a result of subtle career tracking, more women-friendly policies (such as flex time), lack of sponsorship, and negative recruitment experiences.[14] In contrast, nearly two-thirds of men cluster in positions that have profit-and-loss responsibility or are focused on core operations. These jobs are closer to the core of the business, giving these individuals greater access to tangible resources such as staff and budget, and greater visibility to senior leadership. Not surprisingly, a higher percentage of C-suite executives come from core business functions.[15]

Given that White men are much more likely to hold powerful positions in their organizations, women and POC who have mainly homophilous professional networks will have disproportionately fewer relationships with powerful people. The opposite is true for White men's homophilous relationships. When White men have professional relationships with other White men, they are disproportionately likely to connect with powerful people. As a result, *their* social capital is liable to include useful work-related resources, such as jobs, budget, references, and high-visibility projects.[16]

Unlike women and POC, casual interactions among White men are much more likely to include a high-level powerful person. This is why a random group of White men chatting at the company picnic is far more likely to include at least one important organizational decision-maker than is a random group of women and POC at the same event. In the opening story, for example, Jasmine noted that one of her colleagues, Kurt, is a sports nut who enjoys talking about the latest game. And with whom is he "shooting the breeze"? The department head!

Having powerful contacts matters. "Power is a lot like real estate," said Frank Underwood on Netflix Inc.'s *House of Cards*. "It's all about location, location, location. The closer you are to the source, the higher your property value." People with power and status are more likely to have insider information. This explains why job-seekers in male networks receive more relevant job information than do those in female networks.[17] Exclusion from political and strategic knowledge means that navigating and making career decisions is less informed by those who have 'insider' knowledge.[18]

Powerful people use their power to influence others. They can introduce their contacts to other powerful people, for example. Or, they can make a phone call to a prospective employer to put in a good word. One study of 2735 job-seekers found that people who used powerful contacts in a job search were more likely to get hired into high-status jobs. To make matters worse, the same study found that people referred to jobs by male contacts *earned* more than people referred by female contacts.[19]

> Because men are almost always going to have more in common with other men, that's who they're going to default to when it comes time to pass out a tip, a piece of advice, or more noticeably, a promotion...Which is why it's hard to fault them for it entirely—women do the same thing to other women. The problem is that, because so few women are in positions of authority, it creates a terrible cycle where women have to work twice as hard to command the same sort of attention. Otherwise, you'll just get drowned out.
>
> —Ashley Feinberg[20]

Lack of access to powerful people also means that some people have restricted access to senior-level *sponsorship.* Sponsorship can accelerate career advancement, especially among people perceived as outsiders in male-dominated and White-dominated industries, such as the financial or high-tech industries. Compared to men, for example, women have more difficulty finding sponsors, have lower-level sponsors, and have fewer sponsors throughout their career.[21] One study showed that only 10% of senior-level women report that four or more executives had helped them advance in their careers, compared to 17% of senior-level men.[22]

How many sponsors have supported *your* career?

Without consistent sponsorship throughout their career, women and others are forced to increase their internal visibility by finding alternative—often more time-consuming—ways to get on high profile projects. This may be why women generally require 23 years to reach CEO status, whereas men average 15 years, despite having similar qualifications.[23]

Another deeply entrenched dividing line between people who have powerful contacts and those who don't is created by socio-economic background. We all know that lack of money makes it harder to access education and training opportunities, creating a *human* capital disadvantage. But the *social* capital disadvantages are even greater. Here's how one low-income student—on a full scholarship at an elite private college—described the social capital advantages of his mostly affluent peers:[24]

I have a friend whose father owns a WNBA team, and he knows so many people. There was a senator candidate who was running for the US Senate position after Ted Kennedy died, and my friend invited him to speak here...It turns out his father was roommates with this guy at Harvard, and the connections just branch off from that. My former roommate, his dad is a publisher, and he's also Harvard educated. My roommate knows a lot of baseball people and has been able to get a personal tour of the ESPN campus. I don't have those connections.

Compared to people who grew up in higher socioeconomic environments, people in lower socioeconomic situations, tend to have fewer but stronger relationships. Because strong relationships occur most frequently among people who are similar, people from low socioeconomic backgrounds tend to be embedded in small sticky rice networks with others in the same financial situation, making it hard to get even indirect access to powerful people who can provide them with important resources, such as information about job openings and scholarships.[25]

People who lack significant representation in positions of power are in a continuous loop of disadvantage. White men who grew up in affluent households are more likely to support the career advancement of affluent White men and are better positioned to do so. As a result, a greater proportion of affluent White men enter positions of power where they tend to support the career advancement of other affluent White men, making it harder for women and POC to move into positions of power, further reducing the career advancement of women and POC. It's a vicious cycle.

The obvious implication is that women, POC, and other people from historically disadvantaged groups need to develop more *range* in their networks than do their affluent White male counterparts. They need to form professional relationships with people who are *not* like them. In other words, they need to include more White men in their professional networks. And, the research tells us, that's exactly what many of them do.[26]

When it comes to professional networks, White men's networks are more homophilous than the networks of women and POC. White men have predominantly White male networks, while women and POC have more mixed—more diverse!—networks because they also include some White men in their networks.

In previous chapters, we saw the benefits of avoiding homophily in networks and pursuing range instead. So, the fact that the networks of women and POC are *less* homophilous should give them an advantage, right? After all, ties to diverse others are a network strength because it increases the ability to draw upon multiple perspectives and more diverse information.

By that logic, women and POC with diverse networks should do better than White men. Right?

Wrong.

Unfortunately, having diverse networks introduces a *new* problem for women and POC and that has to do with the *strength* of their connections.

The Strong and the Weak

The biggest disadvantage of diverse professional networks for women and POC is that their relationships with White men are relatively *weak*. More than any other differentiators, gender and race/ethnicity shape the way in which we determine who is like us and who is *not* like us. Perhaps because they are highly visible and nearly universal characteristics, gender and race are often core to our identity. We are far more likely to see same-sex and same-race people as similar to us—despite other differences—than we are to see them as different—despite other similarities. Seeing people as similar to us makes it *much* easier to build and nurture strong relationships. The more ways in which we are alike, the easier it is to build a strong relationship. In other words, a White female manager is much more likely to form a strong relationship with another White female—even if she is not a manager—than she is to form a strong relationship with any male manager.

Look at the people in your network. Are most of them the same gender and race/ethnicity as you?

As we know, strong ties have a number of career-enhancing advantages over weaker ties. For example, more information is shared in strong relationships—especially valuable insider knowledge—and what is shared is communicated more easily. But, most relevantly for the present discussion, strong ties build *trust* in a person's competency and character.

> [M]en look at women and think they're all over the place. Whereas with other men they know where they're coming from and know they can trust them.
>
> —Senior civil servant, woman[27]

Trust is a fundamental determinant of career opportunities because trust reduces *uncertainty*. It's always a bit of a risk to hire, promote, or otherwise support someone. You can never truly know if they will perform well in a new position or on a new project. A person who is trusted is a better risk than someone who is less trusted. To some extent, we reduce uncertainty by relying upon documentations of human capital. Trust in a person's capabilities is stronger when they can present evidence such as advanced educational degrees and certificates, impressive resumes, and high test scores.

Decisions to promote or support women and POC are more uncertain than decisions to promote White men. When a company has never had a female CEO—as most have not!—promoting a woman to CEO will seem risky. If a White man has always occupied a particular role, having the role occupied by a White man will come to be seen as "normal" or business-as-usual. A female or POC candidate will be looked at suspiciously. Hiring teams may wonder if this "non-normal" candidate has what it takes to do the job.

Where there is greater uncertainty, there is also greater demand for evidence regarding skills and abilities. That means that women, POC, and other people who are not represented in positions of power need more documentations and measurements of competence as well as a stronger network of professional relationships with people who are themselves trusted—because trust can be transferred—and who are willing to vouch for their competency.[28] More specifically, they need more strong professional relationships with White men from affluent backgrounds.

But this is exactly what they *don't* have.

In short, for women and members of other underrepresented groups, both their homophilous *and* non-homophilous professional networks offer less access to social capital than the professional networks of a typical White man. For women and POC, their homophilous relationships are less likely to connect them to resources and their *non*-homophilous relationships are less likely to be strong which means that they connect them to less social capital. In contrast, the homophilous professional networks of White men from affluent backgrounds are much more likely to include strong connections to resources and power. If you are a woman or member of another underrepresented group, this is definitely bad news...

...but it gets worse.

The barriers that make networking particularly challenging for women and POC are deeply entrenched in our organizations and our larger society. Changing them requires more than instituting a few organizational policies. The only way to truly level the playing field is for members of underrepresented groups to move into positions of power proportional to their share of the work force. Of course, for this to happen, society would have to undergo *major* changes, changes so big that they are expected to take another generation or two or three—or more!

At this point, if you are a woman or POC, you are probably ready to throw up your hands. What's the point of even trying to create an effective network when the deck is stacked against you? Is it even possible to address these challenges on an individual level? Is there a way for you to build, nurture, and leverage more effective networks?

The answer is: *Yes*, but it won't be easy.

Describing *all* the challenges you face is beyond the scope of this book. But understanding a few of the biggest ones will make it easier for you to figure out ways around them. In the next section, I will outline three of the most common barriers facing members of underrepresented groups and suggest some ways to address them.

1. Organization of networking opportunities
2. Pressure and authenticity
3. Personal experience with bridge-building

Barriers to Building Effective Networks

Organization of networking opportunities. In most industries, opportunities to build informal relationships among executives and managers are organized around stereotypically White male interests and activities, especially activities connected to upper middle class backgrounds, such golfing, sailing, skiing, and attending sporting events. Access to these networks is often negotiated outside of the workspace. As one female manager noted,

> I'm not going out to play golf with them, you know in groups or anything, I'm not in a more casual how men get-to-know-each-other and feel-each-other-out kind of a thing. I don't have access to that. And I won't. It's just not the kind of company that's even comfortable with that kind of coed experience.[29]

The affluent White male orientation of many extra-work activities restricts the opportunities that women and others have to participate in relationship-building experiences that combine their passions with interdependence and mutual goals. Moreover, they frequently have little recourse. Employees excluded from a formal organizational network—such as a club or association—can refer to company policy or written job descriptions to argue that they have been unfairly treated. In contrast, employees who are excluded from *in*formal organizational networks—such as weekend ski trips!—have few options for reparation because companies generally do not take responsibility for informal work ties, arguing that employees are free to socialize as they wish outside of work.[30]

Women are particularly disadvantaged by extra-work activities. In addition to being less likely to appeal to their interests, these networking activities are also are more likely to be organized around male schedules that, typically, allow more flexibility for after-work and weekend socializing. Fewer women than men have the time to participate in extra work activities because women are more likely than men to have competing demands in terms of time spent at work balanced with home and childcare duties.[31] A 2017 study by Lean In found that 54% of women (as compared to 22% of men) report doing all or most of the household work, reducing the time they have available for outside-of-work socializing. Women with a partner and child are 5.5 times more likely than their male counterparts to do all or most of the household work.[32] Like Jena in the opening example, women often use their "networking time" to take care of family and household needs.

Men do not shoulder the majority of these unpaid responsibilities, freeing them up mentally and physically to engage in social interactions. This disadvantage grows greater as individuals create families. A 2015 Lean In study found that single women and single men take part just as frequently in the same types of networking activities. Differences only begin to exist when women marry and—more dramatically—become parents.[33]

For those of you who are parents, what percent of the household chores and childcare responsibilities fall to you?

Pressure and authenticity. One of the biggest challenges that members of underrepresented groups face is the tug and pushback from other members of their minority group. There can be strong pressure to be maintain homophilous relationships. To deal with this pressure, many professional women and POC split their professional networks in two, such that they get emotional and social support from their homophilous relationships, and their job- or task-related support from non-homophilous relationships.[34] For example, a woman may reach out to another woman for social interaction and camaraderie but to a man for career advice or information. But one-dimensional networks are weaker than multidimensional networks. To move forward in their organization and careers, women and POC need rich, multiplex, and strong relationships.

The stress of maintaining the two non-overlapping sets of relationships can be emotionally draining. Especially when relations between the two sets of relationships are tense, the networker can find him- or herself thrust into a bridge-building position that is fraught with tension. Pressure to "choose a side" can be intense. POC, for example, may be accused of "acting white" or "talking black" by different colleagues. Women may be accused by both men and women of not demonstrating stereotypical feminine traits. For instance, they may be called "uncaring," "cold," or "unsupportive."

Pressure also comes from within. Unlike most Whites, many POC think about their race on a daily basis; it is often a defining aspect of their identity. This can lead to feelings of inauthenticity when interactions with White colleagues involve submerging cultural identifiers (e.g., dialect) and avoiding behaviors that might trigger racial stereotypes (e.g., exhibiting strong emotion). Whites, in turn, may worry about accidentally saying the wrong thing when interacting with their colleagues of color, making it difficult to have the kind of casual, relaxed conversations that build relationships.[35]

One difference between the issues facing women and those facing POC is that most men have had many social experiences with women whereas a greater proportion of White people have never—or only rarely—experienced ethnic or social class integration outside of a school or professional setting. This sharp division between social and professional interactions can heighten awareness of "cross-border" interactions, and intensify internal pressure. Given that POC are nearly twice as likely as Whites to have grown up in a low-income household, many are at a double disadvantage.[36]

Personal experience with bridge-building. Certain network positions may be more uncomfortable for some people. Being a bridge-builder, for example, may be more stressful for women than it is for men because they may experience being a bridge-builder as being excluded. As one woman said to me, "I hate feeling like I'm on the edge of all these groups at work but never really *in* one." In keeping with the tendency to "accuse" women of demonstrating non-stereotypically feminine traits, research suggests that women who are perceived to be bridge-builders are rated as less warm than other women.[37]

The roots of these negative experiences may go back to childhood. While research in this area is still developing, we know adolescent girls who occupy bridging positions are more likely to think about and actually commit suicide.[38] Research that I conducted with University of Cincinnati Professor of Developmental Psychology Richard Gilman found that high school girls who occupied bridging positions in their school's network felt more socially stressed and had lower levels of life satisfaction than other girls.[39]

When you think about your bridging relationships, do you feel that they connect you to people in other groups or do you feel that they keep you *dis*connected from other groups?

People who were raised in low socioeconomic households are far more likely than people raised in more affluent households to have had limited experience with bridge-building.[40] When you're living on the edge, even small fluctuations in your financial situation can have dramatic effects on the ability to afford adequate food, safe and affordable housing, clothing, and child care. Limited-range, sticky rice networks offer strong relationships among people who can band together to help each other out in important ways. According to The Pew Charitable Trusts' Survey of American Family Finances and the Panel Study of Income Dynamics, people in households that have experienced significant material hardship—such as missing a credit payment—were five times more likely than others to have received money from friends or family.[41]

Living in a sticky rice network is a smart strategy when you're in frequent need of basic resources. But if you were raised in a low socioeconomic household, the short-term gains provided by sticky rice clusters may be outweighed by the long-term losses. While sticky rice clusters can help people avoid dire straits and deviant behavior—perhaps even providing the resources that allow them to build their human capital through education or work—it can also limit their ability to develop the bridging social capital that they need to leverage their human capital.

Without early exposure to networks that incorporate range or bridge-building, people from low-income backgrounds may lack the skills to build effective networks, even when their financial circumstances have changed. Moreover, because our society often downplays the role that social capital plays in our professional advancement, they may not even know the extent to which others are helped by their networks. Even if they do, they may not know what to do about it. As Malcolm Gladwell wrote, "Poverty is not deprivation. It is isolation."[42]

Overcoming the Barriers: The Magnificent Seven

Not everything in life can be changed,
But anything that might be changed must first be faced.
—James Baldwin (1964)

With so many forces working against women, POC, and other historically disadvantaged people, it may seem pointless to network. But when it comes to job and career outcomes, networks and networking *do* matter. They matter for women and POC for the same reasons that they matter for White men. Creating a sustainable, strategic, and effective network leads *everyone* to desirable outcomes such as more job opportunities, higher wages, greater job satisfaction, and faster promotions. But, because of the additional challenges that women and others face, their playbook and their strategies for network-building look a little different.

There are *seven* strategies that women, POC, and other historically disadvantaged people can and have used to successfully create effective networks. They are the *Magnificent Seven:*

1. Leverage diversity.
2. Build a strong external network.
3. Stay open to career opportunities that offer access to resources.
4. Regularly articulate your career goals and strengths.
5. Address the issue of authenticity head on.
6. Proactively cultivate a mentor with whom you identify and a sponsor with power.
7. Support sponsorship programs and informal networking efforts.

These strategies are based on the latest research, as well as on first-hand accounts of successful networkers. The Magnificent Seven strategies apply to anyone who belongs to a historically disadvantaged group, including members of ethnic minority groups, people from working class backgrounds, and others. The main task for all these groups is to increase the power of their networks by connecting directly or indirectly to powerful people.

Leverage diversity. Turn your disadvantage into an opportunity. Network diversity can pay off, even for women and other minorities.[43] As we know, White males—on average—have relatively homophilous networks. In contrast, the networks of women and POC are relatively diverse. Precisely because it is hard to form homophilous relationships, women and other minorities can exploit the relative ease with which they have learned to establish relationships with people who are different. Take advantage of this skill!

Get comfortable with weakening some of your relationships with people like you by increasing your participation in work and non-work events that include people who are *not* like you, especially White men at higher levels in the organization. Reach out to people who are not like you, especially those directly or indirectly connected to resources. Take part in extra-work activities, such as dinners and lunches. If you're a woman and the prospect of a social interaction with male colleagues makes you uncomfortable, invite a trusted third person in any interaction outside of work. To boost the power of your network, choose someone who would also benefit from the interaction, such as a peer or more junior person.

But don't drop all of your same-sex or same-race contacts. Balance your network and maintain its diversity by including people like you among your professional contacts. One study of racial/ethnic minority managers found that those who develop networks that span a broad set of social and corporate circles—including both White *and* POC—were more likely to be identified as "high-potentials" by their organizations than racial/ethnic minority managers who had few, if any, network connections with other members of their minority group.[44] Leverage the diversity in your network to innovate, problem-solve, and transfer knowledge!

Build a strong external network. A study of the networks of star financial analysts recruited by other firms found that women—but not men!—who switch firms maintain their stardom and their new employer's share prices.[45] The reason: star women form strong *external* networks. They don't limit themselves to the individuals within their organization. Men, on the other hand, often rely heavily on their internal networks and so have more trouble when they move into a new organization.

Cultivate relationships with external constituencies—such as customers and mentors—that are not dependent upon your current company. Building a strong external network is a great strategy for someone from an historically disadvantaged background because it makes it more likely that you form a strong connection with a person in a position of power, even if that person is similar to you demographically. While there may only be a handful of women or POC in powerful positions in your company, there are hundreds—if not thousands—in your field or industry!

External connections can also enhance your reputation more effectively than internal contacts. The opinion or recommendation of a respected person who is external to an organization is often weighted more heavily than, say, the opinion of your supervisor or direct report who others might reason have "political" motives for supporting you. These champions can do more for you than you can do for yourself.

> Women are so modest; we tend to not really share and talk about how great we are, how talented we are. So oftentimes, this is the champion's role—our cheerleader—and for women, especially, this is something you really need in your back pocket.
>
> —Christine Power,
> President and CEO, Capital District Health Authority[46]

Develop collaborations outside of work. Possibilities include sitting on boards of local non-profits, getting actively involved in alumni networks, and participating meaningfully in community and industry events. Volunteer to help organize an event for a favorite charity, serve on an industry committee, or coordinate a panel discussion for an industry event. Consider joining a formal network as a vehicle for developing informal relationships.

Stay open to career opportunities that offer access to resources. There are many subtle and not-so-subtle efforts to direct women and other members of underrepresented groups into support functions—which have no profit and loss (P&L) responsibility. Resist them. Powerful positions are at the core of your organization. They offer you closer access to desirable resources—budget, staff, projects—which increase *your* value to others. Anna Capitanio, Vice-President of Organizational Effectiveness and M&A HR, BT Global Services urges, "If you have an appetite for senior roles you need to have the experience of running a business. In line roles you don't get P&L experience and project management is not a substitute."[47]

Having P&L responsibilities also increases the likelihood that your job will require you to interact with high-status people, further increasing the likelihood that you will form relationships with high-status people. Research has shown that when women occupy positions that give them opportunity to interact with high-status employees, they are just as likely as men to include high-status people in their network.[48] As Sheryl Sandburg noted, in her popular book, *Lean In*, don't opt out of high-status career track before you even get on it. Instead, lean in.[49]

Get in the habit of regularly articulating your career goals and strengths. Research shows us that people who highlight their achievements advance further in their careers, are more satisfied with their careers, and had greater compensation growth than those who fail to blow their own horn.[50] So, get comfortable with your assets.

> In my work, I've often heard women express that they're uncomfortable communicating their value, especially early on in business ownership. They say things like, "I don't like to toot my own horn." "I'd rather let the work speak for itself." "I don't like to sing my own praises."
>
> —Casey Brown, Pricing Consultant[51]

Many women are socialized to be modest. They may limit the extent to which they talk about themselves out of a fear of making themselves vulnerable to the negative reactions of others. As a result, sharing professional dreams and ambitions can feel threatening. If directly articulating your career goals and strengths makes you uncomfortable—even when articulated "softly"—try reframing how you think about it. Don't think of it as self-promotion. Think of it instead as giving others the opportunity to understand your strengths. Sharing your achievements helps others see the real you.

If highlighting your professional interests, capabilities, and achievements is simply too daunting for you, seek out opportunities to demonstrate them through action. A great way to do this is to join cross-functional teams and to take advantage of cross-training opportunities. These give women and other members historically disadvantaged groups an opportunity to display their skill, knowledge, and abilities—and build co-worker relation-ships—in everyday work-related interactions. One study of 800 organiza-tions looked at dozens of different types of diversity-enhancing interven-tions— including diversity training and hiring quotas— to see which ones were associated with greater diversity distribution within their organization at all levels. The researchers found that *only* consistent use of cross-func-tional teams and cross-training opportunities significantly increased the di-versity distribution within organizations.[52]

Address the issue of authenticity head on. Ask yourself, How can I feel like I'm being true to myself while interacting with different subcultures? One answer might be to see yourself as having multiple authentic selves, some of which you're still growing into. While I would never encourage you to compromise on your core values, I do believe that you can learn how to present yourself differently—but authentically!—to different audiences. It may help you to find a real or historical person to serve as your role model. Former President Barack Obama, for example, was a master at presenting different "selves" to different audiences while staying authentic.

> At fundraisers in New York, he'd put on his professorial lilt. In front of mostly black audiences in South Carolina, he'd warn them against believing rumors that he was a Muslim. "They try to bamboozle you, hoodwink you," he said, in a deliberate homage to Malcolm X. On the *Ellen* show, he won the week by doing a harmless dance that drove the mostly white audience crazy. After a particularly rough debate in North Carolina, he referenced Jay-Z by brushing dirt off his shoulders and got a standing ovation. In an interview with Steve Kroft, he talked about college football and getting a dog. In an interview with MTV's Sway, he complimented his interviewer— "You look tight"—and emphasized his policy position that "brothers should pull up their pants."[53]

As I've written elsewhere, be careful not to present a *false* self. Present-ing yourself should be a matter of choosing which self you want to bring for-ward in any particular situation. It should never mean fabricating a persona that has no connection with your personal experiences, values, or beliefs.

Proactively cultivate a mentor with whom you identify and a sponsor with power. Successful members of minority racial groups consistently stress the value of same-race contacts in helping them to develop and implement strategies for career success. Same-race and same-sex mentors can help you manage your authenticity because they've had to learn how to manage it, too.[54]

Having a same-race or same-sex sponsor can also be extremely helpful, although they are harder to find them since fewer of them are in positions of power. Instead of focusing on a sponsor who looks like you, focus instead on finding a sponsor who is interested in supporting your advancement.

Unfortunately, as a woman or member of another traditionally disadvantaged group, the onus for forming helpful relationships is on you. Unlike others, you cannot count on bumping into mentors and sponsors in the halls. You also can't expect the few women and POC in positions of power to take on the responsibility of reaching out to you. After all, mentoring and sponsoring take valuable time. Instead, look around. In meetings, pay attention to how higher-ups talk and who might be a good fit for your style and ambitions.

Never ask someone you barely know if he or she would agree to act as your mentor or sponsor. It's a little like asking someone you don't know to be your friend. The other person doesn't know you well enough to make the decision and, besides, you seem like a lot of work. Sponsors in particular don't want to fix something that is broken. Instead, they want to find someone who just needs a little polish to be off and running.

Offer the person something—a relevant piece of information, a comment about a project, or a reaction to something that was said. Make sure that what you offer is likely to be of use to the other person. Keep this first interaction concise and to the point. The idea is to start to establish mutuality and learning—just like you would with any other relationship— through a series of brief interactions. With any luck, it will slowly dawn on the other person that you are worth an investment of time and effort. You are going places and the other person can help you get there.

Support sponsorship programs and informal networking efforts. For those of you who have made it to the C-suite, help your organization and industry include women and other members of historically disadvantaged members in organizational networks. You can't wait for your CEO to take initiative because most literally don't see the need. In one study of 93 female managers, women reported exclusion from informal networks as one of the key obstacles to women's advancement.[55] In contrast, their male CEOs claimed that lack of management experience and too few women in the executive pipeline were the critical barriers faced by women. Nearly 50% of men who work in organizations where only one in ten senior leaders is a woman believe that women are already well-represented in leadership![56]

Organize networking events that take place inside of work hours to accommodate women's schedules, such as lunches, mini-workshops, and workplace book clubs. Invite a high-potential POC to accompany you when you visit clients. Reserve an extra room and babysitters for evening workplace events. Recommend a woman to serve on a conference panel or an industry board. Create opportunities for informal interaction to help members of underrepresented groups build the professional relationships that propel careers. Determine criteria for success and measure outcomes.

Final Note

Understanding some of the challenges facing historically disadvantaged groups seeking to build networks and developing specific networking strategies will go a long way toward leveling the playing field. Networking is a very powerful tool and, when done effectively, *will* increase career opportunities. But I don't want to end this chapter without noting that the challenges facing members of historically disadvantaged groups cannot be addressed solely by individuals. Networks are shaped and constrained by larger societal and organizational forces. It is important to recognize that while networking is an individual activity, it is not *only* an individual activity. While there is some onus on individuals to adapt and change, there is also a need for society and organizations to change.

Many companies understand the importance of networking for women and have implemented a number of programs to help women and POC build professional networks. KPMG, for example, currently has seven national diversity networks that engage nearly 40% of employees. They include Abilities in Motion, African-American, Asian Pacific Islander, Hispanic/Latino, KPMG's Network of Women (KNOW), pride@kpmg (LGBT), and Veterans networks. These networks provide members with "opportunities to participate in career-development programs, broaden professional experiences, and build career-enriching relationships, both within and beyond the firm."[57] General Electric has implemented a version of its *myConnections* talent-spotting and mentoring program for women. Participants are sorted into groups of roughly a dozen members and assigned a coach, typically a rising female star. The groups determine their own agendas but their main goal is to help women connect with one another across levels and functions in the company. So far, the program has been a resounding success.[58]

The efforts of KPMG, General Electric, and other companies are laudable but they're not enough. It is a mistake for company leaders to think that merely creating a formal network will significantly change career opportunities. Believing that ignores very real organizational and societal biases that make it difficult for people from historically disadvantaged groups to build, nurture, and leverage effective professional networks. As Elizabeth Ruske, CEO of Tiara International, a Chicago-based provider of leadership development for women notes, "A minimalist approach will generate some engagement and enthusiasm; it typically does not sustain large-scale change."[59] To truly level the playing field, major changes need to be made in the way our organizations and society function.

To Recap...

Women, POC, and other members of historically disadvantaged groups face significant challenges when seeking to build, nurture, and leverage networks effectively. One the one hand, when they form relationships with people who are like them, they are disproportionately less likely to connect with people who have status and resources. On the other hand, even when they do form relationships with powerful people, those relationships are more likely to be too weak to provide access to a rich stream of social capital. Despite the many barriers facing members of underrepresented groups, there are at least seven strategies that women, POC, and other historically disadvantaged people can and have used to successfully create effective networks.

In the next chapter, we'll drill down deeper into networking challenges by looking at how they change over the course of your career. We'll examine the six key career inflection points at which to analyze—or re-analyze!—your network to make sure that your networking strategy matches your professional career goals

Reflection Questions

What barriers do you face when trying to develop an effective network?

If you are a women, POC, or a member of another underrepresented group, what strategies can you use to develop an effective network?

If you do not belong to an underrepresented group, how can you use what you've learned in this chapter to help diversify your organization?

10

Leverage Your Assets

SELF-ASSESSMENT SNAPSHOT

To answer these questions, please complete the *Organizational Network Exercise* in the Toolbox at the end of this book.

1. Consider the sticky-rice clusters (e.g., functions, departments, units) in your organization that are disconnected from each other. Would it add value to your organization (and to you) if you occupied a bridge-building position between some of these clusters? If so, which ones?

   _____

   _____

2. Which sticky-rice clusters (or individuals) in your organization have the most influence over organizational events? Whose opinions are considered most important when it comes to making decisions?

   _____

   _____

Connect the Dots, pages 175–192
Copyright © 2019 by Information Age Publishing
All rights of reproduction in any form reserved.

3. Think about two sticky-rice clusters that you know well. How would the people in those clusters describe themselves? How would they describe the people in the other cluster?

_____

_____

Roizen to the Rescue

In 1997, Apple Computer ran a full-page advertisement in the *Wall Street Journal*. In the ad, news clippings from dozens of software CEOs declared their commitment to Apple. At the time, Apple was 90 days from bankruptcy. Software developers were abandoning Apple in droves. In those days, Apple was not the major multinational technology company it is today. Many industry commentators, like Stan Dolberg of Forrester Research, confidently predicted its imminent demise. "[W]hether they stand alone or are acquired, Apple as we know it, is cooked."[1] In a few months, Steve Jobs would return to save the company. But when the ad ran in 1997, it was not clear that there would be a company for him to save. Apple desperately needed to keep software developers from jumping off their sinking ship and onto Microsoft's platform. Insiders credit that ad with keeping software developers committed to Apple at a critical moment. Without the public support of those software CEOs, Apple might not have survived.

Who got those all-important quotes?—Heidi Roizen, Apple's new Vice President of Developer Relations.[2] Brian Gentile worked with Roizen at Apple. He noted,

> Heidi *made* each of those quotes happen. If it were not for Heidi, that ad would never have run. And at the time, it was a very big deal for Apple to have these important developers saying, "We still believe in this platform and we're going to stick by Apple."[3]

Roizen had been at her job for less than six months before the ad ran. How had she convinced so many software CEOs to publicly support Apple?

In 1996, Apple Computer teetered on the brink of disaster. While software for the Apple platform once represented a $4 billion market, by 1996, it had declined to a $3 billion market. At the time, Microsoft and Apple were in a fierce competition for market share. Apple had released the popular Apple and Macintosh personal computers that were widely acknowledged to be the most user-friendly on the market but Microsoft still had a strong customer base. Apple dominated the US K-12 institutions and the creative professionals market, which included graphic and Web designers, but Microsoft was considered the default operating program for the much larger business market.

In an attempt to gain market share, Apple made a costly mistake. It licensed the Mac OS to third party hardware vendors such as Radius, Motorola, DayStar, and Power Computing. The Power Computing clones were the fastest personal computers in 1996 but their aggressive pricing undercut Apple's Power Macintosh sales. For example, in December of 1995, the 120 MHz Power Macintosh 9500 cost $6,560. At the same, a Power Computing 120 MHz Mac OS-compatible tower cost $3,344 or roughly half the cost. The worldwide press began to badmouth Apple and sales of Apple's Mac dropped precipitously.

The developer community was worried, and rightly so. Many developers had created their products entirely on the Apple platform, giving an advantage to other developers who had created their products on Windows if Apple failed. Apple users were on the verge of a mass exodus to the safer, seemingly more dependable, Windows program. In 1996, a member of the MacUser community shared this typical story:

> A developer told me recently that the reason his company's new whiz-bang game was coming out on Windows first was due to failed expectations with an earlier Mac title. It seems the distributor told him not to make a hybrid CD-ROM, which would inevitably be placed in the Windows section of the store, but to instead cut a separate Mac package. The developer complied, expecting decent orders for both platforms. But the Mac boxes just sat in the warehouse. During the skittish holiday season, no dealers wanted to order Mac-only units for fear of mounting inventory.[4]

Enter Heidi Roizen. At first glance, Roizen seemed an unlikely person to halt Apple's freefall. She wasn't a programmer, developer, or engineer. In a field dominated by men, she didn't fit the model of sage or savior. But Roizen did have one thing that Apple desperately needed—social capital— and she was willing to leverage it to save Apple.

Roizen hadn't started out with many contacts in the software community. In 1983, recently graduated from a top MBA program, she had almost no experience with technology. But her brother—a computer programmer— did. He had written a software program called T/Maker. T/Maker was a software to develop spreadsheets and so was in direct competition with Lotus 1-2-3. He convinced Roizen to use her business knowledge to help him turn T/Maker into a real company. Without a lot of capital to draw upon and with a well-capitalized competitor like Lotus, T/Maker needed to generate high consumer demand without incurring a lot of costs. But T/ Maker was virtually unknown in the marketplace.

Roizen decided to mount an aggressive campaign to build awareness of the company and its product. She built relationships with members of the press by giving interviews to virtually anyone. It helped that she had an outgoing personality and, as a woman, was an anomaly in the field. She attended numerous industry conferences and events. She joined a handful of well-known technology-oriented groups—such as the Software Entrepreneurs—and took advantage of just about any opportunity to sit on a panel.

After a few years, Roizen joined the board of the Software Publishers Association (SPA)—the largest group dedicated to raising awareness about specific issues relevant to the software industry—where she was able to address issues that were important to software developers and publishers. Later, she was elected president of SPA, which gave her significant industry exposure and the opportunity to meet with industry leaders to discuss the questions and topics that mattered most to them.

At every step, Roizen nurtured her network. She didn't focus on getting to know "important" people. Instead, she built relationships with people she found interesting. "I just like getting to know interesting people," she said. "When you meet interesting people, interesting things happen."[5] Roizen was careful to never take advantage of a relationship or to introduce two people to each other unless both would benefit from the introduction. She hosted eclectic and intimate gatherings at her home that included parents of her children's friends, along with software luminaries such as Bill Gates.

By the time she was tapped by Apple, Roizen was a recognized and respected voice within the developer community. She knew that Apple had to convince developers that it understood their problems and had a battle plan to combat shrinking Mac-software sales. In particular, she needed to appeal to alienated developers who didn't fit tidily into Apple's key markets such as education, graphics, and multimedia.[6] Roizen knew that getting public commitments from software CEOs would be a critical first step in this process.

So what did she do? She *leveraged* her network.

Leverage Your Network

Leveraging networks is the trickiest part of networking. You *leverage* your network when you strategically seek resources through people who are ready and willing to help you. Leveraging your network releases its potential and makes it available to you and others. To leverage effectively, you'll need to develop three critical skills:

1. Knowing
2. Asking
3. Bridging

These leveraging skills can be difficult to master but they are absolutely essential if you want to unleash the power of your network. By the way, if the idea of "using" your network to your advantage arouses complicated feelings and ethical concerns, remember that leveraging your network also benefits *everyone else* in your network, too.

Leveraging Skill 1: Knowing

At its most basic, *knowing* means knowing the human and social capital of the people in your network. It means knowing who has what and who is connected to whom. Knowing who has what will help you know exactly where to turn when you need advice, information, instrumental help, or specific tangible resources. Knowledge of the network increases your ability to leverage it. Roizen knew the important players in her field and whose words would carry the most weight with developers.

Knowing means not only understanding what the individuals in your network have or can do, it also means knowing to whom and to what *they* are connected. Knowing the social capital of the people in your network can help you gauge the additional *indirect* resources that might flow to you through your relationship.

I experienced the benefits of my indirect network the other day when I attempted to analyze some data for a research project. The data were in nearly a thousand Excel worksheets located in 20 different Excel workbooks. Moreover, each worksheet had only one row of data that I needed and it was in a different row in every worksheet. I needed a quick way to gather only the data I needed into one manageable worksheet. I don't normally work in Excel so this seemed like an unsurmountable problem. I reached out to several people I knew but no one had a ready solution.

However, I did know that my colleague Martin had a colleague, Paul, who was an Excel expert. I sent an email to Martin detailing my problem and asked him to forward it to Paul. Within 20 minutes, Martin forwarded Paul's response. Paul had written a few lines of code, and a short series of steps on how to run the code. The code worked and my problem was solved, easily saving me several hours of drudgery. Knowing who Martin knew was key to successfully leveraging my network.

What is the extent, scope, and diversity of *your* indirect network?

Knowing also means knowing the structure of the larger organizational or industry network in which you are embedded. A number of research studies have shown that people who can "see" their organizational network clearly are more likely than others to be identified as powerful leaders.[7] [To capture your organizational network, complete the *Organizational Network Exercise* in the Toolbox.]

To "see" your network better, start by taking a bird's eye view on the relationships in your organization or industry. Note how each person—or team or department or function—fits into the overall social fabric of your organization. How are people and groups connected—or *dis*connected—from each other. Does IT frequently work closely with R&D or is IT more likely to work closely with Accounting? Does HR work more closely with Legal or Marketing? Do union workers socialize with managers or do they tend to stick to themselves? Ask yourself these questions and more to identify opportunities for bridge-building. You can add value to your organization by bridging and then leveraging these gaps, even if the advantage is not immediately apparent.

Once you understand the structure, you can start to create opportunities that will put you in contact with people in different clusters. When building bridges across the "holes," in your organization's network, it is often easiest to connect with the person in the cluster who is most like yourself. That's okay. As we know, it's easier to form relationships with people who are similar.

University of Chicago Professor Ron Burt once said that he makes a point of attending one conference every year on a subject that he knows nothing about. While at the conference, he goes to a variety of presentations and always introduces himself to a few of the speakers whose subject matter most closely relates to his. That is, even though he is surrounded by differences, he seeks out the people with whom he shares the most similarities. These conversations have led this sociology and economics professor to work on projects with physicists and biologists, among others, people he would never have met if he hadn't gone to a conference outside of his area of expertise and initiated conversations with the people there who were most like him. In this way, Burt builds bridges to different sticky rice clusters.

Knowing how people and units fit together in your organization can also help you find people who have power and influence—even though they may not be high on the organizational chart.[8] Figure out how close—or distant!—you are from the most powerful people in your organization or industry. Use this knowledge to leverage opportunities for building targeted relationships with *bridge-builders, gatekeepers*, and *hubs*.

As you know, *bridge-builders* form bridges between otherwise unconnected clusters. People can occupy bridge-building positions for a number of reasons, many of which are accidental or even unwanted. Bridge-builders may not even be aware of the power of their position. Someone who bridges an otherwise yawning abyss between Production and Marketing is in a position of power—whether or not they know how to leverage that power! Forming a relationship with a bridge-builder will give you indirect access to some of the benefits of being a bridge-builder yourself.

Gatekeepers, such as the administrative assistants or trusted advisors of C-suite members, are powerful as a function of their access to power. Their recommendations, suggestions, and goodwill may be highly valued by the high-status people to whom they are connected. Forming a positive professional relationship with a gatekeeper can give you indirect access to those people. Trudy Vitti, for example, was the executive assistant to Kevin Roberts, the former CEO Worldwide of Saatchi & Saatchi. Often when you asked him a question, he'd say, "Ask Trudy." He'd travel for weeks at a time and said that he had complete confidence in Trudy to run the office in his absence.[9]

Another set of influential people are those people who are central in their sticky rice clusters. *Hubs* are particularly influential. Hubs are people in the center of a sticky rice cluster that is itself at the center of multiple clusters. A person who is at the center of a central cluster is likely to have the deepest expertise and insight regarding a particular field, industry, business, or demographic category. These people are not only deep-dive experts but they are the best positioned to distribute information within their cluster or to gather targeted support for an initiative or action.

Unfortunately, seeing your organization's relationship network accurately is hard to do. We humans can't help seeing things in patterns. We all have what is called a *bias toward closure* in that we tend to see connections where none exist. We instinctively connect the dots. For some of us, this tendency is even stronger than it is for others. People who have a strong need for closure (see Chapter 3), for example, have a correspondingly higher bias toward closure. If you think about it from an evolutionary perspective, a bias toward closure makes sense. If a hunter sees a deer partially obscured by trees and brush, she doesn't assume that a half-deer is walking around the forest. Instead, she correctly "connects the dots" to see a whole deer that is half-hidden.

The problem arises when we connect dots that shouldn't be connected. This seems to happen in a consistent way when we think about relationships. For example, if we know that Adam is friendly with Bryan and with Carla, we tend to assume that Bryan and Carla are also friendly with each other, even when they may not be friendly at all. You can train yourself to see relational "holes" in networks—like the one between Bryan and Carla—by looking for evidence of relationships between people or departments that you don't know personally. People who have very few bridges in their professional networks find it even harder to see gaps. In other words, they are more likely than bridge-builders to see connections where none exist.[10]

To guard against a bias toward closure, check your assessment of the organizational network with a "well-connected" colleague. Ask the people in your network who are connected to these people or departments for their perspective. Look also for evidence of collaboration between individuals (e.g., on projects) or between sticky rice clusters (e.g., on new initiatives). The process of "seeing" the larger network in which you embedded is well worth the effort.[11]

How well do you know *your* network?

Leveraging Skill 2: Asking

I have advised you to lead with giving in all of your network relationships for many different reasons, not the least of which is that givers will eventually be on the receiving end of someone else's giving. The research is clear: You'll grow richer if you focus on what you can give.[12] But waiting around for someone to proactively give to you is *not* strategic and may even be crippling you professionally. We all know the person in the office who is always willing to help others but never gets their own work done. This is the networking paradox. You must focus your networking efforts on giving—not receiving—if you want to receive but if *all* you do is give, you will never receive enough to offset the cost of giving. In order to benefit from your network, you need to balance the scales of giving and receiving in your favor.

How can you encourage your network to give *you* more?

The answer is simple: You ask.

Asking is the corollary of giving. Giving without asking will leave you depleted and burnt-out. Asking for as much as you give to others is the primary reason that networking benefits you. Have faith in the concept of generalized reciprocity. As Catalina Girald, founder and CEO of Naja, a San Francisco-based lingerie company that creates upscale-looking women's undergarments at mass-market prices, noted:

In my first company, I didn't ask for help. I was an only child, so I'm used to doing things on my own. I have learned that many successful people are willing to help you because other people helped them.[13]

The key to leveraging the power of your network is to ask *intelligently*. To ask intelligently, build upon your knowledge of the human and social capital of the people in your network. Target your request toward the people in your network who you *know* are both willing and likely to have the resource you need. If you've set up an effective network, all of the people in it should be willing to help you.

Before joining Apple, Roizen had never tapped her network on a large scale. She had personal relationships with most of the industry's top CEOs, some of whom she had met through SPA and many of whom had been guests in her home. People knew her to be ethical and smart. They trusted her. Although she had never cultivated these relationships for the purpose of helping Apple, she was able to turn to her network when she needed it. She explained what she needed—public support of Apple's platform—and because she had created an effective network, she got it.

When you are considering who is likely to have the resource you need, focus first on what you know about the individuals in your network. Who might have the knowledge or resources you need? Target the people who are most likely to be able to help you. This person or group of people are the *first* ones you should turn to. But these are not the *only* people you should turn to.

If your request is urgent, important, or multifaceted—or if the people you asked don't have the resources you need—don't be afraid to widen your search to include people from all areas of your network. The concept of generalized reciprocity means that it may not be clear who can provide you with specific resources.

An excellent exercise, *Reciprocity Ring*®, demonstrates that available resources may be in surprising places. *Reciprocity Ring*® asks individuals to make a personal and then a professional request of other participants— usually less than 25 people—who may be from their industry or organization, but may also be complete strangers. I have run the exercise in numerous workshops and I have personally witnessed many examples of finding resources in unexpected places. I've seen dog-owners find dog-lovers to take care of pets over vacation, a brand manager find in-depth knowledge of launching a locally targeted product from a manager who happened to have launched a similar product in a previous job, and a woman get studio tickets to a specific cooking show—via text exchanges between a participant and his contact while the woman was making her request!

The key to *Reciprocity Ring*® is the key to any resource search: Search widely in terms of *whom* you ask for resources but make *what* you ask for as precise as you can. Your aim is to make it as easy as possible for your connections to provide you with the resources you need. To accomplish this, do three things before asking your network for something:

1. Make your request specific.
2. Make sure that you only request things that you really want.
3. Set a deadline.

Make your request specific. You'd be surprised by how difficult it is for many people to specify what they want or need. Knowing what you want requires some introspection. For instance, you might know that you want advancement opportunities. But asking your network for "help with advancement opportunities" is still pretty vague. What exactly do you want—greater visibility with senior colleagues, knowledge of internal job opportunities, feedback on your current work, or a referral to a trusted recruiter? Hoping that someone else will know what you need better than you do is hopeless. Don't rely upon others to do your thinking for you. Instead, take the time to get very clear on what you need or want. Think as specifically—as narrowly—as you can. What *exactly* do you want?

You may need to do some research. Explore the implications of what you're requesting. For example, perhaps you want to locate a professional to help you prepare for a career change. Before asking your network for a referral, learn the difference between recruiters, career coaches, and career counselors. Investigate the fees that they typically charge and what you are prepared to spend. Make sure that you understand what it is you are requesting. Do your homework.

Make sure that you only request things that you really want. Don't ask your network to help you find a job when you really don't have any intention of taking a new job. Ask yourself, *Is this really what I want?* You are asking people in your network to help you by sharing their human capital or drawing upon their social capital. Use their time and resources intelligently. Be willing to accept or at least follow up on the resources offered to you. For example, if you've asked your network for a job opportunity but what you really want is to know is if your current salary is competitive, then asking for job opportunities is wasting the resources of your network. Instead, ask for what you really want.

Set a deadline. Once you know what you want and you are sure that you want it, set a deadline by which you would like it. Exactly when would you like to receive help? Is it okay if someone knows of a job opportunity that is likely to come up in the next six months or are you hoping to be working at another company within the next two months? Are you ready to seize a job opportunity today or were you hoping to start something next year? The clearer you can be on *when* you want or need something, the easier it will be for people to sift through their resources and social databases to find what you need when you need it.

Roizen's account of seeking an executive board position—long after leaving Apple—is an example of the power of a well-crafted request.[14]

> Several years ago, when I was at a point that I wanted to be considered for board of director positions, I sat down and over the course of eight hours wrote 150-something individual emails to everyone I knew well who was on a board, had served on a board, or was a C-level executive: "Here I am, here are my board qualifications, here's a link to my website that explains more about my board service. If you think I would be an appropriate candidate for a board that you work with, please let me know." That night at a party I ran into someone on the TiVo board, and he said, "I'm so glad you reached out, because I've got an opportunity for you." Even though he already knew me, my request and refresher helped him think of me for this board, which I ended up joining."

Heidi made it easy for her network to help her. Help *your* network help *you* by taking the time to ask intelligently. Identify exactly what you want, if you really want it, and by when you want it.

What do *you* want to receive from your network?

Leveraging Skill 3: Bridging

The bridges you've built are critical levers in your network. Up to this point, we've discussed the value of bridge-building as a fairly passive process. You build bridges across sticky rice clusters and then reap the benefits of being exposed to new and different ways of thinking, as well as increasing your integrative complexity and, with it, your ability to solve problems, innovate, and make higher quality decisions. You can further add value to yourself and your network by connecting two people who don't know each other. The more clusters that a bridge-builder is connected to, the greater the benefits.

But the power of the bridging position goes way beyond these advantages.

In truth, the bridge-building position is really only an *opportunity* for advantages. Returns to bridge-building increase probabilities, they don't predict success. To paraphrase University of Chicago Professor Ron Burt, being a bridge-builder puts you at risk for advantages.[15] Actually reaping those advantages is up to you. You can leverage the value of bridging in three ways, by:

1. *Translating* information between sticky rice clusters
2. *Building coalitions* across a number of clusters
3. *Managing conflict* between clusters

Although in real life, these three activities are usually intermingled, we will consider each separately.

Translating information between sticky rice clusters. One of the ways bridge-builders can leverage their position is through *translating*. Translating skills are difficult to master, which is why they are rare and valuable. Translating starts when you *transfer* a resource from one cluster and share it with another cluster. Transferring goes beyond just thinking about what it going on in different clusters and using those insights to address a problem or decision you yourself are facing. Transferring means literally taking something from one part of the network—money, an idea, a document—and moving it to another part of the network. For example, you might learn about a new project management app at work and then purchase it for your family so that your children can manage their homework better.

Transferring information can be tricky. It's not as simple as, say, picking up a white paper produced by one sticky rice cluster and handing it to another. Instead, you need to recognize specific opportunities. Not only do you have to understand the wants, needs, and resources of different clusters, you have to also understand how a resource in one cluster might fulfill a want or need in another cluster.

But it is not enough to just transfer the information. Information needs to be *translated*, too. *Translating* is reframing and rephrasing the way the information is communicated so that it can be understood by people with different values and perspectives. Skillful translators help people in one part of the network understand the wants, needs, and resources in another.

Recall that each sticky rice cluster has its own language and culture, which can be a comfort to insiders and a source of misunderstanding for outsiders. Translation makes "insider" information comprehensible to "outsiders." By definition, bridge-builders have learned enough of each cluster's culture and language to be able to communicate with at least one member. This competency provides the bridge-builder with the opportunity to serve as translator. Roizen—who had an undergraduate degree in English—was well-known for her skill in taking information developed in one cluster, such as programmers, and sharing it with members of another, such as the press. A bridge-builder who translates information, not only takes it from one sticky rice cluster and brings it to another, she or he also re-packages and reframes the information so that the members of the second sticky rice cluster can truly understand it.

An extreme example of people who translate between sticky rice clusters are language translators. Although they literally make words comprehensible, they are also often interpreting the contextual meaning of words. In Japan, for example, it is considered impolite to state disagreement openly. U.S. managers who don't know this often leave meetings with their Japanese counterparts feeling frustrated. *Why won't they tell me what they want?* is a familiar refrain. But the Japanese have no problem saying *No.* Anyone familiar with Japanese culture will easily recognize "obvious" signs of disagreement: staying silent, changing the conversation, confirming that they understand, or expressing the difficulty of a proposed course of action. A translator can interpret the meaning of information in one culture (or cluster) and share that meaning with someone who is not part of that culture.

Developing your emotional intelligence and interpersonal skills—especially perspective-taking—is key to the translation process. You need to take the perspective of the information source as well as the perspective of the information recipient. Recent research suggests that growing up in a bilingual household or simply being around people who speak another language can enhance perspective-taking.[16] One study explored the worldview of bilinguals by asking them to describe events in different languages and found that they could switch perspectives as fast as they could switch languages. "By having another language, you have an alternative vision of the world," one of the study authors concluded. "You can listen to music from only one speaker, or you can listen in stereo . . . It's the same with language."[17]

Travel is often touted as a way to understand how people may see things differently, especially when you go off the beaten path or are able to connect with locals. But you don't have to visit far-flung places to develop your perspective-taking skills. At its heart, active listening is the process of trying to understand another person's perspective. If you practice active listening and ask good questions, you will develop a global mindset, even if you never leave town.

Of course, it matters how close you are to each person or cluster. It's easier to translate between *strong* connections because they are more likely to understand you and stick with you through the sometimes frustrating process of translating. This is important when you are first using your translation skills to leverage your networks. As you develop your skills, the strength of your connections will become less important.

Why is translating valuable? After all, you can transfer and translate information without deepening your subject matter expertise or creating anything new.

The value of translating lies in the process itself. No one is better positioned than a bridge-builder to transfer and translate. No one knows multiple sticky rice clusters like a bridge-builder, no one has the ability to see how the transfer of information could be useful, and no one else is better positioned to actually translate the information. Bridge-builders offer value by helping others get what they want and need. To get access to that value, you need a bridge-builder. The fact that most people spend their professional lives in sticky rice clusters makes the services of bridge-builders relatively rare and therefore even more valuable.

To the extent that others need their services, bridge-builders can leverage their network to become quite powerful. Given the scarcity of people in the position, bridge-builders can "charge" quite a lot for their services. Sometimes, bridge-builders will literally charge for their service by acting as a broker. Roizen, for example, later entered the field of venture capitalism and became a bridge-builder between start-ups and investors. She used her translation skills to match up companies with promising new technologies to investors looking for good investments.

Other times, the "payment" that bridge-builders receive may be less direct, although just as valuable. As a bridge-builder, you might simply get a reputation for bringing good ideas to the table. You might become the go-to person for the latest organizational gossip and news, boosting your central position in the organizational network, and making you more likely to be tapped to promote organization-wide initiatives or help C-suite executives understand how employees in all areas of the organization are responding to a recent change or event. No wonder bridge-builders earn more and get promoted faster than people who stay embedded in their sticky rice clusters!

What can you do to build *your* translation skills?

Building coalitions across a number of clusters. A second way that bridge-builders can leverage their network position for professional advantage is by *building coalitions.* Coalitions are groups of people who join forces for a common cause. In an industry or organization, a coalition might form to block or support a particular initiative. In the opening example of Apple's Wall Street Journal advertisement, Roizen built a coalition among software CEOs.

Coalitions are powerful because ideas or actions that are supported by more people usually prevail. That's because the sheer number of people who support an idea make the idea seem better. After all, as recent conversations about "fake news" and "alternative facts" attest, facts are simply beliefs that are shared by a lot of people. Remember when everyone "knew" that the sun revolved around the earth? Coalitions validate ideas.

When coalitions are big enough, they can drive action simply because of their size. While a vocal minority can sometimes effect change, a vocal majority nearly always can. Sometimes, it *is* a case of might makes right. Bridge-builders are particularly well-positioned to develop and facilitate change initiatives. A bridge-builder who knows how to reach out to multiple clusters to gain support for an initiative is much more likely than someone embedded in a single cluster to build momentum behind the initiative.

The *process* of reaching out to clusters and building support is also critical to the success of initiatives because it offers an opportunity to test ideas and modify them as needed. As a bridge-builder, you can test new ideas by explaining your ideas thoroughly to your strong connections and getting their endorsement. You can then ask those connections to explain the idea to their sticky rice clusters to get feedback. This feedback will help you understand reactions to the idea as well as potential outcomes and unintended consequences of action. By incorporating the feedback, you can modify her initiative to make it more appealing various constituencies. At the same time, you build commitment to its implementation. By the time you are ready to implement the re-shaped initiative, you will already have strong support for its implementation.

To build coalitions, you need to know—like Roizen did—how the larger network is structured and, more importantly, how power is distributed throughout the network. Who has resources that other areas of the network need? Whose voices are "loudest" in the organization? The vantage point of bridge-builders helps them understand who has what and where in the network. The savvy networker can then target important constituencies and build critical links.

Managing conflict between clusters. Bridge-builders can also help limit the destructiveness of organizational conflict and contribute to the success of mergers, acquisitions, and inclusion efforts. As mentioned earlier, conflict is an unavoidable part of organizational life. Managing it can be costly. Employees spend an average of 2.8 hours per week dealing with conflict, costing US employers over 380 million working days, or over $350 billion dollars, of lost time.[18] Workers who know how to manage conflict effectively can save organizations time and money.

We are all naturally adverse to conflict. It is uncomfortable to intervene when employees or organizational units disagree. It also requires a fair amount of skill to turn a disagreement to into an opportunity for collaboration, problem-solving, and even innovation. Yet, this is exactly what businesses need. When it comes to managing conflict situations, bridge-builders have a number of network advantages that they can leverage to benefit the organization (and themselves!).

Imagine that sales and marketing are eager to offer a new product that responds to what they see as customers' needs. They fear that failure to do so will result in loss of market share and diminished profits. They can't understand why manufacturing is reluctant to change the product line and decide that it is because manufacturing is afraid of trying something new. They also suspect that manufacturing is trying to assert control over sales and marketing.

Manufacturing, on the other hand, is reluctant to change the product line because it would require a costly revision to current processes. They fear that change will result in higher costs and therefore diminished profits. They can't understand why sales and marketing are pushing the product change and decided that they are simply greedy and trying to increase their individual bonuses at the company's expense. Thus, a conversation between members of the two groups might go something like, "Why are you so afraid of change?" and "Why are you trying to ruin the company?"

As a bridge-builder, you have the advantage of already having the positive regard of at least one person in each department and some grasp of their department's goals and challenges. This puts you in a position to communicate the wants and fears of each department to the other in a way that allows them to really "hear" each other without the negative filter of distrust, tension, and suspicion.

Skillful bridge-builders leverage key personal relationships—as well as their translation skills—to broker understanding between parties, thereby reducing destructive conflict. This is what Secretary of State Henry Kissinger did in 1974 when he shuttled back and forth from one Middle Eastern capital to the other to talk with groups in conflict, gathering information from one party and then sharing it selectively with the other party. By using "shuttle diplomacy" to leverage his bridge-builder role, Kissinger facilitated the cessation of hostilities following the Yom Kippur War. Not surprisingly, providing this service to others—formally or informally—enhances the value of the bridge-builder.

Managing conflict well is a difficult skill to master, one of the reasons that it is so valuable. But bridge-builders are not only better *positioned* than others to manage conflicts, they may also be better *prepared*. Ironically, bridge-builder's preparedness for managing conflict arises as function of having to manage their own conflict with different clusters.

Recall that conflicts arise not only between members of different clusters but also between bridge-builders and the members of the clusters they connect. Bridge-builders who occupy a position between two opposed clusters often feel "caught in the middle" rather than "privileged by the middle." Sometimes the anger of each group toward the other is directed at the "traitorous" bridge-builder who refuses to give full loyalty to one side or the other. Bridge-builders who learn how to successfully navigate this difficult position, usually do so by identifying conflict triggers and modifying their actions to avoid setting them off.

Turn this experience into an asset. If you've ever been an accidental bridge-builder or felt caught in the middle, reflect upon the knowledge and skills you've relied upon to manage your position. Start by recognizing what you've learned through your experience. For example, have you learned how different sticky rice clusters perceive each other? Have you learned which aspects of yourself connect you to one cluster and which connect you to another? Have you learned how to get along with very different kinds of people? If you answered "Yes" to any of these questions, they you already have an edge when it comes to perspective-taking and emotional intelligence, two critical components of effective conflict management.

Now, take your reflection a step further. Think about what you did to gain these insights and skills. What did you do—or observe—that helped you figure out how to manage the situation? Use your self-reflection to develop and refine skills that you can then leverage to manage conflict more effectively between *other* sticky rice clusters.

The more bridge-builders learn about different people and different ways of looking at the world, the more they learn *how* to understand—truly understand—different points of view. As a result, bridge-builders usually find it easier to figure out what people *really* want and why. Knowing that, they are better equipped to find resolutions to conflict that satisfy all parties. A bridge-builder with strong conflict management skills can literally build bridges of understanding.

To Recap...

You *leverage* your network when you strategically seek resources through people who are ready and willing to help you. To leverage effectively, you'll need to develop three critical skills: knowing, asking, and bridging. As we saw with the example of Heidi Roizen, each of these skills empowers you to release the full potential of your network for the benefit of yourself and others.

Reflection Questions

How are the people and groups in your organization connected—or disconnected—from each other?

What advice, support, or help would you like to receive from your network? How will you ask for it?

Have you ever been an "accidental" bridge-builder or felt "caught in the middle" by your bridge-building position? If so, can you leverage your bridge-building experience into a tool for managing conflict between other people and clusters?

11

Changing Your Lead[1]

SELF-ASSESSMENT SNAPSHOT

1. Imagine that after a few months (or years) on the job, you have just been promoted to manager. As a first-time manager, what should be your top networking concern and your number one networking goal?

   Networking concern: _____

   Networking goal: _____

2. Fast forward a few years. You have progressed rapidly through the early stages of your career and have recently been identified as a *rising star*. What should be your top networking concern and your number one networking goal?

   Networking concern: _____

   Networking goal: _____

Climbing the Ladder

Detric didn't intend to enter a career in the healthcare industry. He always thought he'd put his marketing degree to work at a consumer goods company but when a representative from a major pharmaceutical company gave a talk at his marketing club, he got hooked. Here was a way to combine his love of science with his communication skills. Immediately after the talk, he contacted alumni from his fraternity who worked in the healthcare industry and asked for their help getting leads. Within six months, he had landed his first job as marketing assistant at a major pharmaceutical company.

Detric loved his job! Although he was in an entry-level position, he felt like a full and important member of his department. His boss praised his work and seemed to value his suggestions. His co-workers were great, too. Every Thursday after the day's work was done, a group of them—including some of the senior managers—would go to a local brew house to drink, eat, and play trivia together. It was a great way to get to know his boss outside of the office. Sometimes, Detric had to work long hours but even that was okay because it meant hanging out with people that he increasingly thought of as friends.

His hard work paid off. After several glowing performance reviews, his manager pulled him aside at one of the Thursday night get-togethers and asked him if he was interested in taking on more responsibility. "Absolutely," replied Detric. His manager encouraged him to apply for the position of Social Media Manager that was opening up in the department. To no one's surprise but his own—and with a strong recommendation from his manager—Detric got the position.

Detric's first big project was the development of a social media page for a new pharmaceutical product, *Alitia*. *Alitia* reduced dry mouth, a common ailment among people taking multiple medications. Detric was determined to create the most impressive social media page he could. His goal was to unveil it at an upcoming regional meeting.

He and his team worked long hours to provide the correct information in an engaging format. The time flew by amidst easy banter and focused teamwork. They called themselves the A-Team. The website they designed had video testimonials, as well as detailed medical information. A chat feature answered common questions. They even created an app that allowed scanned pictures of the inside of someone's mouth and estimated the likelihood that the person's dry mouth would be relieved by the company's product.

Two days before the regional meeting, Detric proudly presented the *Alitia* website to the brand manager. The brand manager clicked through the site for a few minutes. "That's an impressive app," he said finally. "But this will never fly. Most of the people who will visit this page are senior citizens and doctors. The senior citizens won't know how to scan and post a picture and the doctors just want to get the facts as quickly as possible. Back to the drawing board."

Detric was crushed. "It wasn't a career highlight," he said drily. "But eventually I realized my mistake. I should have talked to the brand manager weeks before I did. I was trying to wow him with a finished product but, really, I needed his input earlier in the process." Detric and his team set about redesigning the *Alitia* web site. This time, he met weekly with the brand manager. He also asked each of his team members to reach out to specific other people in the company whose input they needed. The new strategies worked. A few weeks later, the new web design rolled out and was an instant success!

Detric applied what he'd learned about managing team process to subsequent projects and quickly became one of the company's rising stars. He soon became deluged with requests to head up project teams. To deal with the increasing amount of work, Detric soon figured out who in the company could get work done and he turned to them time and time again when forming project teams.

People loved working with Detric, not only because he made things happen, but because he really seemed to care about the people on his teams. He was known for hosting team get-togethers at his townhouse that always included good food and great music. "Detric is a great guy," said one of his frequent collaborators. "We know each other so well that I can almost anticipate what he's going to say before he says it. And I always look forward to his house parties!"

It wasn't long before Detric began to feel overwhelmed. He really wanted to make everyone on his teams feel special but it was becoming a drain. Occasional get-togethers at his townhouse has turned into weekly events. It seemed like every time he opened his email, someone wanted to run an idea by him or "pick his brain" over lunch or coffee.

Finally, Detric's mentor said that he had to make some hard choices. "There's only so much of you to go around," she said. "It's too easy to do what you've always done. You've been pretty successful up to now but, lately, the products your teams have developed have been somewhat staid. Yes, you're getting it done but you are doing it the same old way. Your challenge will be to do things differently."

Detric agreed but he didn't see a way forward. He was swamped by his day-to-day responsibilities and commitments. Where in the world was he going to find time to do things "differently"?

Ripples in a Pond

Networks are in a constant state of change. The dots and lines on a network map can make it seem as if our networks are a set of deeply entrenched pathways, forged to withstand the test of time. But the reality is that a network map is more like a snapshot of ripples in a pond, constantly shifting, churning, and dissipating.

On the one hand networks are dynamic. The exact number of individuals in your professional network probably fluctuates on a near-daily basis. While the core members of your network may change less dramatically over time, collegial contacts are constantly entering and exiting your network as circumstances bring you together and then different circumstances keep you apart.

On the other hand, *networking* is static in that the fundamental principles of relationship building don't change. But the *purpose* of networking changes—at least it *should* change—as your career develops. The networking strategies and goals that were critical to your leadership success in the early stages of your career look markedly different from the strategies and goals that you need to lead in later career stages. Many people make the mistake of continuing to pursue early-stage strategies and goals during later stages of their careers. This common networking mistake traps individuals like flies in outdated networks. Instead of furthering your career, an outdated network keeps you from advancing.

Adapt your network—as well as your networking strategies and goals—to your career stage. There are six key career inflection points at which to analyze—or re-analyze—your network to make sure that your networking strategy matches your professional career goals:

- Your first job
- First-time manager
- Rising star
- Senior Manager
- C-Suite
- Late-stage

Your First Job

The first moment in your career is the very beginning. You're at your first *real* job—the one that you hope will launch your career. Maybe you've landed a summer internship that you hope will turn into a job offer. Or maybe you've taken on a new job at the individual contributor level. You are eager to contribute. You know you need to network but you're not sure where to start. Besides, there's just so much to do. You're still figuring out how to navigate the company intranet server and what you are supposed to be doing each day. Networking feels like too much to add to an already overloaded plate.

Well, get started. Research on newcomer networks suggests that your first year on your job shapes your future career trajectory in the organization. Others go further to say that your first *ninety* days on the job are critical to advancing your long-term professional goals. In one survey of 1,350 senior human resource leaders, nearly three-quarters agreed that "success or failure during the first few months is a strong predictor of failure in the job."[2] As Professor of Leadership and Organizational change at IMD Michael Watkins notes in his book, *The First 90 Days: Proven Strategies for Getting up to Speed Faster and Smarter,* "When leaders derail, their problems can almost always be traced to vicious cycles that developed in the first few months on the job."[3]

Begin by building sticky rice clusters. In contrast to the importance of bridging relationships later in your career, being embedded in sticky rice clusters offer significant benefits for individuals who are in lower positions within the hierarchy of the firm or who are just starting out. For one thing, getting connected to a connected group will help you assimilate faster. Sticky rice clusters can quickly communicate and reinforce organizational norms and job expectations to help you fit in fast. If you're not sure exactly "how things are done around here" or what exactly you're supposed to be doing, embedding yourself within a sticky rice cluster is a good strategy.[4] When Detric first started his job, spending Thursday nights with his co-workers at the local brew house embedded him in a sticky rice cluster.

If you're smart, you'll also take care to embed yourself in a sticky rice cluster that includes particularly helpful or important people.[5] These are usually people who are higher in the organizational hierarchy than you are, like Detric's first boss. The higher ranking people in a sticky rice cluster are more likely to be in a position to help you out and, as a function of embeddedness, more motivated to do so. Detric's first break at the company came when his boss told him about the new social media manager position.

Forming sticky rice clusters with higher status people—especially when those clusters are homophilous in some way—is a smart way to accelerate your understanding of what you should be doing and the best way to do it.[6] Although you may be heavily dependent upon your sticky rice connections, the strength of your relationships is an asset as it makes their help—and access to their social capital—more likely.

First-Time Manager

Congratulations, you've worked hard, networked effectively, and now you've stepped into your first official leadership role! You're a first-time manager. First-time managers are normally first given responsibility for overseeing a group of people, usually a team or department that needs to achieve specific performance objectives. Like Detric, your new role may be complicated by the fact that you're now in charge of people who were formerly your same-level coworkers. The adjustment from co-worker to manager can be stressful because it requires redefining workplace relationships. One study found that nearly 60% of first-time managers said that the transition from co-worker to boss was the biggest hurdle they faced after being promoted into their first managerial role.[7]

A major focus during this stage of your career is leading a team. Up to now, network development meant building mutually rewarding one-on-one relationships. Occasionally, networking might include connecting two unconnected people in your network when it added value to both to do so, usually by making an introduction and then letting the two individuals form their own connection.

But leading a team goes beyond simply making introductions. Team leaders need to build relationships among team members as well as between team members and other stakeholders. In all fields, it is possible be a strong leader without having strong technical skills but it is impossible to be a leader at all without other people. First-time managers need to *proactively* influence the professional networks of their teams.

The optimal team network structure addresses the two primary needs of teams. On the one hand, effective teams develop productive *internal* relationships that support information-sharing, collaboration, decision-making, and coordination. On the other hand, they develop productive *external* relationships with diverse experts and important stakeholders. In networking terms, the internal relationships should form a sticky-rice cluster and the external relationships should build bridges. Your job is to build a team network that looks something like this:

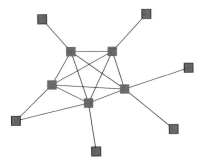

What's new about the first-time manager stage of your career is that—for the first time—you aren't oriented exclusively to your own professional network. You are now in the role of developing the networks of *others* using targeted, directed networking actions. To lead a team, you need to direct your networking efforts toward building the team's *internal* and *external* network.

Internal closure. Internally, your networking goal is to build a sticky rice team network. A sticky rice cluster facilitates coordination, knowledge-sharing, decision-making, and deep collaboration. Whenever a number of stakeholders need to be connected to each other in order to get their work done—such as members of a team, task force, or department—they will work best within a sticky rice cluster. As people grow closer and more comfortable with each other, they develop an internal language—a sort of shorthand—that makes it easier for members to communicate with each other. As they learn more about each other's strengths, challenges, and work preferences, they strengthen their relationships and build trust. And it's not just that sticky rice teams work together more efficiently and more effectively, they also achieve peak performance outcomes.

First-time managers can create a sticky rice team network and boost the effectiveness of their teams by taking three action steps:

1. Build high-quality one-on-one relationships with each member of your team.
2. Build relationships *among* team members.
3. Maintain continued support for relationship-building by creating opportunities for rich, multi-layered interactions.

Build high-quality one-on-one relationships with each member of your team. High-quality relationships are characterized by mutuality, trust, and learning. Research shows that individuals who form high-quality relationships with their leaders are far more committed to group work, work harder to achieve group goals, and demonstrate higher job performance.[8] Team members who have high-quality relationships with their team leader are also more satisfied with their jobs, less stressed, more committed to their organization, more likely to go out of their way to help others, and less likely to leave the team or organization.[9]

If you're a first-time manager and you want to build relationships between you and each team member, start *before* your first team meeting. Take a few minutes to look at each person's company or LinkedIn profile. Make an effort to connect personally with each person, preferably through one-on-one interactions. This is particularly important if you've never met before or if you've had a poor relationship in the past. If possible, avoid setting up a formal "get to know each other" meeting. Instead, interact with each of your future team members in less formal ways. Suggest sharing lunch or a cup of coffee. Stop by offices and cubicles to chat. If your team members are in distant geographic locations, set up a web call.

I know that connecting with individuals one-on-one before the team even meets can seem like a waste of time, especially for first-time managers who lead more than one team. But I guarantee you that the time you invest in building positive relationships with team members before the team launches will be more than balanced by the time you *don't* spend repairing negative relationships and the damage caused by them later. It's a fallacy that all of the problems in a team are the product of so-called "personality conflicts." The truth is that the seeds of cohesion are planted very early. Savvy team leaders know that small gestures in the initial stages of a team's lifecycle—such as making an effort to know each person's professional goals *before* the first team meeting—reap large rewards later.

Build relationships among team members. Building and nurturing high-quality relationships with each of your team members is an important start. But first-time managers also need to build and nurture high-quality relationships *among* the members of your team. As a team leader, it is your responsibility to foster a relationship-building team environment. Start by carefully preparing for the team's launch.

At the first meeting, norms of behavior are set that become very difficult to change. As leader, it is your job to promote positive ways of interacting. You can do this even if everyone on the team knows each other and even if some people already hold negative impressions of each other. Your job is to make it clear that *this* team will work together in a way that works for all.

The key is to plan for success. Create an agenda for the first meeting that includes discussion of task-related objectives (what will we accomplish?) as well as process-related objectives (how will we work together?). Spend at least a quarter to a third of the first meeting discussing how decisions will be made (consensus? majority vote? leader makes?), how information will be shared (team electronic depository, group meetings, subgroup meetings), how often the team will meet (also where and when), and the milestones for the team work and how they will be reviewed. Don't worry if those issues aren't resolved. The critical thing is to have the discussion so that people can understand each other's viewpoints, experience productive disagreement, and gain familiarity with discussing team process issues.

The team might also spend some time sharing what each can contribute to the project as well as opportunities for learning. For example, you might say, "One of my strengths is understanding financial reports but I am challenged by market segmentation metrics." This exchange helps team members identify a strength that they can draw upon and helps the team figure out who knows what. Plus, it builds trust.

These initial discussions about task-related objectives and individual strengths/challenges also serve another purpose. In addition to *what* you say, *how* you say it matters. The way you communicate sets expectations for how the team as a whole should communicate. For example, when one individual suggests that the team decide by consensus and another wants to decide by majority vote, the two individuals are in disagreement. This gives you a perfect opportunity to model productive conflict-handling and decision-making. At the end of the first meeting, ask if there's anything in terms of the team's interaction that could be done differently or that went particularly well.

Maintain continued support for relationship-building by creating opportunities for rich, multi-layered interactions. Continue to look for ways to help team members see each other as individuals. Include a mix of activities to strengthen social bonds among team members. This could be as simple as holding team meetings over lunch, asking members to share something about their life outside of work (*What is something that would surprise others to know about you?*), meeting off site, or engaging in unusual activities together (e.g., sledding, paintball, yoga, etc.).

Continue to set expectations through what you say and do. For example, make it clear that members are responsible for sharing their expertise and for seeking out expertise that they need. Publicly highlight, praise, and reward instances of sharing. Tell stories of others who have shared and the positive impact it had on you or others. Establish a norm of seeking expertise by publicly—and genuinely—by asking one or more team members for their expertise. Be quick to give credit to others for team successes.

To further strengthen relationships among team members, build a unifying team identity. For example, you might ask individuals to verbalize what makes the team unique. Talking about uniqueness reinforces the perception that the team *is* unique. Visible team identifiers also contribute to identity-building. They might include a team name, t-shirts, slogans, a special or consistent meeting room/place, special food that is always present at meetings—trail mix, anyone?—or a particular way of beginning or ending meetings.

> Last summer, for example, I was working with a group of senior executives. The first thing I did when I started off the meeting was to give everybody two toys: a Meeting Network mouse pad and a Meeting Network squeeze ball. The executives played with this stuff throughout the meeting. It was great: One person would say something that another person didn't like, and the second person would throw a ball across the table. Everyone at the meeting had lots of fun. And these were senior executives, by the way—people who are not given to playing at work. A week later, I was in the same room, sitting in as an observer for someone who was presenting to the same group. The executives came in and sat around their table, and as the meeting was about to start, one guy said, "Wait a minute. We can't start yet." Then he ran out— and came back a few minutes later with his squeeze ball!
>
> —Michael Begeman, 3M Meeting Network[10]

Team members should start to see that their contributions to individual members on the team are really contributions to the *team* rather than to any one person.

External bridging. While sticky rice teams are great for getting work done, they risk shutting out critical resources that are external to the team, such as fresh ideas or the support and perspective of external stakeholders. To avoid this, you will need to manage the external boundary of your teams.[11] Failing to manage the team's boundaries is why Detric got blindsided by his brand manager's reaction to the *Alitia* website.

Manage the external boundary of your team by forming bridges between the team and external resources. A common mistake of first-time managers like Detric is to focus entirely on building the team's cohesion and to neglect the team's external environment. One study of 300 self-managing teams at a large manufacturing plant of a Fortune 500 corporation found that leaders who contributed the most to their team's success excelled at managing the boundary between the team and the larger organization.[12]

External bridging has two aspects. One, it's a way of making sure that members of your team bring a diversity of ideas *into* your team. While having shared experiences will make building strong relationships easier, the lack of diversity will limit the range of ideas and perspectives that members can bring to bear on problems. Build bridges with different external groups. Avoid inviting only people from very similar functional and demographic backgrounds onto your team. Instead, advocate for diversity when the team is designed, and then manage the relationships and inherent tensions productively.

The second aspect of external bridging is managing external stakeholders. External stakeholders are people who can influence team outcomes and the implementation of team decisions. As team leader, it is your job to manage external stakeholder relationships. Leaders who fail to form relationships with external stakeholders are vulnerable to being blindsided. This is what happened to the teams at the Palo Alto Research Center (PARC) in Palo Alto, California, in the 1970s.

PARC was Xerox's center for innovation and research.[13] Here, engineers and programmers were protected from management who were headquartered thousands of miles away in Rochester, New York. They were given free rein to research and develop whatever technology they wished.

> "Xerox created this perfect environment," recalled Bob Metcalfe, who worked there through much of the nineteen-seventies... "There wasn't any hierarchy. We built out our own tools. When we needed to publish papers, we built a printer. When we needed to edit the papers, we built a computer. When we needed to connect computers, we figured out how to connect them. We had big budgets. Unlike many of our brethren, we didn't have to teach. We could just research. It was heaven." [14]

PARC teams used their insularity to their advantage to develop essentially all the technology used in today's computer age. They invented laser printers, the Ethernet, and windowed computer applications. One PARC team invented *Alto*, a computer with a mouse and pull-down menus—unlike anything else on the market. The team knew *Alto* had the potential to completely disrupt the field of computer technology. Excitedly, the team pitched the *Alto* prototype to Xerox executives shortly after its initial development in 1973, confident that they too would see its enormous promise for the consumer market.

But the team's very insularity put it at a distance from the people who made decisions about its future. Despite repeated attempts, the team was unsuccessful in persuading its own management to adopt the technology and Xerox missed out on the benefits of its own special research group. In 1981, the Rochester-based executives chose instead to integrate some aspects of *Alto* into a much bigger commercial system—the *Star*—which cost up to $100,000 for a full installation, far too much to appeal to individual users. Within a few years, of course, Apple and IBM introduced personal computers—with *Alto*-like features—to the consumer market, revolutionizing the industry and toppling Xerox's position as industry leader.

What happened?

The *Alto*'s team leader failed to manage the team's network needs.

As a first-time manager, your job is make sure that someone in your team—either you personally or assigned members—has a connection with every important team stakeholder. This is the perfect time to leverage those sticky-rice relationships with high-status individuals who helped propel your career to this point. Ask your network to introduce you to important stakeholders. Identify people who can help you build trust with external stakeholders by vouching—when appropriate!—for your competence and integrity.

Rising Star

Rising stars have led several successful project teams and are increasingly developing a reputation as someone who can "get things done." As a rising star, you are already a relationship-building pro. You've built strategic relationships with stakeholders, mentors, and sponsors. You have close relationships with individual members of your team—perhaps of several teams. You may even stay connected with members of teams that you no longer lead. You know how to nurture relationships over time through casual interactions, electronic updates, joint collaborations, and shared activities inside and outside of work.

All of this relationship-building has fueled your success but now you've got a lot of relationships to manage and less and less time to spend on them. People increasingly seek you out to lead teams and to collaborate on projects. You probably haven't yet gotten to the point where you feel comfortable saying *No* so, not surprisingly, you may find yourself overwhelmed by work. Like Detric, your biggest challenge is managing your workload while continuing to take on the successful, high-visibility projects that will advance your career.

Now is the time to make decisions about which relationships you truly value. You have limited relational energy and many tugs on your time. Which relationships should you nurture with investments of your precious time and effort? As a rising star, your main concern isn't *how* to strengthen relationships, it's knowing *which* relationships to strengthen and which to let lie dormant.

Start by listing your strongest relationships—the people with whom you interact the most or who you identify as your most important professional relationships. If you're like most rising stars, you probably have a large number of these. Evaluate each one by asking yourself two questions (see also Chapter 6):

1. Does this person add *value* to my network?
2. Is this relationship characterized by the three crucial characteristics of mutuality, trust, and learning?

You should be able to answer an emphatic "Yes" to both of these questions for *every one* of your strong relationships. Your strongest *Yes* relationships are your core group of professional connections. They are your inner circle.

Now, think about some of your other, more collegial, relationships. Is there someone who is—or has the potential to be—a strong *Yes* person? Maybe it is someone you got to know when working together on a project but now, because the project is over, you rarely see. Strong *Yes* relationships are rare. When you find a relationship that has the potential to be a strong *Yes*, don't let it fall away. Instead, nurture it so that it grows stronger.

A simple way to strengthen all of your *Yes* relationships is to strategically pick projects that allow you to work with *Yes* people. While it is not advisable to work with only the same people from an innovation and decision-making point of view, strengthening critical relationships through shared projects is smart. As a rule of thumb, try to have about half of each of your project teams composed of people you don't know very well.

On the other hand, if you have someone in your life in whom you invest significant time and energy but who is not a *Yes* person, then it is time to let the relationship weaken or become dormant. It is common for rising stars to hold onto relationships that used to be *Yes* relationships but that are not any longer. These relationships may have been critical to your success as a newcomer and even first-time manager but now those same ties become a burden as you rise up in the organizational hierarchy.[15] Outdated relationships can put rising stars in a very *un*comfortable position.

The sticky rice connections that helped you early in your career become a liability once you no longer are dependent upon their help. For example, junior bankers often benefit from relying on a sticky rice cluster of contacts for obtaining information and support, but these benefits disappear as bankers move up the ranks and require more diverse information and support.[16] As a result, you may have to extricate yourself from the same social ties that helped you advance. Weakening the strength of these relationships will allow you to expand your network strategically. But doing this can be hard.

For one thing, the factors that make it easier to build sticky-rice relationships in the first place—such as similarities you share or the number of projects that bring you together—are the very same factors that make it hard to extricate yourself. Sticky-rice relationships are *sticky* by definition. Perhaps you initiated a relationship because you liked each other and had things to offer each other but then ended up staying in it out of a sense of obligation and inertia. You may not even share the same values anymore but you continue getting together regularly because it's easier to maintain the strong connection than to risk disruption and hurt feelings.

Even when you want to overcome relational inertia, you may find it difficult because of learned behaviors. Although the networking *strategies* that worked earlier in your career don't work as your career develops, the networking *behaviors* that you learned tend to stick. It's hard to unlearn old behaviors. For example, perhaps you've always enjoyed going out in a group with your department on Thursday nights. Now, you'd like to strengthen relationships with colleagues outside of your department. You're not sure that they'll get along with others in your department. Do you invite them anyway and hope for the best? Or, do you go out with the department as usual and think about how to squeeze another after-work get-together into your already crowded schedule? It may be time to think differently about how and when you socialize with work colleagues.

Staying stuck in a sticky rice cluster can happen within teams, too, even top-performing teams. Rather than risking the time and other commitments it takes to seek out new collaborators, rising stars sometimes continue to reuse teams they formed as first-time managers. This is what had happened to Detric and it's easy to see why. You've had positive experiences together and you know you'll enjoy working together again. Why *not* turn to the same old workhorses?

The reason is because familiarity breeds similarity just as similarity breeds familiarity. When we work with the same group of people again and again, we start to become more and more alike in our ways of approaching problems and decisions. This may explain why Detric's mentor told him that the products his teams were creating were becoming staid. Reach out to new collaborators. If new collaborators aren't available, refresh "old" collaborators by assigning new roles. That way each of you can learn new things about each other and also engage in fresh experiences.[17]

Senior Manager

Senior managers are managers of managers. Unlike rising stars who are known for "getting it done," the main task of senior managers is to develop and execute on *strategy*. Senior managers who think and act strategically define the direction in which the organization will go in the long term. But the shift from a focus on short-term implementation to long-term strategy is tough. Every day presents a barrage of tactical issues, organizational missteps, and urgent but trivial problems. As a senior manager, it's easy to fall back on what you know and do well—short-term implementation—and avoid the "big picture" stuff of developing strategy.

Failing to think strategically is one of the biggest career stumbling blocks of senior managers. As one CEO told me, "Worrying about our leadership pipeline keeps me up at night. We have a lot of good senior managers but hardly any good strategic thinkers." He's not alone in his concern. One poll found that more than 80% of CEOs felt that less than half of their managers were strong at strategic thinking.

So, how can you become a better strategic thinker?

By developing a strategic network.

Many people mistakenly think that strategic thinking is something you can learn by taking a class, reading a book, or watching TED talks. Sure, you can memorize theories and models of strategy. But strategic *thinking* is not something you can memorize because each organizational situation is fluid and unique and includes factors that aren't part of established models. According to Julia Sloan, author of *Learning to Think Strategically*, learning to think strategically evolves out of confronting experiences and perspectives that first throw us off balance and then force us to figure out how to regain balance. She compares the process to travel.

> [W]hen we intend to take a trip, we begin by making plans. As plans progress, we may experience imbalance if the ticket gets misprinted, and when we arrive on a stormy night only to find that the hotel reservation has been inadvertently cancelled. The sense of imbalance persists when we get food poisoning, when we address a meeting where our language is not fully understood and our objectives are misinterpreted, and when we assess financial reports that have been "fudged for foreigners." The very success of our travel depends on other people and things we cannot control. The same is true of strategy making as we attempt to seek balance from our imperfect, incomplete, and infinitely complex world.[18]

Creating a strategic network exposes you to diverse perspectives and associated experiences. Without ever having to leave town, you can improve your strategic thinking by "traveling" through your network. Seek out different perspectives. Develop your strategic thinking by trying to create a single story. What do the differing perspectives tell you about what the future might hold and how you can adapt to it?

A common mistake when you get to this stage in your career is to focus primarily on strengthening your relationships with key stakeholders. Key stakeholders are the people you trust to get work done. But you need to start thinking about developing forward-thinking strategic initiatives. And for that, you need bridges.

Direct your energy toward building bridges, extending range, and managing churn. Don't stagnate in the same sticky rice clusters of managers who can execute. Refresh your mentors and sponsors. Now is the time to (re)analyze the organizational network and make sure that you are connected to disparate parts of the organization.

A great way to build strategic relationships with people in functions and at hierarchical levels to which you have no connections is to ask for business advice. In particular, reach out to colleagues in the same or similar job role. They face similar challenges so natural questions to ask are, *How did you handle that issue?* and *What did you do?*. People in similar roles also have similar pressures on them and, often, similar goals that they're working toward. Having so much in common will make it easier to connect and transfer knowledge.

A final note to senior managers: *Allocate time for networking.* A significant portion of your day-to-day work should be spent building, nurturing, and leveraging relationships—as much as 65%! Allocating time for networking is especially hard at this stage of your career because time may feel like your most limited resource. But building effective networks is essential if you are to advance to the C-suite. Delegate lower-level tasks and use the time instead to engage in strategic thinking and—of course!—more networking.

C-Suite

C-Suite.[19] You made it! You're in the C-suite. You've worked hard and leveraged your network to accelerate your career. It may be tempting to think that you have finally moved beyond the need to network. After all, you've already made a lot of connections. Networking is for those rising through the ranks, not for those who've made it to the top.

Right?

Well, not quite. Although you've developed an effective network for a senior manager, you have different needs now. As a member of the C-suite, you will be increasingly associated with organizational performance. As the company's stock price rises, so does your personal position in the company—and the industry. Of course, the flip side is also true. As the company's stock plummets, so does yours. "The short-termism of shareholders and the shame of not being able to make your numbers can be relentless, especially in publicly traded companies," says Manfred Kets de Vries, an executive coach and management professor at INSEAD business school in Fontainebleau, France.[20]

In the face of ever-greater pressure to perform, it is natural to rely upon your tried and true. It makes sense to turn to people you've known for years and whose advice you trust, especially when you need to make so many important and pressing decisions every day. These trusted co-workers probably include members of the executive team as well as select senior managers that have proven their value to you over the years.

Unfortunately, the very relationships that have served you so well in the past may now prevent you from accessing the new, the negative, and the sometimes unpleasant information you desperately need to make good decisions. Often with the best of intentions, this internal group may now form a shield, buffering you against unpleasant truths and emerging issues.

> As you get more senior in your career, people often don't want to tell you the truth because they want to please, and they want to handle things so that they're not bringing you just the problems.[21]
>
> —Beth Comstock
> Vice Chairwoman of General Electric

Even your tried and true set of informal advisors—your inner circle—may inadvertently keep you isolated from new and ground-breaking developments in your industry and others. Much of the cutting-edge work in any field is done by outsiders and novices. People at the top often find themselves far removed from the creativity and pioneering energy of those wrestling with unconventional solutions and ways of thinking. But to stay on the top, C-suite leaders need to stay connected with new ideas in order to develop innovative strategy. Your network can help you do that.

So, how do you stay connected when you're in the C-suite? In two ways: by connecting with people at all levels in your organization and by connecting with new ideas.

Connect with people at all levels in your organization. Don't build a sound-proof wall of executives around you. Your reports—especially as you move into the C-Suite—can give you insight into different areas in the organizations. You need to understand first-hand what's going on at all levels vertically.

Leaders set the tone and culture of organization, and your responsibility increases the further you go up the formal hierarchy. If you project a closed door policy or don't-come-to-me-with-bad-news impression, you can shut down information flow, not just to you but between others in your organization who are looking to you for clues as to how to act.

One networking strategy is to build relationships with "key influencers." For example, when John W. Rowe, MD, became Aetna's fourth CEO in five years in late 2000, the company was struggling with a negative reputation and poor financial performance.[22] Rowe could have chosen to rely solely upon his senior management team to determine the way forward. Instead, Rowe identified a core group of *influencers* at all levels of the organization, people who were central in the organization's network, well-respected, and sensitive to company culture.

Rowe began interacting with roughly two dozen of these influencers and, within a few months, expanded the group to include close to a hundred. These discussions not only gave him insights about the staff but created a rapport between him and a respected group that disseminated his message both formally and informally. As a result, Rowe was able to determine and implement a successful change strategy that not only was embraced by employees but also moved the operating income from a $300 million loss to a $1.7 billion gain, and the stock price from $5.84 to $48.40 a share.

Connect with new ideas. While it is critical to stay connected to the pulse of your organization, it is also important to stay connected to new ideas. Here are four suggestions to start building those connections:

1. *Spend time at a start-up within your business sector.* Get unfiltered access to people and information.[23]
2. *"Outsource" your networking.* Start using your staff to find you new and interesting ideas outside your organization. Reid Hoffman, co-founder of LinkedIn and author of several books on professional networking, suggests maintaining an "interesting person fund" for employees to pay for coffees and meals with interesting people in their network. The only requirement? To report back on what they learned.[24]
3. *Seek out board positions outside of your industry.* Leverage your functional expertise or related industry experience (e.g., with a custom-

er or supplier) on a board outside of your industry. You'll develop your network and provide the board with a different perspective.

4. *Tap into your dormant network.*[25] Reach out to thought-leaders both inside and outside of your industry with whom you once had a positive connection.

As a C-suite member, you also bear a responsibility to support the effective design of your organization's overall network. Help others network up and down the hierarchy, as well as across sticky-rice clusters and demographic differences. Encourage employees to make targeted investments in their social capital. Conferences, meetings, social events all provide opportunities for people to connect. Take care that these opportunities are not biased to fit only men's interests or the schedules of non-parents.

Your behavior can start to shape and strengthen the professional networks of people throughout the organization. Members of the C-suite in particular have the power to shape norms of behavior by explicitly—or implicitly—rewarding some behaviors and punishing others. Build networking time into your schedule, value it when other people take that time, and reward people for building positive relationships. Develop a culture of mentorship and sponsorship. At Allstate, for example, the CEO personally coaches and supports people who are serving as mentors to others, sending a strong signal about the importance of the program.[26]

Late-Stage

At some point, you will begin to think about retirement and, possibly, a second career. With people living longer and healthier lives, many people continue working, full or part-time, for 10, 20, or even 30 years past "retirement." If you've followed advice and stretched beyond your profession and into your community, you are likely to have developed a network that reaches into many different areas that might appeal to you.

Here's where you reap the rewards of a life well-lived. You probably have a core of trusted professional contacts, many of whom have become close friends over the years. These are people you can turn to for advice, counsel, and future-planning. Along the way, you've created hundreds—if not thousands or even hundreds of thousands—of dormant relationships. You can strategize your next steps with your core group and then identify the people in your extended network who are likely to be able to help you.

Dormant relationships are more valuable to older people than they are to younger ones, mostly because you have so many of them and because—if you've developed a strategic network throughout your life—they are likely to tap into many different industries, functions, geographies, and sectors. Moreover, if you've followed the principles in this book and networked strategically, then you've formed mutuality, trust, and learning relationships with every one of your professional contacts. As a result, your dormant contacts will want to help you as best they can.

Now is the time to activate your dormant relationships. Thoughtful and targeted reactivation can set you on the path to your "second act."

To Recap . . .

In this chapter, we explored networking for leaders at six critical career stages: first job, first-time manager, rising star, senior manager, C-suite member, and late-stage. Each stage requires a different network structure and different networking behaviors. Your goal is to select the network strategy that best matches your current professional career stage and goals.

Reflection Questions

Diagnose your career stage. Where are you in your career?

Look at your network. Does it reflect the characteristics of an effective network for your career stage?

What steps can you take *today* to align your network with the goals and needs of your current career stage?

12

In Conclusion...

In this book, we explored networks and networking as they relate to the fulfillment of *your* career goals. We learned exactly how and why networks and networking matter and what you can do to develop a network and networking approach that fits *your* personal style and professional needs, according to where you are in your life and career.

The principles and methods discussed in this book were designed to help you develop your ability to build, nurture, and leverage effective networks. By taking the self-assessment snapshots at the beginning of each chapter, answering the reflection questions presented at the end of each chapter, completing the *Toolbox* exercises, and by following the simple steps and guidelines presented throughout the book, you have begun to create a personal action plan for networking effectiveness.

We are all unique individuals with unique gifts, experiences, skills, and knowledge. Your networking strategy won't look like anyone else's because no one is exactly like you. Pick and choose what works for you to develop an ethical, effective, and empowering networking strategy that will unleash the potential of your network.

Connect the dots to make your network work for *you.*

Professional Support Network Exercise

Most people have two sets of people in their professional network: people who support your development as a professional (i.e., *supporters*) and people who have a stake in your current projects (i.e., *stakeholders*). In this exercise, you are going to identify the people who are in your *professional support network.*

Start by looking at the following table. You will be filling in the three columns: "Who?"; "What?"; and "How Close?" You might find it helpful to copy the table into a spreadsheet.

If you want to create a visual representation of your network, the Social Media Research Foundation makes a free and relatively easy to use visualization software that works with Excel. To try it, go to https://www.smrfoundation.org/nodexl/ and download NodeXL Basic. Several youtube videos and online documents are available to show you how to input your *Who* people as "vertices" and the *Whats* as "labels."

Some people like to use their LinkedIn networks as a starting point for visualizing their network. Socilab is one free tool to help you do that. To try it, go to http://socilab.com/#home. Once you've visualized your network, go to https://ryzeapp.co/what-to-do-after-you-visualize-your-linkedin-network -with-socilab/ for ideas on how to do additional analyses.

Who?	What?	How Close?

Column 1: "Who?"

In the left-most column, list the names of all the people in your life who you turn to for career advice or guidance. Within your current organization, this list will include people who help you understand organizational priorities, how your contribution supports those priorities, and your possible career paths within and outside of the organization. They are people who you might contact to figure out a new organizational initiative, understand a recent organizational event, or learn about career opportunities.

Outside of your organization, this list should include people—from inside and outside your industry—who help you understand trends in your industry and job roles, your possible career paths, and/or how you can develop as a professional. These are people you might check with to figure out if you're on the right track professionally or to learn about new opportunities. For many of you, this group might include family members, friends, teammates, and other members of the various social, community, religious, and other nonwork organizations to which you belong.

Include people on the list who you haven't talked with for a year or more (e.g., a high school coach). It may help to break down your life into 5-year chunks, starting around the beginning of high school. Within each chunk, who offered or provided you with meaningful career advice or guidance?

Take some time writing this list. You may want to do it over a couple of hours or days. Try writing down an exhaustive list and then coming back to the list in a day or two. Chances are, you will think of new names in the interim.

Column 2: "What?"

In this column, and next to each person's name, list a couple of words that describe the person. For the purposes of this exercise, avoid describing each person's personality and focus instead on more demographic or group-based attributes. For example, a partial list might include each person's gender, race/ethnicity, age, sexual orientation, disability status, marital status, geographic location, functional area, job role, educational level, organizational or industry affiliation, and political affiliation. It's okay if you don't know too much about the person. Just do the best you can.

Column 3: "How Close?"

This is the easiest of the three columns to complete. For each person, put a checkmark in the column if you consider yourself to be "close" to the other person. Obviously, feeling close is a matter of interpretation. In general, close means feeling connected, relatively intimate (e.g., feeling like you can confide in the other person), mutually supportive (i.e., you'd do what you could for the other person and s/he would do the same for you), and interacting on a fairly frequent basis. But you can determine what close means to you. This is your network; identify close contacts using your definitions.

This list comprises the *supporters* in your professional network. To identify the *stakeholders* in your professional network, go to Toolbox B.

Professional Stakeholder Network Exercise

Most people have two sets of people in their professional network: people who support your development as a professional (i.e., *supporters*) and people who have a stake in your current projects (i.e., *stakeholders*). In this exercise, you are going to identify the people who are in your *professional stakeholder network*.

Start by looking at the following table. You will be filling in the four columns: "Goals," "People," "Need," and "Inclination."

Inclination	Need	People	Three Goals

Column 1: "Goals"

In the left-most column, write down three specific business goals that you hope to achieve in the next year. When you write your goals, focus on the results that you intend to produce, not the processes that you will undertake to reach your goals. For example, "reduce overhead" is an intended result whereas "track costs" is a process to achieve results. Effective goals follow SMART goal principles; they're specific, measurable, aggressive, realistic, and time-bound. For example, you might set this goal: "The October 15th quarterly report will demonstrate that my department spent 15% less on paper than was reported on the April 15th quarterly report."

If you have more than three goals on your plate, select the three that are your top priority. If you have fewer than three goals, that's fine, too. For those of you who are currently seeking a job or even an internship, set the business goal of finding a particular job/internship in a particular industry. For example, you might set this goal: "By October 15th, I will have received at least one job offer to work as a market analyst at a small biotech firm located in a major U.S. city."

Column 2: "People"

In the second column, list the names of all the people whose help or support you need in order to accomplish your goal. If you don't know the name of a particular person, simply write down the job role (e.g., Carolina's administrative assistant, someone in IT who can sign off on new purchases, career counselor). Make an exhaustive list. You will almost certainly have more than one person whose help or support you need in order to accomplish each of your goals. It will help you if you think through the process of achieving your goal. Whose help or support do you need at every step?

These people are your professional stakeholders because they have a stake in work that you need to undertake in order to accomplish your business goals. Some of the people in your stakeholder network may also be in your supporter network.

Column 3: "Need"

In the third column, record the extent to which you need each person's help or support to accomplish your goal. Write:

- "Collaborate" if you need the person to work with you in order to accomplish the goal. For example, you might write collaborate next to Jonathan, Meryl, and Kayla because they are your teammates and you need your entire team to help you think of creative ways to market the company's new product.

■ "Comply" if you merely need the person to complete a specific task in order for your project to move closer to accomplishing the goal. For example, you might write comply next to Ira, who you merely need to process a shipping request.

Column 4: Inclination

In the final column, make a check mark next to every person that you think is inclined to collaborate or comply with what you need to do in order to accomplish your goals. For example, if you listed Meryl as someone you need to collaborate, put a check mark next to her name if you also think she is likely to collaborate.

In order to accomplish your goal, *everyone* on your list should have a check mark next to his or her name. If someone does not have a check-mark next to his or her name, you have two choices. Either find a way to accomplish your goal *without* this person's help or start cultivating—or re-pairing—the relationship so that the person will provide the help you need. You need all of your stakeholders to collaborate or comply in order to accomplish your goal.

This list comprises the *stakeholders* in your professional network. To identify the *supporters* in your professional network, go to Toolbox A.

TOOLBOX **C**

Organizational Network Exercise

This exercise will help you to understand opportunities for action within your organization. Your organization—like all organizations—is almost certainly a collection of sticky-rice clusters. Within each cluster, all members have something in common (e.g., functional background, same client/product on a project team, production line workers, salary grade, etc.). The main defining feature of the sticky-rice cluster is that relationships within each cluster are tighter and more connected than the relationships between clusters. Each cluster will form its own subculture with insider language and norms of behavior.

To begin, identify the important sticky-rice clusters of informal relationships within your organization. This may take some thought. Consider the size and formal structure of your company when identifying clusters.

Size

If you belong to a relatively small organization (i.e., less than 250 employees), most clusters are likely to be the teams or departments in your

Connect the Dots, pages 223–226
Copyright © 2019 by Information Age Publishing
All rights of reproduction in any form reserved.

organization. In organizations of this size, you are likely to know most of the people by name and all of the departments by name.

If you belong to a medium-sized company (i.e., between 250 and 500 employees), clusters are more likely to be determined by departments or other organizing clusters (e.g., geographic location) in your organizations. In organizations of this size, you are likely to have heard of most of the departments or other organizing clusters by name and interacted with many of them.

If you belong to a larger company (i.e., greater than 500 employees), consider only the departments or organizing clusters with which you interact on a regular basis or with which you have first-hand knowledge. For example, if you belong to a large multinational organization, you might normally only interact with people in your geographic location or mainly with people in your functional area (e.g., human resources).

Formal Structure

Sometimes the reinforcement of skills, interest, background, and day-to-day interactions mean that formal departments are the main clusters in an organization. In a research and development organization, for example, field of study is an important basis upon which clusters form.

Sometimes, of course, the sticky-rice clusters have nothing to do with the organizational chart. For example, many defense contractors work side-by-side with other members of military units but when it comes to professional relationships, the strongest ones are often among the contractors and among the military members, and not between the two groups regardless of the work units. Similarly, the strongest connections might be among members of a particular nationality or within acquired companies. If you live in a flat organizational structure, groupings might be project/client teams, functional background, nationality, or level/type of education.

Create a name for each sticky-rice cluster. If the clusters align with the formal structure of the organization, use the formal names for the clusters (e.g., accounting, B2B, etc.). If they don't align with the formal structure of the organization, use a name that captures the key descriptors of each cluster (e.g., original company, Singapore, etc.).

Put the name of each sticky-rice cluster in a bubble. Fill in as many bubbles as you want adding more bubbles as needed.

Once you have created an exhaustive list of clusters, do the following:

▪ Circle any clusters to which you belong.
▪ Put a check mark next to those clusters that have more power in the organization.
▪ Draw a line connecting clusters that share a lot of members or who tend to get along fairly well (e.g., work on new initiatives together, composed of people with similar backgrounds, etc.).
▪ Draw a dotted line between clusters that don't get along very well.

Your map offers at least three opportunities for action. You can add value to your organization by:

1. *Forming a connection with a member of a powerful cluster.* Here, you can add value by gaining and sharing insights into organizational politics and priorities.
2. *Forming a bridge between clusters that are currently disconnected.* Here, you can add value by translating information between sticky-rice clusters and building coalitions.
3. *Forming a bridge between clusters that don't get along very well.* Here, you can add value by managing conflict between clusters. You can perform this important function whether or not you are a member of one of the clusters.

About the Author

An award-winning instructor, Inga Carboni, PhD, has been developing leaders for many years through executive education, graduate and undergraduate courses, and academic writings. Her teaching and research interests include leadership, networks and networking, diversity and inclusion, and building effective working relationships. Her work has appeared in numerous journals and books, such as *Human Resource Management, Group Dynamics, European Journal of Work and Organizational Psychology*, and the *Journal of Management Education*. Grants from the National Institute for Health, the National Institute of Justice, the William T. Grant Foundation, and the Fulbright Program have supported her scholarship.

Prior to entering academia, Inga Carboni worked in different capacities in industry, including management consulting and project development.

Inga Carboni lives with her husband and their two daughters in Williamsburg, Virginia.

Endnotes

Chapter 1

1. Bell, M. (2016, January 21). The importance of networking (and how to do it well). *Huffington Post*. Retrieved from https://www.huffingtonpost.com
2. Dowley, K.M. & Silver, B.D. (2002). Social capital, ethnicity and support for democracy in the post-communist states, *Europe-Asia Studies, 54*, No. 4 (2002): 505–527. Temin, P. (2017). *The vanishing middle class*. Cambridge: MIT Press.
3. See, for example: Forret, M. L., & Dougherty, T. W. (2001). Correlates of networking behavior for managerial and professional employees. *Group & Organization Management, 26*(3), 283; Wolff, H., & Moser, K. (2009). Effects of networking on career success: A longitudinal study. *Journal of Applied Psychology, 94*(1), 196–206.
4. As quoted in Bensaou, B. M., Galunic, C., & Jonczyk-Sédès, C. (2014). Players and purists: networking strategies and agency of service professionals. *Organization Science, 25*(1), 29–56, p. 44.

Chapter 2

1. Palm Beach Post. (2008, December 12). Madoff's arrest in billion-dollar fraud case shocks Palm Beach investors. Retrieved from http://www.palmbeachpost.com
2. Assad, M. (2015, October 20). Madoff scam still cuts local victims. Retrieved from http://www.mcall.com
3. Collins, D. (2011, p. 440). *Bernie Madoff's Ponzi Scheme: Reliable Returns from a Trustworthy Financial Adviser*. Retrieved from http://dcollins.faculty.edgewood.edu/pdfdocuments/Madoff%20Case.pdf.

Connect the Dots, pages 229–248
Copyright © 2019 by Information Age Publishing

4. Creswell, J., & Thomas, L., Jr. (2009, January 24). The talented Mr. Madoff. *The New York Times*. Retrieved from http://www.nytimes.com.

5. Bandler, J. & Varchaver, N. (2009, April 30). How Bernie did it. *Fortune*. Retrieved from http://archive.fortune.com.

6. Varchaver, J. B. (2009, April 24). How Bernie did it. *Fortune*. Retrieved from http://archive.fortune.com.

7. Feuer, A., & Haughney, C. (2008, December 12). Standing accused: A pillar of finance and charity. *The New York Times*. Retrieved from http://www.nytimes.com.

8. Creswell & Thomas (2009).

9. Henriques, D. B. (2009, January 9). New description of timing on Madoff's confession. *The New York Times*. Retrieved from http://www.nytimes.com.

10. Wolf, A. A. (2008, December 15). Trustee appointed by court; SIPC taking action to protect customer assets. Retrieved November 03, 2009, from http://www.madofftrustee.com.

11. Creswell & Thomas (2009).

12. Gendar, A. (2009, October 30). Bernie Madoff baffled by SEC blunders; compares agency's bumbling actions to Lt. Colombo. *Daily News*. Retrieved from http://www.nydailynews.com.

13. Creswell & Thomas (2009).

14. Casciaro, T., Gino, F., & Kouchaki, M. (2014). The contaminating effects of building instrumental ties: how networking can make us feel dirty. *Administrative Science Quarterly, 59*(4), 705–735.

15. Tonge, J. (2008). Barriers to networking for women in a UK professional service. *Gender in Management: An International Journal, 23*(7), pp. 484–505, https://doi.org/10.1108/17542410810908848.

16. Cohen, S., Blades, E., & Tacopino, J. (2017, March 27). Investor burned by Madoff leaps to death from luxury hotel balcony. *New York Post*. Retrieved from http://nypost.com.

17. Covert, J. (2015, December 1). Mark Zuckerberg just created the biggest charity in the world. *New York Post*. Retrieved from http://nypost.com.

18. https://www.nytimes.com/2015/12/04/business/dealbook/how-mark-zuckerbergs-altruism-helps-himself.html

19. Kraft, T. L., & Pressman, S. D. (2012). Grin and bear it: The influence of manipulated facial expression on the stress response. *Psychological Science, 23*(11), 1372–1378.

20. Seitz, L. (2010). *Student Attitudes Toward Reading: A Case Study* (2nd ed., Vol. 3, Journal of Inquiry & Action in Education). Retrieved from http://digitalcommons.buffalostate.edu.

21. Casciaro, Gino, & Kouchaki. (2014).

22. Ibid.

23. (n.d.). Retrieved from https://www.youtube.com/watch?v=Z1T3h4e53PQ.

24. Ariely, D., Bracha, A., & Meier, S. (2009). Doing good or doing well? Image motivation and monetary incentives in behaving prosocially. *American Economic Review, 99*(1), 544–555. doi:10.1257/aer.99.1.544

25. Baker, W. E., & Bulkley, N. (2014). Paying it forward vs. rewarding reputation: mechanisms of generalized reciprocity. *Organization Science, 25*(5), 1493–1510, p. 1504. doi:10.1287/orsc.2014.0920.

26. Franklin, B. (1954 edition, p. 126). *The autobiography of Benjamin Franklin*. New York, NY: Pocket Books.

27. Grant, A. M. (2014). *Give and take: why helping others drives our success*. New York, NY: Penguin Books.

28. Dweck, C. S. (2012). *Mindset: Changing the way you think to fulfil your potential*. London: Little Brown Book Company.

29. Cohen, A.R. & Bradford, D.L. (2005). *Influence without authority*. Hoboken, New Jersey: John Wiley & Sons, Inc.

30. Anderson, K. (2010, July 12). Looking back at Live Aid, 25 years later. Retrieved October 22, 2016, from http://www.mtv.com/news.

31. McIlhenney, B. (1984, December 8). Feed the world. *Melody Maker*, 24–25.

32. Morgan-Grampian Publications. (1984, December 1, p. 1). Stars rally round. *Music Week*.

33. Jones, G. (2005, July 6). Live Aid 1985: A day of magic. Retrieved May 22, 2011, from http://www.cnn.com.

34. Bensaou, B. M., Galunic, C., & Jonczyk-Sédès, C. (2014). Players and purists: networking strategies and agency of service professionals. *Organization Science, 25*(1), 29–56. doi:10.1287/orsc.2013.0826

35. (n.d.). Retrieved from Stnfd.biz/xTXhc

36. Pondy, L. R. (1992). Reflections on organizational conflict. *Journal of Organizational Behavior, 13*(3), 257–261.

Chapter 3

1. Adapted from Levy, Paul (2001). The Nut Island effect: When good teams go wrong. *Harvard Business Review 79*(3), 51–59.

2. Levy, p. 55.

3. Levy, p. 55.

4. Levy, p. 55.

5. Levy, p. 51.

6. Levy, p. 55.

7. Levy, p. 58.

8. Long, T. (2004, October 27). A.D. Mazzone, judge who led harbor effort, dies at age 76. *The Boston Globe*.

9. Levy, p. 55.

10. Hallinan, M. T., & Hutchins, E. E. (1980). Structural effects on dyadic change. *Social Forces, 59*(1), 225–245.

11. Granovetter, M.S. (1973). The strength of weak ties. *American Journal of Sociology, 78*(6), 1360–80.

12. Janicik, G. A., & Larrick, R. P. (2005). Social network schemas and the learning of incomplete networks. *Journal of Personality and Social Psychology, 88*, 348–364.

13. Flynn, F. J., Reagans, R. E., & Guillory, L. (2010). Do you two know each other? Transitivity, homophily, and the need for (network) closure. *Journal of Personality & Social Psychology, 99*(5), 855–869.

14. Howard, J. (1978). *Families*. New Brunswick: Transaction Publishers, p. 234.

15. Wisman, A., & Koole, S. L. (2003). Hiding in the crowd: Can mortality salience promote affiliation with others who oppose one's worldviews?. *Journal of Personality & Social Psychology, 84*(3), 511–526. doi:10.1037/0022-3514.84.3.511

16. McFarland, D., & Pals, H. (2005). Motives and contexts of identity change: A case for network effects. *Social Psychology Quarterly, 68*(4), 289–315. Retrieved from http://www.jstor.org/stable/4150489

17. Smith, K. P., & Christakis, N. A. (2008). Social networks and health. *Annual Review of Sociology, 34,* 405–429.

18. Berkman, L. F., Melchior, M., Chastang, J., Niedhammer, I., Leclerc, A., & Goldberg, M. (2004). Social integration and mortality: A prospective study of French employees of electricity of France-gas of France: The GAZEL cohort. *American Journal of Epidemiology, 159*(2), 167–174.

19. Ertel, K. A., Glymour, M. M., & Berkman, L. F. (2009). Social networks and health: A life course perspective integrating observational and experimental evidence. *Journal of Social & Personal Relationships, 26*(1), 73–92.

20. Berkman, L. F. (1995). The role of social relations in health promotion. *Psychosomatic Medicine, 57*(3), 245–254.

21. Wang, H., Karp, A., Winblad, B., & Fratiglioni, L. (2002, June 15). Late-life engagement in social and leisure activities is associated with a decreased risk of dementia: A longitudinal study from the Kungsholmen Project, *American Journal of Epidemiology, 155*(12), 1081–1087.

22. Holt-Lunstad J., Smith T. B., Layton J. B. (2010) Social relationships and mortality risk: A meta-analytic review. *PLoS Med 7*(7): e1000316.

23. Storrs, C. (2016, January 15). We get by with a little help from our friends. Retrieved from http://www.cnn.com.

24. Semuels, A. (2015, December 1). How poor single moms survive. *The Atlantic.* Retrieved from https://www.theatlantic.com.

25. Haines, V. A., Beggs, J. J., Hurlbert, J. S. (2002). Exploring the structural contexts of the support process: social networks, social statuses, social support, and psychological distress, in Judith A. Levy, Bernice A. Pescosolido (ed.) *Social Networks and Health* (Advances in Medical Sociology, Volume 8). Emerald Group Publishing Limited, pp. 269–292. Totterdell, P., Wall, T., Holman, D., Diamond, H., & Epitropaki, O. (2004). Affect networks: A structural analysis of the relationship between work ties and job-related affect. *Journal of Applied Psychology, 89*(5), 854–867.

26. McCarthy, J. M., Trougakos, J. P., & Cheng, B. H. (2016). Are anxious workers less productive workers? It depends on the quality of social exchange. *Journal of Applied Psychology, 101*(2), 279–291.

27. Andersen, J. P., & Papazoglou, K. (2014). Friends under fire: Cross-cultural relationships and trauma exposure among police officers. *Traumatology, 20*(3), 182–190. http://dx.doi.org/10.1037/h0099403

28. O'Net. (2014). National Center for O*NET Development. 33-3051.01. *O*NET OnLine*Retrieved from http://www.onetonline.org/link/summary/33-3051.01

29. McCarthy, Trougakos, & Cheng (2016).

30. Kalish, Y., & Robins, G. (2006). Psychological predispositions and network structure: The relationship between individual predispositions, structural holes and network closure. *Social Networks, 28*(1), 56–84.

31. Sampson, R. J., Raudenbush, S. & Earls, F. (1997). Neighborhoods and violent crime: A multilevel study of collective efficacy. *Science* 277: 918–924.

32. Balkundi, P., & Harrison, D. A. (2006). Ties, leaders, and time in teams: strong inference about network structure's effects on team viability and performance. *Academy of Management Journal*, 49(1), 49–68. doi:10.5465/AMJ.2006.20785500

33. Ruef, Martin. 2010. *The entrepreneurial group: Social identities, relations, and collective action*. Princeton: Princeton University Press. See also http://10years. firstround.com/.

34. Sheridan, P.M. (2014, June 28). GM's 'culture' blamed for current crisis. Retrieved from http://money.cnn.com.

35. Gargiulo, M., & Benassi, M. (2000). Trapped in your own net? Network cohesion, structural holes, and the adaptations of social capital. *Organization Science, 11*(2), 183–196.

36. Levy, p. 58.

37. Latkin CA, Forman V, Knowlton A, Sherman S. (2003). Norms, social networks, and HIV-related risk behaviors among urban disadvantaged drug users. *Social Science & Medicine, 56*, 465–476. Liu H., Feng T, Liu H, et al. (2009). Egocentric networks of Chinese men who have sex with men: network components, condom use norms, and safer sex. *AIDS Patient Care STDs 23*(10), 885–893.

38. Shakya, H. B., Nicholas A. Christakis, N.A., & Fowler, J.H. (2014). Association between social network communities and health behavior: an observational sociocentric network study of latrine ownership in rural India. *American Journal of Public Health 104*(5), 930–937.

39. Smith, J. (2013, July 25). How to deal with cliques at work. *Forbes*. Retrieved from http://www.forbes.com

40. Fox, S., & Stallworth, L. E. (2005). Racial/ethnic bullying: Exploring links between bullying and racism in the US workplace. *Journal of Vocational Behavior, 66*, 438–456.

41. Renn, R., Allen, D., & Huning, T. (2013). The relationship of social exclusion at work with self-defeating behavior and turnover. *Journal of Social Psychology, 153*(2), 229–249.

42. Thau, S., Aquino, K., Poortvliet, P. M. (2007). Self-defeating behaviors in organizations: The relationship between thwarted belonging and interpersonal work behaviors. *Journal of Applied Psychology, 92*, 840–847.

43. Maurer, R. (April 16, 2005). Onboarding key to retaining, engaging talent. Retrieved from https://www.shrm.org.

44. Cacioppo, J. T., Fowler, J. H., & Christakis, N. A. (December 1, 2008). Alone in the crowd: The structure and spread of loneliness in a large social network. Available at SSRN: https://ssrn.com/abstract=1319108.

45. Gargiulo & Bernassi (2000).

Chapter 4

1. Adapted from Narasimhan, A. (2012). Restoring the British Museum, case IMD595. Lausanne: International IMD.

2. Rushe, D. (2000, November 19, p. 11). Whiz-kid's dust-up at British Museum. *The Sunday Times*. Retrieved at https://www.thetimes.co.uk.

3. Dowle, J. (1999, April 1, p. 24). The British Museum should recognise that the hold of history operates more subtly than the geewhizzery of science. *The Times*. Retrieved at https://www.thetimes.co.uk.

4. Ellis, W. (2000, October 29, p. 17). Heritage: Troubled scenes at the British Museum–What has happened to the BM? An eyesore of a new building and populist exhibitions suggest it has abandoned its scholarly calling. *The Independent on Sunday*. Retrieved at http://www.independent.co.uk.

5. Brooks, R. (2001, November 18). Gallery boss to take on British Museum 'hell.' *The Sunday Times*. Retrieved at https://www.thetimes.co.uk.

6. Interview with Dr. Robert Anderson, Director of the British Museum [Interview by A. Gardner & C. Kleinitz]. (2000, June 15). *Papers from the Institute of Archaeology, 11*(2000), 7–16.

7. Narasimhan, A. (2012). Restoring the British Museum, case IMD595. Lausanne: International Institute for Management Development.

8. Rushe, D. (2000, November 19, p. 11). Whiz-kid's dust-up at British Museum. *The Sunday Times*. Retrieved at https://www.thetimes.co.uk.

9. Brooks, R. (1999, April 4, p. 9). Museum peace? *The Sunday Times*. Retrieved at https://www.thetimes.co.uk.

10. Brooks, R. (2001, September 9, p. 3). British Museum chief warns of exhibition cuts to save cash – Interview. *The Sunday Times*. Retrieved at https://www.thetimes.co.uk.

11. Brockes, E. (1999, April 1, p. 11). Arts: That'll do nicely; The British Museum is now being run by a banker. How will that go down with the old guard? Emma Brockes investigates. *The Guardian*. Retrieved at https://www.theguardian.com.

12. Interview with Dr. Robert Anderson, Director of the British Museum [Interview by A. Gardner & C. Kleinitz]. (2000, June 15). *Papers from the Institute of Archaeology, 11*(2000), 7–16.

13. Damian, W. (2007, May 5, p. 28). National treasure. *The Times*. Retrieved at https://www.thetimes.co.uk.

14. Ibid.

15. Narasimhan, p. 8.

16. Tait, S. (2004, March 5, p. 2).Voyage of rediscovery. *The Independent*. Retrieved at http://www.independent.co.uk.

17. Burt, R. S. (2007, p. 8). *Brokerage and closure: an introduction to social capital.* Oxford: Oxford University Press.

18. Burt, R. S. (2004). Structural holes and good ideas. *American Journal of Sociology, 110*(2), 349–399.

19. Burt, R. S., & Ronchi, D. (2007). Teaching executives to see social capital: Results from a field experiment. *Social Science Research, 36* (2007), pp. 1156–1183.

20. Burt (2004).

21. Battilana, J., & Casciaro, T. (2012). Change agents, networks, and institutions: A contingency theory of organizational change. *Academy of Management Journal, 55*(2), 381–398.

22. 1876/1937, p. 172.

23. Rahtz, D. (2017, January). Personal communication.

24. Mitchell, A., Gottfried, J., & Matsa, K. E. (2015, June 01). Millennials and political news. *Pew Research Center.* Retrieved from http://www.journalism. org/2015/06/01/millennials-political-news/

25. Jeppesen, L. B., & Lakhani, K. R. (2010). Marginality and problem-solving effectiveness in broadcast search. *Organization Science, 21*(5), 1016–1033.

26. Wharton, R. (2014, February 28). Don't call it fusion cuisine. *Wall Street Journal.* Retrieved from http://www.wsj.com/

27. Burt (2007).

28. Borowski, S., Zeman, J., Thrash, T., Carboni, I., & Gilman, R (2016). Adolescent controversial status brokers: A double-edged sword. *School Psychology Quarterly,* 31(3).

29. Kleinbaum, A. M. (2012). Organizational misfits and the origins of brokerage in intrafirm networks. *Administrative Science Quarterly, 57*(3), 407–452.

30. Kleinbaum, p. 442.

31. London Sunday Times. (2007, September 23, p. 19). The cultural braveheart who gets the world rallying to him. *The Sunday Times.* Retrieved at https:// www.thetimes.co.uk.

32. Kai Chi, Y., Fehr, R., Keng-Highberger, F. T., Klotz, A. C., Reynolds, S. J., & Yam, K. C. (2016). Out of control: A self-control perspective on the link between surface acting and abusive supervision. *Journal of Applied Psychology, 101*(2), 292–301.

33. George, B. (2016, November 17). What does authentic leadership really mean? *Huffington Post.* Retrieved from http://www.huffingtonpost.com.

Chapter 5

1. Lacy, L. (2017, April 5). The spectacular implosion of Pepsi's in-house Kendall Jenner ad could mark a win for agencies. *The Drum.* Retrieved from http:// www.thedrum.com/news/2017/04/05/the-spectacular-implosion-pepsi-s-house-kendall-jenner-ad-could-mark-win-agencies.

2. Schultz, E.J. & Diaz, A. (2017, April 5). Pepsi is pulling its widely mocked Kendal Jenner ad. *Ad Age.* Retrieved from: http://adage.com/article/cmo-strategy/pepsi-pulling-widely-mocked-kendall-jenner-ad/308575/.

3. Hooton, C. (2017, April 5). Pepsi ad review: A scene-by-scene dissection of possibly the worst commercial of all time. *Independent.* Retrieved from http:// www.independent.co.uk/arts-entertainment/tv/reviews/pepsi-ad-advert -commercial-kendall-jenner-police-protest-black-lives-matter-review-a7667486 .html

4. https://twitter.com/berniceking/status/849656699464056832?lang=en

5. Eborn, A. & Hillgrove, R.J. (2017, April 5). It's just not the real thing – Pepsi and the Kendall Jenner 'protest' ad controversy. *The Drum.* Retrieved from: http://www.thedrum.com/opinion/2017/04/05/its-just-not-the-real-thing-pepsi-and-the-kendall-jenner-protest-ad-controversy.

6. McCarthy, J. (2017, April 5). Pepsi mentions up 7,000% as Kendall Jenner's soft drink civic dispute solution stuns social media users. *The Drum.* Retrieved from: http://www.thedrum.com/news/2017/04/05/pepsi-mentions-up-7000-kendall-jenner-s-soft-drink-civic-dispute-solution-stuns.

7. Schultz, E.J. & Diaz, A. (2017, April 5). Pepsi is pulling its widely mocked Kendal Jenner ad. *Ad Age*. Retrieved from: http://adage.com/article/cmo-strategy/pepsi-pulling-widely-mocked-kendall-jenner-ad/308575/.

8. Colbert, S. (2017, April 6). The Late Show. *CBS*. Retrieved from: www.cbs.com.

9. Fallon, J. (2017, April 6). The Tonight Show. *NBC*. Retrieved from: https://www.nbc.com/the-tonight-show.

10. Elizabeth, D. (2017, April 4). Why people are NOT happy about Kendall Jenner's Pepsi commercial. *Teen Vogue*. Retrieved from: https://www.teenvogue.com/story/pepsi-commercial-kendall-jenner-reaction.

11. Batchelor, T. & Hooton, C. (2017, April 5). Pepsi advert with Kendall Jenner pulled after huge backlash. *Independent*. Retrieved from: http://www.independent.co.uk/arts-entertainment/tv/news/pepsi-advert-pulled-kendall-jenner-protest-video-cancelled-removed-a7668986.html.

12. Adams, C. & Telling, G. (2017, April 6). How many millions could Pepsi's pulled Kendall Jenner ad cost the company. *People*. Retrieved from: http://people.com/food/kendall-jenner-pepsi-commercial-company-cost/.

13. Kimmel, J. (2017, April 6). Jimmy Kimmel Live! *ABC*. Retrieved from: http://abc.go.com/shows/jimmy-kimmel-live.

14. Florida, R. (2016, May 9). The racial divide in the creative economy. *Citylab*. Retrieved from: https://www.citylab.com/life/2016/05/creative-class-race-black-white-divide/481749/

15. Robson, S. (2017, April 6). Team behind controversial Pepsi ad accused of 'lack of diversity' as it emerges 'ALL those credited are white'. *Mirror*. Retrieved from: https://www.mirror.co.uk/news/world-news/team-behind-controversial-pepsi-ad-10169148

16. Fratiglioni, L., Pallard-Borg, S., & Winblad, B. (2004). An active and socially integrated lifestyle in late life might protect against dementia. *Lancet Neurology, 3*, 343–353.

17. Helgeson. V.S., Cohen S, Fritz H.L. (1998). Social ties and cancer. In: Holland JC, Breitbart W, editors. *Psycho-oncology*. New York: Oxford Press, 99–109.

18. Maddux, W. W., Bivolaru, E., Hafenbrack, A. C., Tadmor, C. T., & Galinsky, A. D. (2014). Expanding opportunities by opening your mind: Multicultural engagement predicts job market success through longitudinal increases in integrative complexity. *Social Psychological and Personality Science, 5*(5), 608–615. doi:10.1177/1948550613515005

19. Burt, Ronald S. (2002). The social capital of structural holes. In *The New Economic Sociology*, edited by Mauro F. Guillén, Randall Collins, Paula England, and Marshall Meyer. New York: Russell Sage Foundation, 148 - 192.

20. Levine, S. S., Apfelbaumc, E. P., Bernard, M., Bartelte, V. L., Zajacf, E. J., & Starkg, D. (2014). Ethnic diversity deflates price bubbles. PNAS Proceedings of the National Academy of Sciences of the United States of America, 111(52), 18524–18529.

21. Levine, S. S., & Stark, D. (2015, December 09). Diversity makes you brighter. *New York Times*. Retrieved from https://www.nytimes.com

22. TADStaff. (2012, November 5). 10 Celebrities You'd Never Guess Studied to be Accountants. Retrieved from https://www.topaccountingdegrees.org/celebrity-accountants/.

23. McPherson, M., Smith-Lovin, L., & Cook, J. M. (2001). Birds of a feather: Homophily in social networks. *Annual Review of Sociology, 27*, 415–429.

24. Brooks, D. (2003, September 01). People like us. *The Atlantic.* Retrieved from https://www.theatlantic.com

25. Godsil, R., Tropp, L., Goff, P.A., & Powell, J. (2014, November). The science of equality. *Addressing Implicit Bias, Racial Anxiety, and Stereotype Threat in Education and Health Care, 1.* Perception Institute.

26. Shih, M. J., Stotzer, R., & Gutiérrez, A. S. (2013). Perspective-taking and empathy: Generalizing the reduction of group bias towards Asian Americans to general outgroups. *Asian American Journal of Psychology, 4*(2), 79–83.

27. Pettigrew, T. F., & Tropp, L. R. (2006). A meta-analytic test of intergroup contact theory. *Journal of Personality and Social Psychology, 90*(5), 751–783.

28. University of Virginia (Producer). (2014, July 9). *The untapped power of the weird.* [Video file]. Retrieved from https://ideas.darden.virginia.edu/2014/07/the-untapped-power-of-the-weird/

29. University of Virginia (Producer). (2014, July 9). *The untapped power of the weird.* [Video file]. Retrieved from https://ideas.darden.virginia.edu/2014/07/the-untapped-power-of-the-weird/

30. Bureau of Labor Statistics USDL-17-1158 (2017, August 24). Number of jobs, labor market experience, and earnings growth among Americans at 50: Results from a longitudinal survey. *U.S. Department of Labor.* Retrieved from: https://www.bls.gov/news.release/pdf/nlsoy.pdf.

31. Berger, G. (2016, April 12). Will this year's college grads job-hop more than previous grads? *LinkedIn Official Blog.* Retrieved from: https://blog.linkedin.com/2016/04/12/will-this-year_s-college-grads-job-hop-more-than-previous-grads.

32. Harter, J.K., Schmidt, F.L., Agrawal, S., Plowman, S.K., & Blue, A. (2016). The relationship between engagement at work and organizational outcomes: 2016 $Q^{12®}$ Meta-Analysis: Ninth Edition. *Gallup, Inc.* Retrieved from: http://news.gallup.com/reports/191489/q12-meta-analysis-report-2016.aspx.

33. Society for Human Resource Management. (2015, April 28). 2015 Employee job satisfaction and engagement: Optimizing organizational culture for success. Retrieved from https://www.shrm.org

34. Labianca, G., & Brass, D. J. (2006). Exploring the social ledger: negative relationships and negative asymmetry in social networks in organizations. *Academy of Management Review, 31*(3), 596–614.

35. Sparrowe, R. T., Liden, R. C., Wayne, S. J., & Kraimer, M. L. (2001). Social networks and the performance of individuals and groups. *Academy of Management Review, 44*(2), 316–325.

36. Chua, R. Y. J., Ingram, P., & Morris, M. W. (2008). From the head and the heart: Locating cognition- and affect-based trust in managers' professional networks. *Academy of Management Journal, 51*(3), 436–452. Venkataramani, V., & Dalal, R. S. (2007). Who helps and harms whom? Relational antecedents of interpersonal helping and harming in organizations. *Journal of Applied Psychology, 92*(4), 952–966.

37. Casciaro, T., & Lobo, M. S. (2008). When competence is irrelevant: The role of interpersonal affect in task-related ties. *Administrative Science Quarterly, 53*(4), 655–684.

38. Yuan, Y. C., Carboni, I., & Ehrlich, K. (2010). The impact of awareness and accessibility on expertise retrieval: A multilevel network perspective. *Journal of the American Society for Information Science and Technology, 61*(4), 700–714.

39. Cavailoa, A, & Lavender, N. (2000). *Toxic coworkers: How to deal with dysfunctional people on the job.* Oakland, CA: New Harbinger Productions.

40. House, J. S., Landis, K. R., & Umberson, D. (1988). Social relationships and health. *Science, 241*(4865), 540–545. Gilman, R., & Huebner, E. S. (2006). Characteristics of adolescents who report very high life satisfaction. *Journal of Youth and Adolescence, 35*, 311–319.

41. Lincoln, K. D. (2008). Personality, negative interactions, and mental health. *Social Service Review, 82*(2), 223–252. Lincoln, K. D., Chatters, L. M., & Taylor, R. J. (2005). Social support, traumatic events, and depressive symptoms among African Americans. *Journal of Marriage and Family, 67*(3), 754–766.

42. Grant, A. (2017, January 3). Are you a giver or a taker? Retrieved from https://www.ted.com.

Chapter 6

1. A pseudonym

2. McPherson, M., Smith-Lovin, L., & Brashears, M. E. (2008). Social isolation in America: Changes in core discussion networks over two decades. *American Sociological Review, 73*(6), 1022.

3. Krackhardt, D. (1992). The strength of strong ties: The importance of philos in organizations. In N. Nohria & R. G. Eccles (Eds.), *Networks and organizations: Structure, form, and action* (pp. 216–239). Boston, MA: Harvard Business School Press.

4. McCarthy, H. (2004). *Girlfriends in high places: How women's networks are changing the workplace.* London: Demos, p. 53.

5. Eisner, M. & Cohen, A. (2010). *Working together: Why great partnerships succeed.* New York City: Harper Collins.

6. The Creative Group (2015). Retrieved from https://www.prnewswire.com/news-releases/coworker-sabotage-nearly-one-third-of-execs-say-colleagues-have-tried-to-make-them-look-bad-300130235.html.

7. Carmon, I. (2016, February 13). What made the friendship between Scalia and Ginsburg work. *Washington Post.* Retrieved from https://www.washingtonpost.com

8. Cross, R., & Thomas, R. (2011). A smarter way to network. *Harvard Business Review, 89*(7/8), 149–153.

9. Zeggelink, E. (1994). Dynamics of structure: An individual-oriented approach. *Social Networks, 16*, 295–333.

10. Kalish, Y. & Robins, G. (2006). Psychological predispositions and network structure: The relationship between individual predispositions, structural holes and network closure. *Social Networks, 28*(1), pp. 56–84

11. Tweney, D. (2012, May 29). Tim Cook: What I learned from Steve Jobs. Retrieved from https://venturebeat.com.

12. Nan, L. (1999). Social networks and status attainment. *Annual Review of Sociology, 25,* 467–487.

13. Merton, Robert K. (1968). The Matthew effect in science. *Science. 159* (3810): 56–63.

14. Marcinkus, W., & Kram, K.E. (2010). Understanding non-work relationships in developmental networks. *Career Development International, 15*(7), 637–663.

15. Marcus, B. (2014, June 09). Advice from top women leaders about finding a mentor. *Forbes.* Retrieved from https://www.forbes.com.

16. Pareles, J. (2016, January 13). Iggy Pop on David Bowie: 'He Resurrected Me'. *New York Times.* Retrieved from https://www.nytimes.com.

17. Kilduff, M., & Krackhardt, D. (1994). Bringing the individual back in: A structural analysis of the internal market for reputation in organizations. *Academy of Management Journal, 37*(1), 87–108.

18. Burt, R. (2010). *Neighbor networks: Competitive advantage local and personal.* Oxford: Oxford University Press, p. 1.

19. Hewlett, S. A., Marshall, M., & Sherbin, L. (2011). The relationship you need to get right. *Harvard Business Review, 89*(10), 131–134.

20. Ibid.

21. Ibid.

22. Ibid.

23. Dunbar, R. I. M. (1992). Neocortex size as a constraint on group size in primates. *Journal of Human Evolution, 22* (6): 469–493.

24. Gourlay, C. (2010, January 24, p. 7). OMG: brains can't handle all our Facebook friends. *The Sunday Times.* Retrieved from https://www.thetimes.co.uk.

25. Lebowitz, S. (2017, April 21). Ask yourself a question from a behavioral economist to make your schedule less stressful. *Business Insider.* Retrieved from http://www.businessinsider.com.

26. Granovetter, M.S. (1973). The strength of weak ties. *American Journal of Sociology* 78 (6), 1360–1380.

27. Cox, D., Navarro-Rivera, J., & Jones, R. (2016, August 03). Race, religion, and political affiliation of Americans' core social networks. Public Religion Research Institute. Retrieved from https://www.prri.org/research.

28. Kamenetz, Anya (2011). Most innovative companies: LinkedIn CEO Reid Hoffman on network intelligence. Fast Company. https://www.fastcompany.com/1723301/most-innovative-companies-linkedin-ceo-reid-hoffman-network-intelligence.

29. Simmons, M. (2014, June 24). Open relationship building: the 15-minute habit that transforms your network. *Forbes.* Retrieved from: http://www.forbes.com/sites/michaelsimmons/2014/06/24/open-relationship-building-the-15-minute-habit-that-transforms-your-network/3/#7ca1c2c15faf.

30. Farr, C. (2012, May 8). When Harvard and Stanford teach networking, they look to Heidi Roizen. Here are her top tips. *The Next Web.* Retrieved from: https://thenextweb.com/insider/2012/05/08/when-harvard-and-stanford-teach-networking-they-look-to-heidi-roizen-here-are-her-top-tips/.

31. Vilkomerson, S. (2015, November 25). Jennifer Lawrence: 'My bullsh— detector is phenomenal'. *Entertainment Weekly*. Retrieved from: http://ew.com/article/2015/11/24/jennifer-lawrence-bullsh-t-detector-friends/.

Chapter 7

1. Loosely based on Skinner, C. W., Krackhardt, D., & Casciaro, T. (2003). Elizabeth Parker (A). Harvard Business School Cases.
2. Aldred, T. (2016, December 2). What are the benefits of shared office space for SMEs? *The Telegraph*. Retrieved from http://www.telegraph.co.uk/connect/small-business/business-networks/benefits-of-sharing-office-space/.
3. Feld, S.L. (1981). The focused organization of social ties. *The American Journal of Sociology, 86*(5), 1015–1035.
4. Mooney, L. (2014, June 11). Heidi Roizen: "Today Everything Is Relationship-Driven". *Insights by Stanford Business*. Retrieved from https://www.gsb.stanford.edu/insights/heidi-roizen-today-everything-relationship-driven.
5. Inam, H. (2015, July 15). How women can succeed by networking authentically. *Forbes*. Retrieved from https://www.forbes.com/sites/hennainam/2015/07/14/how-women-can-succeed-by-networking-authentically/#2d673faf17eb.
6. Schawbel, D. (2014, September 01). Judy Robinett: How entrepreneurs can become power networkers. *Forbes*. Retrieved from https://www.forbes.com/sites/danschawbel/2014/09/01/judy-robinett-how-entrepreneurs-can-become-power-networkers/#b4bc18c243a6.
7. Ambady, N. & Rosenthal, R. (1992). Thin slices of expressive behavior as predictors of interpersonal consequences: A meta-analysis. *Psychological Bulletin, 111*(2), 256–274.
8. See, for example, Ambady, N., & Skowronski, J. (Eds.) (2008). *First impressions*. New York, NY: Guilford Press.
9. Paterniti, M. (2016, October 13). The world's happiest man wishes you wouldn't call him that. *GQ*. Retrieved from https://www.gq.com/story/happiest-man-in-the-world-matthieu-ricard.
10. Personal communication.
11. Cross, R., Baker, W., & Parker, A. (2003). What creates energy in organizations?. *MIT Sloan Management Review, 44*(4), 51–56.
12. Townsend, H. (2011, p. 34). The Financial Times guide to business networking: How to use the power of online and offline networking for business success. *Financial Times*. Retrieved from https://www.safaribooksonline.com/.
13. Casnocha, B. (2017, April 09). 10,000 Hours with Reid Hoffman: What I Learned. Retrieved from http://casnocha.com/reid-hoffman-lessons#helpfirst.
14. Williams, J. C.; Dempsey, R. (2014, p. 294). *What works for women at work: four patterns working women need to know*. New York, NY: NYU Press.
15. Charan, R. (2012, June 21, p. 4). The discipline of listening. HBR.ORG. Retrieved from https://hbr.org/2012/06/the-discipline-of-listening.
16. Carnegie, D. (1936). *How to win friends and influence people*. New York: Simon & Schuster, p. 52.
17. Bamburger, P. (2009). Employee help-seeking: Antecedents, consequences and new insights for future research. In Liao, H. (Ed.) *Research in Personnel*

and Human Resources Management, Volume 28 (pp. 49–98). Bingley: Emerald Group Publishing Limited.

18. Ibarra, H. (2015). The authenticity paradox. *Harvard Business Review, 93*(1/2), 52–59.

19. Ibid.

Chapter 8

1. Robben, B. (2015, October 8). Bill Clinton's networking skills won the white house. Retrieved from https://www.takeyoursuccess.com/networking-skills-got-clinton-the-white-house/.

2. Maraniss, D. (1992, December 28). A weekend with Bill friends. *Washington Post.* Retrieved from https://www.washingtonpost.com/archive/lifestyle/1992/12/28/a-weekend-with-bill-friends/2dfea45a-b45d-42fa-a4d1-9ac63438284a/?utm_term=.1c6e96c5857c.

3. McAuliffe, T., & Kettmann, S. (2008, p. 202). *What a party!: My life among democrats: presidents, candidates, donors, activists, alligators, and other wild animals.* New York, NY: Thomas Dunne Books.

4. Ferriss, T. (2007, August 13). Networking tips from the white house. Retrieved from https://tim.blog/2007/08/13/networking-tips-from-the-white-house/.

5. Walker, M. (1992, November 8). Clinton's European ties—networking before the term was invented: Politics: The President-elect maintains fast friendships with a wide-ranging group. Many Europeans are included among these 'FOBs', or 'Friends of Bill.' *Los Angeles Times.* Retrieved from http://articles.latimes.com/1992-11-08/opinion/op-181_1_clinton-family.

6. Ibid.

7. Clinton, B. (2004). *My Life* (p. 107). New York, NY: Alfred A. Knopf.

8. Maraniss, D. (1995, chapter 9). *First in his class: The biography of Bill Clinton.* New York, NY: Simon & Schuster. Retrieved from https://www.amazon.com/.

9. Waldsee (camp). (2017, September 3). Retrieved from https://en.wikipedia.org/wiki/Waldsee_(camp).

10. Walker (1992).

11. Rangwala, S. (2012, October 09). Networking 101: Build relationships and advance in your career. *Washington Post.* Retrieved from https://www.washingtonpost.com/jobs_articles/2012/10/09/dbb7d628-121d-11e2-be82-c3411b7680a9_story.html?utm_term=.97c4908f4be9.

12. Bender, R. G. (2016, June 22). 7 ways to maintain your professional network without annoying your contacts. *Fast Company.* Retrieved from https://www.fastcompany.com/3061118/7-ways-to-maintain-your-professional-network-without-annoying-your-contacts.

13. Edmiston, D. (2017). Personal communication.

14. Gordon, I. (2016, October 26). Ilene Gordon [Personal interview].

15. Pfeffer, J., & Walker, R. (2013, location 28). *People are the name of the game: How to be more successful in your career—and life.* Cork: BookBaby. Retrieved from https://www.amazon.com/.

16. Ibid, location 40.

17. Botelho, E. L., Powell, K. R., Kincaid, S., & Wang, D. (2017). What sets successful CEOs apart. *Harvard Business Review, 95*(3), 70–77.

18. McCullough,M.E.,Kilpatrick, S.D., Emmons,R.A., & Larson,D.B.(2001). Is gratitude a moral affect? *Psychological Bulletin, 127*, 249–266.

19. Stephenson, S., & Robbins, A. (2009, p. 44). *Get off your "but": How to end self-sabotage and stand up for yourself.* San Francisco, CA: Jossey-Bass. Retrieved from https://www.amazon.com/.

20. Grant, A. & Gino, F. (2010). A little thanks goes a long way: Explaining why gratitude expressions motivate prosocial behavior. *Journal of Personality & Social Psychology, 98*(6), 946–955.

21. Aron, A., Melinat, E., Aron, E. N., Vaollone, R., & Bator, R. (1997). The experimental generation of interpersonal closeness: A procedure and some preliminary findings. *Personality and Social Psychology Bulletin, 23*, 363–377.

22. Lee, A. (2017, December 18). Christopher Plummer reveals how he shot 'all the money in the world' in just 9 days. *The Hollywood Reporter.* Retrieved from https://www.hollywoodreporter.com/news/christopher-plummer-reveals-how-he-shot-all-money-world-just-9-days-1068726.

23. Cross, R. & Gray, P. (2013). Where has the time gone? Addressing collaboration overload in a networked economy. *California Management Review, 56*(1), 50–66.

24. Eichler, L. (2017, March 24). Collaborative overload: When work gets in the way of doing your job. *The Globe and Mail.* Retrieved from https://www.theglobeandmail.com/report-on-business/careers/career-advice/life-at-work/collaborative-overload-when-work-gets-in-the-way-of-doing-your-job/article30821954/.

25. Cross, R., Rebele, R., & Grant, A. (2016). Collaborative overload. *Harvard Business Review, 94*(1), 74–79.

26. Staples Study Finds Over Half of Employees Are Burned Out. (2015). *Report on Salary Surveys, 22*(12), 16.

27. Corcoran, J. (2015, May 19). The Bill Clinton guide to networking. Retrieved from http://smartbusinessrevolution.com/bill-clinton-guide-to-networking/.

28. Buffet, M. and Clark, D. (2006, p. 114). *The Tao of Warren Buffett: Warren Buffett's words of wisdom: quotations and interpretations to help guide you to billionaire wealth and enlightened business management.* New York, New York, NY: Scribner.

29. King, M. (2018, January 09). Why working hard is not enough to get ahead. *Forbes.* Retrieved from https://www.forbes.com/sites/michelleking/2018/01/09/why-working-hard-is-not-enough-to-get-ahead/#16ae58bd4b67.

30. Pfeffer & Walker (2013), location 18.

Chapter 9

1. Ibarra, H., Ely, R., & Kolb, D. (2013). Women rising: The unseen barriers. (cover story). *Harvard Business Review, 91*(9), 60–67.

2. Annis, B., & Gray, J. (2013). *Work with me: 8 blind spots between men and women in business.* New York, NY: St. Martin's Press.

3. Rider, C. I., Wade, J., Swaminathan, A., & Schwab, A. (2016). *Racial disparity in leadership: Performance-reward bias in promotions of national football league*

coaches (Georgetown McDonough School of Business, Research No. 2710398). SSRN. Retrieved from https://papers.ssrn.com/sol3/papers.cfm?abstract_id=2710398.

4. Belson, K. (2016, January 20). Among N.F.L. coaches, a lack of diversity trickles up. *New York Times*. Retrieved from https://www.nytimes.com/2016/01/21/sports/football/among-nfl-coaches-a-lack-of-diversity-trickles-up.html?mtrref=www.google.com&gwh=25D0E2602ED5F50FCF4B5AC4D57CC21E&gwt=pay.

5. McKinsey&Company, & Lean In. (2015). *Women in the workplace*. Retrieved https://womenintheworkplace.com/2015.

6. McKinsey&Company, & Lean In. (2017). *Women in the workplace*. Retrieved https://womenintheworkplace.com/.

7. Miller, D., James, M., & Christensen, K. (2017, October 21). How Harvey Weinstein used his fashion business as a pipeline to models. *Los Angeles Times*. Retrieved from http://www.latimes.com/business/hollywood/la-fi-ct-weinstein-fashion-models-20171021-htmlstory.html.

8. DeWolf, M. (2017, March 1). 12 Stats About Working Women. Retrieved from https://blog.dol.gov/2017/03/01/12-stats-about-working-women.

9. Feintzeig, R. (2016, June 14). Another study shows little progress getting women on boards. *Wall Street Journal*. Retrieved from http://www.wsj.com/articles/another-study-shows-little-progress-getting-women-on-boards-1465876862.

10. Bureau of Labor Statistics. (2017). Employed persons by detailed occupation, sex, race, and hispanic or latino ethnicity. Retrieved from https://www.bls.gov/cps/cpsaat11.htm.

11. Peterson, C., Snipp, C. M., & Cheung, S. Y. (2017). State of the union 2017: Earnings. *Pathways*, 32–35. Retrieved from https://inequality.stanford.edu/sites/default/files/Pathways_SOTU_2017.pdf.

12. Bureau of Labor Statistics. (2016). Median weekly earnings of full-time wage and salary workers by detailed occupation and sex. Retrieved from https://www.bls.gov/cps/cpsaat39.htm.

13. Ibid.

14. Brands, R. A., & Fernandez-Mateo, I. (2017). Leaning out: How negative recruitment experiences shape women's decisions to compete for executive roles. *Administrative Science Quarterly, 62*(3), 405–442. doi:10.1177/0001839216682728.

15. McKinsey & Company, & Lean In (2015).

16. Ibarra, H. (1993). Personal networks of women and minorities in management: A conceptual framework. *Academy of Management Review, 18*(1), 56–87. doi:10.5465/AMR.1993.3997507.

17. Lutter, M. (2015). Do women suffer from network closure? The moderating effect of social capital on gender inequality in a project-based labor market, 1929 to 2010. *American Sociological Review, 80*(2), 329–358. doi:10.1177/0003122414568788.

18. Durbin, S. (2011). Creating knowledge through networks: A gender perspective. *Gender, Work & Organization, 18*(1), 90–112. doi:10.1111/j.1468-0432.2010.00536.x.

19. McDonald, S. (2011). What's in the "old boys" network? Accessing social capital in gendered and racialized networks. *Social Networks, 33*(4), 317–330. doi:10.1016/j.socnet.2011.10.002.

20. Evans, D. (2015, November 15). On gawker's problem with women. Retrieved from https://medium.com/matter/on-gawker-s-problem-with-women-f1197d8c1a4c#.14kf0ibct.

21. Ibarra, H., Carter, N. M., & Silva, C. (2010). Why men still get more promotions than women. *Harvard Business Review, 88*(9), 80–85.

22. McKinsey & Company, & Lean In (2015).

23. McKinsey & Company, & Lean In (2015).

24. Hopkins, L. E., & Adams, M. (2014, p. 143). *Beyond the pearly gates: White, low-income student experiences at elite colleges* (Doctoral dissertation, UMass Amherst). Amherst: Scholar Works. Retrieved from https://scholarworks.umass.edu/cgi/viewcontent.cgi?article=1038&context=dissertations_2.

25. Campbell, K. E., Marsden, P. V., & Hurlbert, J. S. (1986). Social resources and socioeconomic status. *Social Networks, 8*(1), 97–117. Also, Oishi, S., & Kesebir, S. (2012). Optimal social-networking strategy is a function of socioeconomic conditions. *Psychological Science (0956-7976), 23*(12), 1542–1548. doi:10.1177/0956797612446708.

26. Ibarra, H. (1992). Homophily and differential returns: Sex differences in network structure and access in an advertising firm. *Administrative Science Quarterly, 37*(3), 422–447. Also, Ibarra, H. (1997). Paving an alternative route: Gender differences in managerial networks. *Social Psychology Quarterly, 60*(1), 91–102.

27. McCarthy, H. (2004, p. 28). *Girlfriends in high places: How women's networks are changing the workplace.* London, England: Demos.

28. Hua Fang, L., & Huang, S. (2017). Gender and connections among Wall Street analysts. *Review of Financial Studies, 30*(9), 3305–3335. doi:10.1093/rfs/hhx040.

29. Bierema, L. (2005). Women's networks: A career development intervention or impediment?. *Human Resource Development International, 8*(2), 207–224. doi:10.1080/13678860500100517.

30. McGuire, G. M. (2000). Gender, race, ethnicity, and networks. *Work & Occupations, 27*(4), 500–523.

31. Thompson, L., & Walker, A. J. (1991). Gender in families: Women and men in marriage, work, and parenthood. In A. Booth (Ed.), *Contemporary families: Looking forward, looking back* (pp. 76–102). Minneapolis, MN: National Council on Family Relations.

32. McKinsey & Company, & Lean In (2017).

33. McKinsey & Company, & Lean In (2017).

34. Ibarra, H. (1992). Homophily and differential returns: Sex differences in network structure and access in an advertising firm. *Administrative Science Quarterly, 37*(3), 422–447. Also, Ibarra, H. (1997). Paving an alternative route: Gender differences in managerial networks. *Social Psychology Quarterly, 60*(1), 91–102.

35. Richeson, J. A., & Trawalter, S. (2005). Why do interracial interactions impair executive function? A resource depletion account. *Journal of Personality & Social Psychology, 88*(6), 934–947. doi:10.1037/0022-3514.88.6.934.

36. Institute for Research on Poverty. (2016). Who is poor? Retrieved from https://www.irp.wisc.edu/faqs/faq3.htm.

37. Brands, R. A., & Kilduff, M. (2014). Just like a woman? Effects of gender-biased perceptions of friendship network brokerage on attributions and performance. *Organization Science, 25*(5), 1530–1548. doi:10.1287/orsc.2013.0880.

38. Bearman, P. S., & Moody, J. (2004). Suicide and friendships among American adolescents. *American Journal of Public Health, 94*(1), 89–95.

39. Gilman, R., Rice, K. G. and Carboni, I. (2014), Perfectionism, perspective taking, and social connection in adolescents. *Psychology in the Schools, 51*(1), 947–959. doi:10.1002/pits.21793.

40. Granovetter, Mark (1983). The strength of weak ties: A network theory revisited. *Sociological Theory* 1 (1983):201–233.

41. The PEW Charitable Trusts. (2016, March 02). Extended family support and household balance sheets. Retrieved from http://www.pewtrusts.org/en/research-and-analysis/issue-briefs/2016/03/extended-family-support-and-household-balance-sheets.

42. Gladwell, M. (1999, January 11). Six degrees of Lois Weisberg. *The New Yorker*, 52. Retrieved from https://www.newyorker.com/magazine/1999/01/11/six-degrees-of-lois-weisberg.

43. Ibarra, H. (1997). Paving an alternative route: Gender differences in managerial networks. *Social Psychology Quarterly, 60*(1), 91–102.

44. Ibarra, H. (1995). Race, opportunity, and diversity of social circles in managerial networks. *Academy of Management Journal, 38*(3), 673–703. doi:10.2307/256742.

45. Groysberg, B. (2008). How star women build portable skills. *Harvard Business Review, 86*(2), 74–81.

46. Marcus, B. (2014, January 6). Advice from top women leaders about finding a mentor. *Forbes.* Retrieved from https://www.forbes.com/sites/bonniemarcus/2014/01/06/advice-from-women-leaders-about-finding-a-mentor/#5b08ec8768d3.

47. Wichert, I. C. (2011, p. 78). *Where have all the senior women gone? Nine critical job assignments for women leaders.* London, England: Palgrave Macmillan.

48. McGuire, G. M. (2000). Gender, race, ethnicity, and networks. *Work & Occupations, 27*(4), 500–523.

49. Sandberg, S., & Scovell, N. (2013). *Lean in: Women, work, and the will to lead.* New York, NY: Alfred A. Knopf.

50. Lang, I. H. (2011). Co-opt the old boys' club: Make it work for women. *Harvard Business Review, 89*(11), 44.

51. Brown, C. (2015, May). Know your worth, and then ask for it. Retrieved from https://www.ted.com/talks/casey_brown_know_your_worth_and_then_ask_for_it/transcript.

52. Kalev, A. (2009). Cracking the glass cages? Restructuring and ascriptive inequality at work. *American Journal of Sociology, 114*(6), 1591–1643.

53. Beam, C. (2010, January 11). Code black. Retrieved from http://www.slate.com/articles/news_and_politics/politics/2010/01/code_black.html.

54. Ibarra (1995).

55. Schuck, K., & Liddle, B. J. (2004). The female manager's experience: A concept map and assessment tool. *Consulting Psychology Journal: Practice & Research, 56*(2), 75–87. doi:10.1037/1061-4087.56.2.75.

56. McKinsey & Company, & Lean In (2017).

57. KPMG. (2018). Inclusion and diversity. Retrieved from https://home.kpmg.com/us/en/home/about/corporate-responsibility/diversity-and-inclusion.html

58. Hewlett, S. A., & Rashid, R. (2010). The battle for female talent in emerging markets. *Harvard Business Review, 88*(5), 101–106.

59. Nance-Nash, S. (2015, October 2). Strategic support. Retrieved from http://hreonline.com/HRE/view/story.jhtml?id=534359348&.

Chapter 10

1. Lewis, P. H. (1996, January 25). What is an Apple worth?; ailing innovator's luster as an acquisition dims. *New York Times*. Retrieved from http://www.nytimes.com.

2. Ziff-Davis Publishing Company. (1996, June). Full text of "MacUser June 1996". Retrieved from https://archive.org/stream/MacUser9606June1996/MacUser_9606_June_1996_djvu.txt.

3. McGinn, K.L., & Tempest, N. (2000, Revised 2010, p. 5). Heidi Roizen. *Harvard Business School Case, 800-228.*

4. Ziff-Davis Publishing Company (1996).

5. McGinn, K. L. (2001, November). An Interview with Heidi Roizen. Harvard Business School Video Supplement 902-804.

6. Ziff-Davis Publishing Company (1996).

7. Krackhardt, D. (1990). Assessing the political landscape: structure, cognition, and power in organizations. *Administrative Science Quarterly, 35*(2), 342–369.

8. Ibid.

9. Duncan, M. J. (2011, May). The case for executive assistants. *Harvard Business Review*. Retrieved from https://hbr.org.

10. Janicik, G. A., & Larrick, R. P. (2005). Social network schemas and the learning of incomplete networks. *Journal of Personality & Social Psychology, 88*(2), 348–364.

11. Burt, R. S., & Ronchi, D. (2007). Teaching executives to see social capital: Results from a field experiment. *Social Science Research, 36*(3), 1156–1183.

12. Grant, A. M. (2013). *Give and Take: A Revolutionary Approach to Success*. London: Phoenix / Orion Books.

13. Ekiel, E. B. (2014, April 17). Catalina Girald: "I Want to Change Women's Lives." *Insights by Stanford Business*. Retrieved from https://www.gsb.stanford.edu/insights.

14. Mooney, L. (2014, June 11). Heidi Roizen: "Today Everything Is Relationship-Driven". *Insights by Stanford Business*. Retrieved from https://www.gsb.stanford.edu/insights/heidi-roizen-today-everything-relationship-driven.

15. Burt, R. S. (1995). *Structural Holes: The Social Structure of Competition*. Cambridge, MA: Harvard University Press.

16. Athanasopoulos, P., Bylund, E., Montero-Melis, G., Damjanovic, L., Schartner, A., Kibbe, A., & Thierry, G. (2015). Two languages, two minds: Flexible cognitive processing driven by language of operation. *Psychological Science (0956-7976), 26*(4), 518–526.

17. Weiner, N. (2015, March 17). Speaking a second language may change how you see the world. *Science*. Retrieved from http://www.sciencemag.org/.

18. Lawler, J. (2010, June 21). The real cost of workplace conflict. *Entrepreneur*. Retrieved from https://www.entrepreneur.com.

Chapter 11

1. This chapter draws upon research reported in Wilburn, P. & Cullen, K. (2014). A leader's network: How to help your talent invest in the right relationships at the right time. Greensboro: *Center for Creative Leadership*.

2. As reported in Watkins, M. D. (2009). *Your next move: the leader's guide to navigating major career transitions*. Boston, MA: Harvard Business Press.

3. Watkins, M. D. (2013, p. 1). *The first 90 days: Proven strategies for getting up to speed faster and smarter*. Boston, MA: Harvard Business Review Press.

4. Morrison, E. W. (2002). Newcomers' relationships: the role of social network ties during socialization. *Academy of Management Journal, 45*(6), 1149–1160. doi:10.2307/3069430

5. Podolny, J.M., & Baron, J.N. (1997). Relationships and resources: Social networks and mobility in the workplace. *American Sociological Review, 62*(5), 673–693.

6. Burt, R.1992. *Structural holes: The social structure of competition*. Cambridge, MA: Harvard University Press.

7. Gentry, W. A., Logan, P., & Tonidandel, S. (2014). Understanding the Leadership Challenges of First-Time Managers: Strengthening Your Leadership Pipeline. Retrieved from https://www.ccl.org.

8. Dulebohn, J. H., Bommer, W. H., Liden, R. C., Brouer, R. L., & Ferris, G. R. (2012). A meta-analysis of antecedents and consequences of leader-member exchange: Integrating the past with an eye toward the future. *Journal of Management, 38*(6), 1715–1759.

9. Dulebohn, J. H., Bommer, W. H., Liden, R. C., Brouer, R. L., & Ferris, G. R. (2012). A meta-analysis of antecedents and consequences of leader-member exchange: Integrating the past with an eye toward the future. *Journal of Management, 38*(6), 1715–1759.

10. Imperato, G. (1999, March 31). You Have to Start Meeting Like This! Retrieved from https://www.fastcompany.com.

11. Ancona, D., & Caldwell, D. (1992). Bridging the boundary: External activity and performance in organizational teams. *Administrative Science Quarterly, 37*(4), 634–665.

12. Druskat, V. U. & Wheeler, J. (2004). How to lead a self-managing team. *MIT Sloan Management Review, 45*(4), 65–71.

13. Gladwell, M. (2011, May 16). Creation Myth. New Yorker, 44-52.

14. Ibid, p. 49.

15. Gargiulo, M., & Benassi, M. (2000). Trapped in your own net? Network cohesion, structural holes, and the adaptations of social capital. *Organization Science, 11*(2), 183–196.

16. Ibid.

17. Sanders, A. (2014, March 25). Daniel McFarland: What Is the Secret to a Happy Collaboration? *Insights from Stanford Business.* Retrieved from https://www.gsb.stanford.edu/insights.
18. Horwath, R. (2018). What CEOs Think About Strategy. Retrieved from http://www.strategyskills.com.
19. Sloan, J. (2013, p. 51). *Learning to Think Strategically.* Oxford, UK: Routledge.
20. Ansink, J. (2013, September 10). C-suite suicides: When exec life becomes a nightmare. *Fortune.* Retrieved from http://fortune.com.
21. Bryant, A. (2016, June 17). Beth Comstock of General Electric: Granting Permission to Innovate. *New York Times.* Retrieved from http://www.nytimes.com.
22. Katzenbach, J. R., Steffen, I., & Kronley, C. (2014, July 31). Cultural Change That Sticks. Retrieved from https://hbr.org.
23. Wilburn, P. & Cullen, K. (2014, p. 13). A leader's network: How to help your talent invest in the right relationships at the right time. Greensboro: *Center for Creative Leadership.*
24. Hoffman, R., & Casnocha, B. (2012). *The Start-Up of You: Adapt to the Future, Invest in Yourself, and Transform Your Career.* New York, NY: Crown Business.
25. Wilburn & Cullen, p. 13.
26. Cohn, J., Katzenbach, J., & Vlak, G. (2008). Finding and grooming breakthrough innovators. *Harvard Business Review, 86*(12), 62–69.